The Roots of Excellence

Ronnie Lessem is a graduate of Harvard Business School. He has been a corporate planner, the managing director of a small supermarket chain and, more recently, a businessman, consultant and academic. He is Director of the only university-based programme in business development in the UK, and has consulted with leading companies in the areas of networking, innovation and entrepreneurship. While also having helped some five hundred people to start businesses of their own, he has written *Enterprise Development* (1985) and *The International Entrepreneur* (1986).

Bob Garratt is a management consultant and Honorary Secretary of the Association of Teachers of Management.

Other Books for the Successful Manager

Managing Your Own Career, Dave Francis
Manage Your Time, Sally Garratt
Managing Yourself, Mike Pedler and Tom Boydell

Ronnie Lessem

The Roots of
Excellence

Fontana/Collins

First published in 1985 by Fontana Paperbacks,
8 Grafton Street, London W1X 3LA

Set in Linotron Times
Made and printed in Great Britain by
William Collins Sons & Co. Ltd, Glasgow

Contents

Acknowledgements   7
Preface   9

1. To Grow or to Die   19
2. Business Development   31
3. A Cast of Excellent Characters   38
4. The Foundations of Excellence   58
5. Sinclair Research   68
6. F International   111
7. Habitat/Mothercare   141
8. ICI   198
9. The Tree of Business Life   283
10. Economic Recreation: a Future for Britain   297

Index   309

Acknowledgements

For my own business roots I have to thank my father, and his Lithuanian ancestors before him. For my intellectual roots I have to thank my mother, and her Austrian ancestors before her. For my emotional roots I have to thank Africa, and my wife Joey, who is even more firmly rooted in African soil than I am. For allowing me to bring all these roots together I have to thank Great Britain, for tolerating individuality and diversity.

The roots of this particular book are manifold. First there was Mike Tull, a management consultant in New York with a great sense of humour, and Mark Bernadi, a Californian business executive with great entrepreneurial flair. They suggested I write the book, and even provided me with the title. Then there is Bob Garratt, who contains all the best British qualities within him, and who set the whole proposition up. Helen Fraser at Fontana took it on from there, and provided the most constructive sort of criticism, which stirred me emotionally and intellectually into re-action. Malcolm Stern, at Gower Press, kindly gave me permission to quote excerpts fom my book *Entesrprise Development*.

In fact I owe a tremendous intellectual debt to three people in Britain, Holland and America. In Britain Kevin Kingsland, through his *Spectral Theory of Personality* (Metavision, 1985), has provided me with continuing inspiration. In Holland Bernard Lievegoed, through *The Developing Organization* (Celestial Arts, 1980), has developed my organizational insight. Thirdly, I do owe a debt to Thomas J. Peters and Robert H. Waterman Jr, authors of the bestselling *In Search of Excellence* (Harper and Row, 1982), both because of and in spite of my criticism of them. After all, they set us all on the road to excellence.

Finally, and perhaps most importantly, I am indebted to that long list of businessmen and women who form the whole basis for

The Roots of Excellence's being. To start with there is Fred and Nelli Eichner at Interlingua. Theirs is a family business and lifestyle *par excellence* (although, sadly, Fred died while I was writing the final chapter). Then there are the excellent companies themselves. At Sinclair I have Nigel Searle, in particular, to thank for opening the doors. At F International Steve Shirley gave me invaluable amounts of her precious time. At Habitat/Mothercare I have Sir Terence Conran to thank for giving me time and lessons in business mastery, and at ICI, Sir John Harvey-Jones. In all four companies, and in several others, many, many people other than the above mentioned gave me the basis on which to write this book. My appreciation to them is equally great. I can only hope that I have done them all justice.

Preface

This book is about business. An excellent business, with strong roots, never dies. It has a beginning, a middle, and no end. It enters youth, middle age, and then maturity, when it successfully transforms itself. In the end is its recreation!

How does all this come about? The question has haunted me for twenty-one years, the full extent of my adult life. In that time I have been to Harvard Business School, become a corporate planner, and run a family business. I have created three businesses of my own and helped hundreds of budding entrepreneurs to create theirs. I have worked with multinational corporations to help them create new ventures, and to exercise their corporate responsibilities more effectively. I have taught at business school since 1970, and have been taught myself by business masters. Yet it is only now, after a twenty-one-year quest for the holy business grail, that I have perhaps found it. The question I have asked myself is: how do successful businesses grow and develop?

THE BUSINESS TREE

Where then must we begin? I have to start by removing the most inhibiting aspect of the conventional business wisdom. So the familiar organization chart, or so-called 'family tree', has to be cast aside. For it is truly lifeless. It lies limply in an office drawer, or hangs suspended on someone's office wall. It has no roots. It is ungrounded.

In its place I want to establish the 'business tree of life'. First, it is firmly planted in the *ground*, preferably in fertile soil. Second, it *grows* in stages; three of them. Its growth and development infuses the whole business organism with life. Not to grow is to die, whether as a tree or as a business. Third, as the organism grows, it becomes more strongly *rooted* in the soil. Fourth, a main stem or

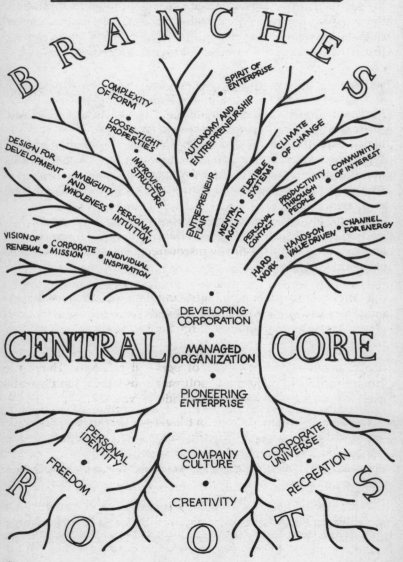

The TREE of BUSINESS LIFE

BRANCHES

SPIRIT OF ENTERPRISE

COMPLEXITY OF FORM

AUTONOMY AND ENTREPRENEURSHIP

LOOSE-TIGHT PROPERTIES

CLIMATE OF CHANGE

DESIGN FOR DEVELOPMENT

FLEXIBLE SYSTEMS

IMPROVISED STRUCTURE

COMMUNITY OF INTEREST

AMBIGUITY AND WHOLENESS

PERSONAL INTUITION

ENTREPRENEUR FLAIR

MENTAL AGILITY

PERSONAL CONTACT

PRODUCTIVITY THROUGH PEOPLE

CHANNEL FOR ENERGY

VISION OF RENEWAL

CORPORATE MISSION

INDIVIDUAL INSPIRATION

HARD WORK

HANDS-ON VALUE DRIVEN

CENTRAL

DEVELOPING CORPORATION

MANAGED ORGANIZATION

PIONEERING ENTERPRISE

CORE

PERSONAL IDENTITY

COMPANY CULTURE

CORPORATE UNIVERSE

FREEDOM

CREATIVITY

RECREATION

ROOTS

10

tree trunk develops from it, giving the tree or business a growth *centre*. Fifth, the tree sprouts *branches*, seven of them, giving the tree business character. Finally, the fruit or foliage, in other words the products or services, emerge, and these in their turn produce the *seeds* of renewal. As a combined result, the business can be suitably grounded, developed, rooted, centred, characterized (excel) and renewed. Let's start down on the ground.

FERTILE GROUND FOR DEVELOPMENT

Professor Reg Revans, the founder of 'action learning', has said, 'If we are looking for a country's economic salvation, we have to find it within its own shores.' The American authors Peters and Waterman went out in search of excellence and came back with a treasure-trove of business insights. But their treasure was found in American soil. So their findings cannot take firm root outside their own country.

In order to discover fertile ground for the development of British business I decided to take a brief trip through Britain's social and economic history. I finally discovered four particularly fertile grounds.

1. Prolific *recreational* grounds, including widespread hobbies, outdoor pursuits and voluntary activities, represented in many a gifted amateur. Therein lie the roots of Sinclair.

2. Strong grounds for *individuality*, even to the point of eccentricity, combined with a love of personal freedom. Therein lie grounds for F International, a software house which has dedicated itself to shaping work around individual lives.

3. A *creative* tradition, both in the arts and in the sciences, which has served Britain well in the basic sciences, and has recently led to her reemergence in industrial and commercial design. Terence Conran and Habitat/Mothercare are obviously grounded in this tradition.

4. A *tolerance for diversity* which is reflected in the many different nationalities that have settled in this country, and the number of businesses which have been created here by foreigners

seeking refuge from persecution or prejudice. ICI, one of whose founders was Ludwig Mond who came to this country to escape from German prejudice against Jews a hundred years ago, is a prominent example.

NOT TO GROW IS TO DIE

Fertile soil stimulates growth. A developing business, drawing on fertile ground, never stops growing, qualitatively as well as quantitatively. The seed of an idea falls to the ground, and roots grow; the developing individual and corporate identity. Then the stem, branches and first leaves follow. The business, its activities and products begin to take shape. The shape of each leaf, or product, is a manifestation of the original seed pattern. The process of development involves the unfolding of identity, structure, activity and product from the seed idea, which contains the original business blueprint. This seed is the joint creation of a person or company and their environment.

The stages in a process of development can be distinguished from one another. A business grows, unfolding to the point when the original structure can no longer be maintained. There is an inevitable crisis as the architects of change create chaos in the old structure. This painfully necessary process paves the way for the emergence of a more complex organization, one that is capable of undergoing further evolution. If no more development is considered possible or desirable, the organism grows rigid and gradually disintegrates.

For the healthy and growing business, there are three major development phases. In the first, pioneering phase, the organism develops as one entrepreneurial whole. With continuing growth the entrepreneur finds himself unable to cope. A crisis point is reached. The survival of the business is at stake. So, in the second stage, specialization of function sets in, to deal with advancing complexity. Each function or subsidiary is now in a position to make decisions independently. A hierarchy of command is established, one above the other, covering each separate part of the whole, constraining individual freedom.

With further growth comes another crisis: lack of motivation, integration and innovation leads to stagnation. There is a need for regeneration, for renewal. The third development stage calls for interdependence and, for the first time, the conscious development of people, business and organization. A new centre, a new vision emerges, one that is a transformation of the old technology and organization. A return to the roots and underlying ground is called for, but one that involves the discovery of higher, transcendent corporate intention: 'We are no longer in the transport business; we're in communications!'

In summary, there are three growth stages: pioneering, expansive and integrative. As the business develops from one stage into the other, it undergoes a crisis, sheds one skin and dons another. If it fails to evolve it will become extinct. The 'hero' of the first stage is the individual entrepreneur, and of the second, structured management. The heroes of the third stage are a variety of 'intrapreneurs' inspired and integrated by a corporate leader. That brings us back to roots.

IN SEARCH OF ROOTS

A developing business, like a tree, grows from its roots upwards. The roots draw from, and contribute to, the fertile ground below. In the process they establish the identity of the business, in between itself and its environment. For the young roots *personal* and *business* identity are as one, as is the case with Sinclair. Clive Sinclair has drawn on electronics and recreation from the fertile British soil and is contributing back his own fertile brand of inspiration and individuality.

As they develop, the personal roots are outgrown. In their place emerges the *cultural* identity of the company as a whole, separate from, and yet related to, the founders' individual personalities. Habitat/Mothercare, through Terence Conran, draws on the creative talent of this country and contributes back its design and management skills. F International, through Steve Shirley, draws on the British propensity for freedom and individuality, and contributes back flexibility of workstyle.

Finally, as a company matures, it outgrows its own cultural roots. They become too confined, too limited and limiting. In fact the deeper the roots grow into the soil, the closer the attachment to their underlying foundations. Company culture, with its distinct and convergent values, turns into a *corporate universe* with a multicultural, multifunctional, multidisciplinary approach. Its universal values are catholic and cosmopolitan, embracing a very wide range of individuals, technologies and cultures. Unlike Peters and Waterman's closed culture, it is open, and unlike their converging myths and rituals, it is open to diversity of scientific and cultural exchange. ICI draws on its rich and widespread heritage and contributes a diversity of knowledge and wealth back to it.

THE GROWTH CENTRE

As the roots grow, so does the trunk, the main stem of the business. For the pioneering business, *personal enterprise* is the central core, arising out of the founder's personal identity. For the middle-aged company it is the *managed organization* which emerges, reflecting its specialized product or service. For the mature business a purposeful and *developing corporation* takes over. Whereas Sinclair's enterprises are distinctive and personalized, and both Conran's Habitat/Mothercare and F International have an entirely distinctive image, the direction in which ICI is developing is not yet altogether clear. ICI has still to complete its transformation. For more clues we need to turn towards the branches of excellence.

THE BRANCHES IN CHARACTER

We have now looked at the underlying grounds, the roots and the central core of business. From roots we extract business identity, but not overall character. The word 'excellence', in fact, comes originally from the Greek *arete*, meaning 'the sum of good values that makes up character'. In Britain, as far as business is concerned, they are likely to be different from those in America. I have focused on seven of these characteristics, which also develop in three stages. At each stage of their development they shed their former existence, but retain links with it. Why, then, are there seven attributes?

The seven branches, or business attributes, are an extension of our own human personality. Every one of us, in varying degrees, and in differing combinations, has the following:

- physical prowess
- social ability
- intellectual skill
- willpower
- analytical ability
- intuitive awareness and
- creative imagination

These capacities are reflected in a different character, but one that retains the same underlying form, at each stage of development.

PIONEERING

The pioneering entrepreneur, such as Clive Sinclair, excels when he combines:

- hard *work*
- personal *connections* (close customer)
- mental *agility*
- *entrepreneurial* drive
- improvised organization (*simple form)*
- market *instinct* and
- technical *inventiveness*

MANAGING

If the enterprise passes successfully through its growth crisis, from an improvised to a professionaly managed organization, and purposefully transcends its original character, it becomes an F International or a Habitat/Mothercare. The business evolves from birth and infancy into youth and adulthood. It becomes more complex, organizationally, than a Sinclair Research.

The managed attributes now involved, which retain the form but not the character of personality traits, are as follows:

- physical hard work turns into *hands-on* activity

- social connections become *productivity* through *people*
- intellectual skill and mental ability turn into *flexible systems*
- willpower and entrepreneurial flair become *autonomy* and entrepreneurship
- analytical ability and simple organizational form turn into '*loose-tight*' structural properties
- intuitive awareness and market insight become design-based sensitivity and a feel for *ambiguity* and *paradox*
- creativity and imagination turns from inventiveness into business *mission*

This is where Peters and Waterman's *In Search of Excellence*, and most other business texts, come to a halt. They leave us with a false and dismal picture of maturity. The truly evolved and mature corporation has transcended, rather than replaced, both its infancy and younger adulthood. In coping with its 'mid-life' crisis, it emerges out of a period of encroaching bureaucracy and stagnation into a new era of development. In so doing, it retains the form of our original personality attributes, but provides them with new character.

DEVELOPING

The developing corporation, like ICI, is neither entrepreneurial nor should it be a managed organization. Its reason for being is, for the first time in its history, to consciously develop, in the sense described above, its products and markets, its people and organization. More specifically:

- hard work and hands-on activity is turned into a *channel* for *physical energy*, both material and human (physical)
- connections and people's productivity is transformed into a *community* of *interests* (social)
- mental agility and flexible systems are turned into an overall *climate* for *change* (intellectual)
- willpower and entrepreneurial flair become an all-pervading *spirit* of enterprise (wilful)
- simple form and loose-tight properties are turned into *complexity* of organizational *form* (analytical)
- market instinct and design awareness are transformed into a

design for *development* of people and organization as well as products and markets (intuitive)
- technical inventiveness and business mission become an all-encompassing *vision* of *renewal* (imaginative)

In developing and even transforming itself, the self-renewing corporation both draws on its ever-deepening roots and returns 'seed corn' to the fertile soil in which it stands. This brings us on to the seeds of renewal.

THE SEEDS OF RENEWAL

The branches of business, whether young or old, are not the actual goods or services, which is, after all, what business is there to provide. The foliage coming from the branches comprises these products. For Sinclair they are electronically based, for F International based on computer services; for Habitat/Mothercare they are well-designed products for the person and the home, and for ICI, they are chemically based products for the home and industry.

The products and services emerge from the combination of branches rather than from any one in particular. If one branch is weak, all the foliage will suffer. As the tree matures, so the fruit grows more abundantly, if occasionally overripe.

If all the fruit is plucked, or milked like 'cash cows', no new seeds will return to the underlying ground. Seeds that are returned may or may not be absorbed. In the early stages of the business it is up to the individual entrepreneur, a Sinclair, to be receptive and to cross-fertilize. In the intermediate stage, the company culture needs to be receptive to new product ideas. In the mature stage, the whole corporate universe needs to partake in nourishing its own 'seed corn' with fertilizer from the surrounding soil.

THE ROOTS OF EXCELLENCE

The four excellent companies that I have selected are obviously more than 'good performers' in the conventional sense. For not only do they span the three stages of business development, but they are also strongly grounded in British soil, and firmly rooted within a personal or corporate identity. Each, therefore, fits the following four criteria:

1. Reasonably and consistently, though not necessarily excessively, *profitable*.

2. In a position to capture the public *imagination*, socially and culturally as well as technically and commercially.

3. Closely in touch with, and responsive to, the social and industrial *evolution* of this country.

4. Able to play a significant part in *transforming* Britain's cultural and economic foundations.

In other words, as excellent companies with roots they are grounded in fertile soils, they act their age, they have a full repertoire of appropriate behaviours, and they have a strong personal, cultural or corporate identity. I selected the four companies analysed here in depth for that combination of reasons. Sinclair in some shape or form, F International, Habitat/Mothercare and ICI are the kinds of organizations that will survive in the truly long term.

1. To Grow or to Die

George Land, an American biologist and organizational psychologist, wrote a fascinating book in the seventies. He called it *To Grow or to Die*. The gist of his argument was 'Today's successes are tomorrow's failures. Not to grow is to die.' My own roots have made me very familiar with that particular point of view.

I was born in Rhodesia, part of the old British Empire. Rhodesia failed to grow up, politically, until it was eventually forced to do so in becoming Zimbabwe. My father was, and is, a successful businessman, a self-made man. He has lifted himself up by his own bootstraps. Like my mother, he fled from persecution in Eastern Europe, and landed in Africa in the 1920s. After spending a few years drifting from job to job, as storekeeper, book-keeper and teacher, he started up in business. Last time I visited him in Africa, I asked my father to give me the full story of how he created his business from the very beginning.

Pioneering

'Well,' he said, 'you had to be prepared to *work* damn hard. In those early days, back in the thirties, Rhodesia was virgin territory. We lived out in the bush, and made *contact* with the locals, through barter. We became part of their culture and they became part of ours. We laughed and joked and sang together. Brother Jack and I opened our first general store, selling mainly clothing in exchange for grain. We made very little profit in the beginning, and made all the mistakes under the sun. But we *learnt* from them, quickly. Gradually we entered the cash economy and our deals became more complicated. Jack bought and sold cattle, and made enough profit to be able to finance the stocking of our

19

store. My brother was a real wheeler-dealer. He loved to
negotiate. I suppose you might have called him an instinctive
entrepreneur. But he had no idea about finance or organization.
That's where I came in, during those early days. Gradually we
were able to finance the opening of one clothing store after
another. I started taking a few calculated risks along the way, like
buying a fleet of lorries for a fair old price, and then selling them
for even more. I was beginning to trust my instincts, more, my
market *intuition*. Even the occasional glimmer of *inspiration* was
beginning to show itself. That decision to travel up to South Africa
to purchase the lorries was an inspired one. I wasn't a natural
entrepreneur, like Jack,' my father insisted. 'I grew into it.
Necessity started me off, and then ambition took over. No sooner
had I become an entrepreneur, though, than I had to grow into
something else!'

Managing

Hard work, an affinity with the local people, the ability to learn
quickly from his mistakes, and the inclination – which his brother
had first, and then my father grew into – to take calculated risks,
turned my father into an entrepreneur. After seven years, they
had built up twenty-five stores, dotted around the Rhodesian
countryside. But time never stands still. In fact, all too quickly, the
business outgrew brother Jack's raw entrepreneurial instincts. 'To
succeed in business,' my father told me, 'you have to be more than
a rugged adventurer, an enthusiastic salesman, or even a risk-
taking entrepreneur. The time inevitably comes when you have to
grow up or else you die! In other words, you have to learn how to
manage money, and people. Ten years after we had opened our
first store we went into wholesaling. It made economic sense,
providing us with access to a wider range of merchandise at a
better price. Three years after that we built our own factory:
Concorde Clothing. That really required management and organization, the kind of thing you teach in business school. I had to
learn the hard way, especially how to manage people. It wasn't
long before we had five hundred working for us.'

So my father had to 'grow up', and turn himself out of the purely entrepreneurial mould into a managerial one. The business was transformed from African Trading Company into Concorde Clothing Ltd. Abe and Jack Lessem were transformed into a limited liability company with a quality-product image. The identity of the business shifted. Production planning and control, financial analysis and management, sales strategy and promotion, took over from the improvised structure that had existed before. Though the organization retained a *simple form* and lean staff – only three of them at a managerial level – separate functions were identified and allocated. A business administration was established.

Developing

At that point our economic and commercial imagination often comes to a halt. After an MBA, what? We can conceive of the pioneering enterprise, whether it is welcomed or is discarded by the powers that be. We can comprehend the formal organization with its managed hierarchy and impersonal control systems. But is there life thereafter? How does the excellent company develop beyond the point of structured management? Does the whole basis for excellence change, from one point of a company's development to the next?

My father had a point to make. 'Once we had built up the factory into a viable concern my emphasis began to change. I now saw myself no longer as a businessman, or even an executive, but as part of a wider community. I became chairman of the Rhodesian Chamber of Commerce, and played an active part in the establishment of the local university. I also took time off to lecture on courses at the technical college. I became non-executive director of the country's largest milling company, and took an interest in agriculture. I spread my wings. I no longer had to struggle to survive. The company was now running smoothly. I wanted now to *develop* myself and my country.'

As I listened to my father, it all seemed to make some kind of sense. Yet, what did it all mean for business and management? 'Where did you go from there?' I asked him.

'That's the strange thing,' he answered, 'I don't know. I was

21

offered a safe seat in parliament, in the fifties, but I turned it down. Somehow, I didn't see myself as a politician. From time to time I had this dream that I would combine our farms, our factory and our retail stores into a self-sufficient community. Remember, in Russia we Jews were totally isolated. In Rhodesia I had the chance to create a new and integrated community, where black man and white man, Jew and Gentile, could work happily together. But it never happened. I got diverted. In the mid-sixties, as you know, your mother and I left the country, and here I am in South Africa, now in the property business, while brother Les looks after the factory in Zimbabwe.'

It seems to me now, with hindsight, that my father has been left with unfinished business. Abe Lessem had spent his youth creating a pioneering enterprise. The business had been hands-on, value driven, close to the customer, action oriented, and entrepreneurial in its approach. In his thirties and forties my father established a managed organization. He secured productivity through people, kept a simple form of business operation, and basically stuck to the corporate mission. While growing into wholesaling and manu-facturing, from a retail base, he stayed with clothing all the way. Then, in his maturity, he spread his wings, and became more integrated within the economic community. His own development became interwoven with that of his country. At this point my father, in the good company of most business academics, became lost for words.

It is as if the stages of the development of his business had happily mirrored the phases of his own life, until he had got diverted. Perhaps, having initially lost touch with his roots in Eastern Europe he wasn't able to rediscover them, to the full extent of realizing his dream. This problem, writ large, faces many of our mature business corporations today. They have lost touch with their roots, and are therefore unable to fulfil their vision. This is a subject to which I shall return in the final chapter. Now I need to probe a little further into roots and excellence, although re-maining, for the time being, with the smaller business. After all, I could hardly have put forward a whole new theory of business, based on the sample of one. I needed more evidence. I also needed to uncover the roots of a business more thoroughly than I had my own father's. I felt that I needed at least one more small business, as an example, and then selected excerpts from middle- and large-sized companies. Without hesitation my choice of a small business was Interlingua.

THE INTERLINGUA STORY

Pioneering

ROOTS

There is no other business besides my own that I have studied more closely. Interlingua is a small but international company, involved in the interpreting and translation of all the languages under the sun.

It all began on a little farm in Czechoslovakia, where Nelli Eichner was born seventy years ago. 'Some prisoners of war', she told me, 'had been working on our farm. Some were Italian and some were Russian. These lonely men were only too glad to tell the stories of their homelands to a little four-year-old, who loved sitting on their laps and listening. Gradually, I started to under- stand the legends of old mother Russia, full of werewolves, and the Italian stories about the singing mermaids of Venice. In the evening I repeated these stories in Czech to my little sister. With- out knowing it I had become a translator!'

Those are the roots of Interlingua, on Nelli's side. She lives in her country cottage, right next door to Interlingua's headquarters. Nelli's home is a mixture of farmhouse, social centre, music room and computer bureau. Ducks, children, electronic signals and business clients mingle together. In her 'retirement', Nelli runs a language school, a greenhouse, an extended family, and computer courses. Her husband, Fred, founded the business with her. For him, it all started happening in his youth.

'It was at fifteen or sixteen that I first became aware of myself. The great time of questioning had begun, and I didn't feel that religion could supply the answers.' As a student of life Fred pursued two early paths. From his home base in Eastern Europe he travelled abroad, and he also studied chemistry. 'Being very

23

curious I wanted to know how others lived, so I hitch-hiked around Europe. I was interested in the people rather than the buildings. That's how I learnt to communicate with other nationalities. I was curious about things as well as people, especially molecules. I loved chemistry from a young age. To work out the theory behind chemical reactions was a great challenge. I put two things together and I got a third. That was one form of communication. Love is another form of communication. If you look at Nelli and I as partners, as a wife she helped, supported me, and built up my ego as a man. I was a natural innovator. Nelli appreciated what I was doing and turned vision into action. I always assured her of my continuous love.'

HARD WORK

The birth of Interlingua did not take place all of a sudden. It was long and protracted. Both Fred and Nelli fled from Nazi-ridden Europe and found a refuge in Britain. During the war years they battled to survive. They were obliged to move out of London into the countryside, when their second son contracted polio. 'We were by then buried in the depths of rural Sussex,' Nelli told me. 'We had to find a way of earning more cash so that we could afford the repairs on our new house. Fred had to give up his job in north London as a chemist, and my bit of translating was not bringing in enough. One of our florist friends told Fred, while he was cutting our cypress hedge, that the clippings were in demand. That's how we started supplying Covent Garden flower market with greenery. At the same time we raised and bred chickens. At Christmas time we had to pluck 110 of them, draw out their innards and truss them. It was tremendously hard work.'

PERSONAL CONTACT

All those efforts brought in cash the hard way, but never enough. There were soon five children to feed! Nelli, meanwhile, had been discovering several local women, trained in modern languages, but equally tied down by their families. 'Together we tackled languages that I could not have coped with on my own. There was enough money at last for the down payment on our first, second-hand, electronic typewriter. One of the mums did the typing.

'The word then got around Crawley New Town that we were in business. Many new export-minded companies had been setting up shop there. We were called on to do highly technical translations. So we needed more technical translators, more dictionaries, more typewriters. In a small way we were now in business, but still broke!'

The hard work, and the personal involvement with the surrounding community, were as much in evidence with the Eichners as they were in the early days of my father's business, yet it seemed as if still more had to be learned before they could begin to make real money.

MENTAL INGENUITY

Nelli went on:

By now our translation jobs included aeroplanes, flight simulators, harvesters and diving gear. We were learning about anything and everything. It was also when the construction of Concorde was being planned in this country. It was going to be an Anglo-French effort. One of our clients phoned: 'How would you like to translate all the specifications for us from English into French?' Would we, oh boy! What a lovely job this was going to be. We were all delighted but . . .

IMPROVISED ORGANIZATION

This was a government job. We couldn't supply sundry boffins with invoices in triplicate, under the name Fred and Nelli Eichner. The contract was to be signed the next day. So, the whole family sat down, drank tea together, and cooked up a respectable-sounding name, suitable for a company with government contracts. Interlingua was born.

Fred and I were by now a properly constituted and registered partnership. Our little Interlingua had grown into a reputable, but still only local, company. Our children were as proud of

Interlingua as we were. They felt part of it, having worked with us since they were babies.

PERSONAL CREATIVITY

There was, of course, more to tell, a breakthrough to come as Fred the innovator made his first significant mark on the developing business. Nelli described it thus.

In our pride and boundless enthusiasm we were always thinking and forward planning. That's when Fred had a brainwave. Instead of fetching, carrying and delivering our translations on bicycles, why didn't we install a telex machine? The idea was new. Telexes were still regarded as a rare and costly installation which was used only by large, well-heeled industrial companies. There was a good reason why we, little Interlingua, could not install a telex. The reason was a fifty-pound down payment! A quarter of a century ago the pound was still worth a pound and fifty pounds was an awful lot of money. But we did scrape it up and gambled it all on a telex machine. It was a gamble. Would it ever pay?

The new machine, a huge noisy monster, was installed in our lounge! Yes, no other location would have been elegant enough. It stood on one side of the fireplace in front of the piano – and a new carpet was purchased in order to set it off to best advantage.

Then we all, yes *all*, including the children, learned how to use the telex machine. When we were almost sure what we were doing, I started to send out short messages to other telex subscribers, informing them that: 'Interlingua provide instant translations by telex.' Our very first telex translation job was a paper mill in the Midlands. It was just a few lines, an urgent message about a pulp shipment. I translated it, typed it, and sent it back to the client in minutes.

MARKET RESPONSE

He was surprised. No, he was amazed. No, he did not believe it was possible. It could not be done! He sent another translation by telex just to see if we could do it again. We did. He told all his

26

friends in the club about Interlingua. They all tried out the new service. Yes, it really worked. Within a couple of weeks the local newspaper got to hear about us. Yes, one could send a message in Rumanian to Sussex, via telex, and have the translation back in Scotland within the hour. The story made headlines in 42 papers. The *Daily Mirror* gave it centre page spread. Newspapers in many European countries picked up the story of the telex in Sussex woods. Enquiries came pouring in. Work as well. At long last . . . money!

That was the turning point. Within months Interlingua expanded from a local to an international company. Visitors came to see the Eichners from all over the world, asking to become telex translation subscribers. The sweat and toil of the early days, nourished by family and friends, and upgraded by learning and ingenuity, had finally resulted in a profitable business, involving trade with innumerable countries.

For a further fifteen years Interlingua continued as a loose-knit family business. In the meantime, the eldest son Michael had become an accountant with a love for electronic gadgetry and ancient musical instruments. Iona, the eldest daughter, had travelled the world before she took over the Far Eastern office. Claudia, the younger daughter and guitar teacher, took over the local music shop that Fred had originally purchased. Claudia was soon joined by the youngest son Mark, who now has two more music shops of his own.

All five children, at one stage, had set up a new kibbutz together in Israel. It was while they were there that Fred had a stroke, and Michael had to return home and take over as managing director. Mike now lives fifty yards away from Interlingua's headquarters, though he spends four months of the year travelling around the globe. Mike is a musician and would-be engineer who has business in his blood and knows the company finances like the back of his hand. This is how he described the takeover from his mother and father.

Managing

My sister Iona and I took over five years ago, at a time when the business was not in particularly good shape. The problem was, basically, one of poor financial control. In a sense, my parents were seat-of-the-pants people. They had sales figures and that was that. We had to make some drastic changes. We started producing internal accounts, chopped the Brighton office, and formed a management team.

In that way, Interlingua developed from a pioneering enterprise into a managed organization. But no sooner had this been accomplished, albeit somewhat hurriedly, than it was time for a further evolutionary step.

Developing

INTERDEPENDENCE

This is how Michael saw it.

By 1983 we needed to change the formula. Our business had been changing all the time. The big cloud on the horizon was machine translation. Within two to three years, it seemed, companies would be able to buy a translation system on a computer. That led us in three directions. First, we decided to collaborate with Rank Xerox. They're the first ones to have installed translations equipment. So we're working with them to evaluate the results. At the moment, for us, it's more of an education than an immediate business prospect. Secondly, we are slowly changing our product. In fact we're working with several British manufacturers of microcomputers to develop training programmes, for computer users, in foreign languages. Only a small proportion of the work is straight translation. The majority of it is something called versioning. This involves a lot of programming, to adapt to the nuances of foreign languages.

In essence we have had to evolve our product range in collaboration with associated companies, both large and small. Thirdly, we're cooperating with British Telecom on the teleconferencing side. There are all sorts of new developments in which several of us companies have a shared interest, and it is my job to keep up with them.

For Interlingua then, the managed organization has already been superseded, though not replaced, by a pattern of business integration. A series of franchised outlets have recently been set up in this country, as well as in Europe and the Far East. The introduction of electronic communications into the company's worldwide operations has resulted in the creation of a so-called 'Linguanet'.

The new form of economic and technological interdependence has also developed in a cultural direction, as Iona Eichner told me.

> Just in the last few months something new has happened. I joined the Association of Professional and Business Women, in Hong Kong and then Singapore. For the first time I have started to measure myself up against fellow women. It has given me an enormous boost. In the past I have tended to disregard women in business and the professions, and to measure myself up against men. Yet I'm not a man. Now I'm a woman among like-minded women, and I stand up very well. We've started to run courses for women who want to start up in business. We planned for 70 people, on the first of ten evenings, and got 350!

RE-VISION

For a vision of the future, interestingly enough, I had to turn back to Interlingua's roots, to Fred and Nelli, rather than to their children. Fred put it this way.

> We are in the middle of a communications revolution. There'll be a great dispersal of production facilities. People will be able to work full blast from the country. Communications will be via modem and facsimile. This should all serve to increase our mutual understanding of one another. If it doesn't turn out that way, we shall all cease to exist as a species.

Nelli's vision, of course, is more personal, more homely, based more upon her own extended family, than upon the family of man. 'During one of Fred's inspired moments,' Nelli said, 'he bought twenty acres of beautiful Sussex countryside, surrounding an elegant mansion. This is now our head office. On the same plot of land, each of our five children have built their own house. . . . Our grandchildren play in the pool. The older children come into the office to help and leave when the job is done. These children are my greatest blessing. They fill my heart with pride and joy. There is no happiness like shared happiness.'

2. Business Development

The Interlingua story and my own father's, duly reinforced by the formidable cast of business characters you will meet in later chapters, have given me the confidence to draw up my 'phase' theory. The theory goes like this. Excellence, or outstanding performance, is acquired in cumulative stages. Unless a business realizes the potential of each stage it cannot fully excel. Both my father's business and the Eichners' excelled at the pioneering stage, but only partially thereafter. They remained, therefore, small.

The 'phase' theory is not new, though my application of it is. A leading Dutch management consultant, Bernard Lievegoed, conceived of 'developing organizations' in the sixties. Man and organizations, he claimed, have a time to learn, a time to expand, and a time to grow wise. So excelling at one stage is different from doing so at another. To excel, overall, is a progressive process.

A large and mature corporation, like IBM or ICI, will contain businesses at varying stages. Whereas the whole company will be a mature one, cumulatively speaking, its new venture groups will be youthful, and some recently acquired subsidiaries may be middle-aged. So excellence, for the mature business, comes in three stages.

Pioneering

Nelli and Fred Eichner, like thousands of others in this country before and after them, started out as business pioneers. First and foremost, they had the capacity to work hard. They stayed up late at night, plucked chicken feathers, clipped cypress hedges, and translated lengthy documents. But, as business pioneers, hard work was never enough. My father, Fred and Nelli were more than workers. They made personal contacts. They got to know the locals, and the locals got to know them. Their personal approach, direct style of communication, closeness to the customer, and the family feeling that they often generated among employees, were clearly apparent in both cases. 'There is no happiness like shared happiness' – Nelli Eichner's words capture that social sensibility.

Hard work and personal contact can get a business moving. But neither trait can guarantee that the enterprise will survive. In order for it to endure, physical and social skills must be combined with mental agility, including the ability to learn from experience, and to adapt to change. The way Fred Eichner adapted their translations business, to accommodate telex, is a perfect example.

Yet, quintessentially, the pioneering enterprise will develop, not only because of physical, social and mental faculties, but also because of entrepreneurial flair. The pioneer's ability and inclination to take a calculated risk, to do a good deal, to make an instinctive judgement, and to pursue profit single-mindedly, is paramount. The Eichners risked everything they had to invest in their first telex machine. My father and uncle accumulated resources, initially, through astute bartering. Entrepreneurs have stamina, enthusiasm, the ability to think on their feet, and the inclination to take a calculated risk. But there is more to come.

Pioneering enterprises, if they are to succeed, need minimal structure, but adequate organization and control. In fact, Peters and Waterman's terms, 'simple form and lean staff', are entirely appropriate. I was always intrigued by the way my father managed to run a factory, having a workforce of five hundred, with only three people in management. The simplest of financial and production controls, combined with good housekeeping, kept things in good order.

My father's internal organization, albeit of a minimal nature, was matched by his sensitivity to the external environment. For the pioneering enterprise that grows and develops draws heavily on the founder's *market intuition*. In the Eichners' case, they somehow found themselves in the right place, by Crawley New Town, at the right time. Fred sensed the way the market was going, and that involved more than Nelli's ability to make personal contact with people. He had an ability to anticipate, some kind of insight into the future. In his case, too, this intuition was accompanied by *creative imagination*. He saw himself as an in-novator. That trait has since taken Interlingua into a leading position in the machine-translation age.

In summary, the pioneer, and the pioneering enterprise that truly excels, have the following qualities:

- a capacity to *work hard*
- an inclination to make *personal contacts*
- *mental agility*
- *entrepreneurial flair*
- *simple form and lean staff*
- market *intuition*
- the gift of *imagination*

Managing

The manager has become an accepted part of the business estab-lishment. Yet in the nineteenth century he did not exist, and, until the 1950s in Britain and America, did not hold the pride of place he now occupies. In developing from the pioneering to the man-aged organization, a company undergoes a transformation, and usually a crisis to go with it. Michael Eichner had to 'revive' Interlingua from his parents' purely instinctive approach. He re-placed their improvised organization with a properly managed organization, including delegated managerial functions and tight financial and cost controls. In fact, for the first time, financial control and sales management were separated out as defined functions. Michael had not trained as an accountant for nothing!

A properly managed organization provides the central thrust for the second stage, whether in Interlingua or my father's Concorde Clothing. As circumstances change, the pioneer, and his en-terprise, lose their innocence, the spontaneous enthusiasm and instinctive judgement that goes with it. If he is able to make the transformation, and this is often not the case, he becomes man-aging director rather than entrepreneur. He is no longer as deeply involved in everything, all of the time.

The Eichners took time off to travel. Their continuing presence was often more important symbolically than physically. Inter-lingua became, to use the classic Peters and Waterman phrase, 'hands-on, value driven'. The Eichners were there to provide physical continuity as well as tangible examples of their values at work. Nelli built up the company from a close-knit group into a veritable family of nations. At one point, some thirty different nationalities were working together in their Sussex headquarters. Through newsletters, celebrations, lively bulletin boards and a homespun personnel management, she achieved productivity through people within a cohesive culture.

By the 1970s, Interlingua was beginning to come to grips with the new computer technology. As new branches were opened overseas, flexible structures were created to allow for the speedy transfer of information, and to adapt to change. It was no longer enough to rely on Fred's mental agility. At the same time, the children were becoming more active in the business. However, because of Nelli's enlightened attitude, each branched off on their own first. Unusually, for a family business, the Eichners en-couraged autonomy and entrepreneurship within their own family.

While Michael Eichner has turned a pioneering enterprise into something of a managed organization, he has only partially done so. He retains his own desire for autonomy, as well as for entre-preneurship. On the one hand, the combination of centralized control and franchised overseas operations does provide the balanced loose-tight structure required. On the other, the in-tegration of the business, and its product line, is still incomplete. Michael continues to excercise his market intuition rather than cultivating a design for wholeness which would give the company a coherent image. If anything, he is disinclined to 'stick to the knitting' – or the corporate mission – and is always itching to diversify, whenever business opportunities present themselves. Fred and Nelli's personal inspirations remain in the background, as the company responds to an increasingly international and computerized environment.

In summary, the managed organization, albeit incompletely so in the Interlingua case, excels when it successfully transforms:

- hard work into *hands-on*, value-driven management

- personal contacts into *productivity through people*
- mental agility into *flexible systems* and structures
- entrepreneurial flair into *autonomy and entrepreneurship*
- simple form, lean staff into *loose-tight properties*
- hunch and intuition into a *design for wholeness*
- personal inspiration into a distinctive company image, one which involves '*sticking to the knitting*'

Developing

Here we enter into almost virgin territory. Beyond the entrepreneur, beyond the manager, lies what? Ironically, the mature corporation, while it dominates our industrial and commercial landscapes, has not yet found a style of operation that befits its stage of development. This is perhaps the major issue which this book addresses. To my mind cohesive culture, the shared values that are advocated so strongly elsewhere, are more appropriate to the second, managed phase than to the third. So what is the so-called 'developmental' phase about?

We can start with my father's business and Interlingua, although they never became large corporations. On a Rhodesian scale, Concorde Clothing was a big business. As my father and his company matured, he became very active in the community. His business became woven into the fabric of the economy and society. Concorde Clothing and the Rhodesian economy became increasingly interdependent. As a result my father became active in the Chamber of Commerce, and in the newly emerging system of higher education. He partook in the evolution of the clothing industry and the Rhodesian economy.

In the Eichners' case, the major evolution in which they have partaken is a technological one. They have now created a 'Linguanet' which links their worldwide operations through electronic communications. Interlingua has become involved in a series of joint ventures, with larger corporations, to develop new forms of language and machine translation. The company is becoming more interdependent, engaging in long-term partnerships with its customers and suppliers. Interlingua often acts, too, on behalf of the interpreting and translations establishment as a whole, to further their cause worldwide.

Interlingua is also teetering on the edge of fundamental transformation, in technological and social terms. Fred Eichner's idea of communication between all nations and races, suitably updated to accommodate modern technology, sits there in the background. Certainly the potential is there, within the company's 'Linguanet' and worldwide operation. However, the company has not passed successfully enough through the second and third stages to fully harness this potential.

If Interlingua is to develop fully, then hard work and hands-on activity has to be turned into physical and human energy. In other words, health- and fitness-based activities as well as electronic technology would set rural Sussex alight! The cohesive culture that Nelli developed would become a genuine community of interest linking customers and suppliers, collaborators and competitors, employees and franchisers, and Interlingua worldwide. Flexible structures would be transcended until the enabling of technological, social and economic change became recognized as a corporate activity. Adaptable plans to accommodate change would be created.

The spirit of enterprise, so strong in the Eichner family, would infuse all of the Interlingua staff and associates. New ventures would be spawned throughout Europe, America and the Far East, where their operations are based. Finally, the multinational organization would take on a complex form, one that accommodated the pioneering, managerial and developmental functions, and that accelerated the interdependence between people and technology.

In summary, the developing, mature corporation would advance from:

- sticking to the knitting to *transforming* a whole industry
- design for wholeness to *conscious evolution* of products, of people, of technology, of organization
- loose-tight properties to *complex organizational form*
- entrepreneurship and autonomy to an all-pervading *spirit of enterprise*
- flexible structures to the more conscious *enabling of change*
- an inward-looking culture to an outward-looking *community of interests*

- hands on management, to the release of physical and human *energy*

While the pioneering enterprise is person centred and implicitly run, the managed organization is company centred and explicitly structured. Finally, the developing corporation is environment centred – both internal and external – and consciously evolved. Excellence is therefore a layered set of qualities as is demonstrated in the Table 2.1 :

Table 2.1   **Stages of Excellence**

STAGE Quality	Pioneering (person centred)	Managed Organization (product centred)	Developing Corporation (environment centred)
Physical	Hard work	Hands-on, value driven	Physical/human energy
Social	Personal contact	Productivity through people	Community of interests
Mental	Mental agility	Flexible structures	Enabling change
Emotional	Entrepreneurial flair	Autonomy and entrepreneurship	Spirit of enterprise
Conceptual	Simple form, lean staff	Loose-tight properties	Complex form
Aesthetic	Hunch and intuition	Design for wholeness	Conscious evolution
Creative	Personal imagination	Corporate mission	Industrial transformation

3. A Cast of Excellent Characters

Now that we have caught a glimpse of the stages of business development, both in theory and practice, I want to extend their application. Specifically, I shall be uncovering the roots of excellence for youthful, middle-aged and mature companies in turn. I want to draw initially on examples other than the four case studies central to this book. This gives us a broader base of application. I shall begin with the best-known millionairess in this country!

WORK/HANDS ON/ENERGY

HARD WORK

Anita Roddick is a fireball of a woman who has created a chain of some one hundred franchised outlets in Britain, Scandinavia and Canada. She was born in the UK of Italian stock, and, as Anita told me, 'I've always worked terribly hard. From the age of ten, when my father died, there was no alternative but to work for survival. That never leaves one.' In fact, being very conscious of the physical wear and tear that a hard life can produce, Anita has gone into natural skin and hair products wholeheartedly. She constantly travels to the remotest parts of the globe, picking up new and indigenous recipes. Her company is called 'Body Shop'. Hard work, accompanied by both physical stress and relaxation, is intrinsic to her business. She is physically active, her products are earthy, and she serves her customers' physical needs, for both health and beauty.

HANDS ON

The action bias and hands-on management activity to which Peters and Waterman refer is as much symbolic as it is physically real. Anita's physicalness is, both literally and figuratively, more basic, and it has more to do with physical presence than with physical strength or dexterity. Ann Sayer, Habitat/Mothercare's publicity manager, put it this way when describing the preparations for the opening of the new Habitat/Heal's complex of stores in London.

> On 23 May the Habitat store still had a long way to go, but help was on its way. A burly figure dressed in sweat shirt and jeans climbed out of a Mercedes and made a bee line for a pot of paint. At 2 a.m., on the 24th, he was still there.

It was Terence Conran, the company chairman.

This combination of physical and symbolic action will often have a theatrical touch to it. John Mellersh, who heads ICI's Electronic Chemicals Group, described himself like this: 'My style is theatrical. I walk around the lab, call in the evening from New York and want things done yesterday.' A sense of speed and urgency is combined with a desire to create an effect on his 'audience', like an actor. In fact the theatrical analogy is particularly apt when it comes to something like a store opening. Oliver Gregory, Habitat's design director, has been involved with the opening of every one of their fifty-odd stores. 'The opening day is just like the opening of a play. It is not word perfect, but the show must go on. The invitations have gone out, and there's a lot of theatrical excitement. The doors must open.' A sense of imminence and immediately is therefore added to the speed and urgency that Mellersh conveys. Hard work, the bias towards action and a sense of urgency can, in fact, be built into an organization's overall ethos, so that it even becomes a central feature of it. I got the same impression from Sinclair Research's production director, David Southward: 'Clive has installed a unique R and D philosophy among us. If you come out with a new product, you know it has a limited life. So if you can bring forward the launch date by even a day, you're effectively increasing turnover by £100,000.' Not surprisingly, Sinclair is known for running some seven miles a day, and he keeps his personal energy level running high. This energy pervades his entire organization.

ENERGY

For the small businessman or woman hard work is of the essence.
First in to work in the morning, and last away at night, the Anita
RT BECOMES MORE IMPORTANT. The sense of urgency,
immediacy and even drama sets the business stage alight for all to
see. Finally, in the large and mature corporation, energy, as a
feature of excellence, needs to be represented, not only personally, but also mechanically and electronically. Human, natural,
mechanical and electrical energy all have their part to play, in a
sense that Nobel previewed a hundred years ago (see page 210).

FAMILY/CULTURE/COMMUNITY

FAMILY FEELING

Energy usually moves things, people or information physically,
but not individuals emotionally. Nelli Eichner has a habit of
moving me, emotionally, telling me: 'We became one family, one
group of people who pulled together for the common good.' Not
surprisingly, Clutterbuck and Goldsmith in *The Winning Streak*
have come up with the 'family factor' as a significant and common
denominator in their excellent British companies. The family influence has always provided a cohering force in business, as is
evident from companies such as Marks and Spencer and J.
Sainsbury. But it is the smaller family enterprise which quite
genuinely makes suppliers and customers, as well as employees,
feel part of a family-like community. I remember Mary Quant's
husband telling me, 'There are just twenty of us in the building,
and we're a very close-knit group. Our cleaner joined us when she
was sixty and she is now eighty-five. She still wears a pair of Mary's
high-fashion boots.'

COHESIVE CULTURE

The next step beyond the family identity, as a company grows, is
towards a cohesive 'culture'. David Potter, who is founder and
managing director of Psion, the very successful software house, is

a physicist with a difference. David and I were at school together in Rhodesia, and I remember him as a late developer who, very suddenly, towards the end of secondary school, rose to academic heights. He also turned out to have a head for business, and left academia in 1980 to seek business fame and fortune. He has recently landed a massive order with Marks and Spencer, who will be using his pocket computer, the Organizer, to control their new chargecard system.

David made the following comments about his organization, which currently employs about one hundred people:

> The way we develop our people is interesting. ICL did a quality-assurance check on us before teaming up on the production of Xchange business software. They spoke to one of our junior people, who had been with us for one year. 'It's like this,' he said. 'They don't tell us what to do. What they do is they show you the project, get you used to the idea, and then ask you to sign up. Effectively, you are asked to undertake the project. If you say you're committing yourself, you're doing it in the context of the next guy. If I don't do my bit I lose face. Worse than that, if they're doing their bit and I'm not doing mine, it becomes totally apparent. There's a whole youth culture here.

This kind of cohesive culture is not exclusive to the smaller business. Terence Conran remarked that 'An incredible team spirit and atmosphere was built up as the final preparations were being made' for the recent opening of a Habitat store.

COMMUNITY OF INTERESTS

Of course, it's one thing to foster team spirit amongst thirty or even one hundred people at a time. It is quite another to bind people within an entire, large corporation. That is the kind of task to which Sir Peter Parker addressed himself when he took over the chairmanship of British Rail. Parker is a man of enormous charm who exudes a great passion for life, and who you could imagine building up a community of interest, one that could bind manager and worker, customer and supplier, even industry and gov-

ernment. 'So much of business', he said, 'comes down to personal
relationships. There was myself, the permanent secretary, and the
secretary of state for industry. They're like the jewels in the
movement of ideas and exchange of hopes. There were good times
and bad. We laughed and cried. . . . 'You can't run an international business through an imperial web. I used to encourage my
board at British Rail to read novels. They thought I was a bit
kinky, but you've got to understand the imaginative life of people
if you're wanting to do business with them, or to relate to them as
fellow members of the company.'

A community of interest, linking people within and without the
corporation, is not something easily come by. Even Parker had his
problems at British Rail, as vibrant a person as he is. Sir John
Harvey-Jones, chairman of ICI, has certainly given this kind of
task top priority. 'You've got to be approachable,' he told me. 'I
like being called by my first name. I loathe being called
"Chairman".'

Yet, to create a binding culture, and a community of interest
that transcends the corporate boundaries, requires more than enthusiasm, vitality, charm and a sense of fraternity. It also requires
something that Brian Mills, chairman of F International (UK) said
to me, in earnest:

> A highly personalized organization, like this one, needs a queen
> bee, or a Henry V-type figure, who awards pats on the back and
> medals. The role is almost a mystical one. It's not necessarily a
> noisy or drum-beating role. Steve Shirley, our founder, is rather
> like the Black Prince in relation to Edward I. Edward, in his
> later years, withdrew into the sidelines, but he was always
> there.

As the business evolves, so the almost instinctive family feeling
develops, from a cohesive corporate culture into a wide-ranging
community of interest, embracing customers and suppliers, as well
as staff and line. To hold together that breadth of human
capability and attitude takes not only charm and affability, but also
elements of mystery and even magic! Peters and Waterman refer
us to the 'rich tapestry of myth and anecdote' that characterizes

the excellent corporations. My conclusion is that if you have the kind of richness and variety in product that, for example, Habitat/Mothercare possesses, the myth and anecdote becomes secondary. In other words, the products become part of the family. They become 'user friendly', which brings us on to flexibility, learning and information systems.

AGILITY/FLEXIBILITY/CHANGE

A community of interest binds people together. It provides tradition and continuity rather than flexibility and change. Stable communities learn slow!

FLEET OF FOOT

Jack Dangoor came from nowhere to set up a computer company that, at the last count, was turning over tens of millions. A Jewish refugee from Iraq, Jack dropped out of his physics degree at London University because it wasn't taking him in the direction he wanted. So he went into the electronic watch business for a few years and learnt fast about both the marketplace and the technology. It was then that he decided to get out of watches, into computers, and whatever he developed had to be IBM compatible. So he hired some talented design and engineering consultants, gave them the specifications, and set them to work. Two years later the Advance computer was created, and, through amazing acts of dexterity, the completely unknown 'Jack of all trades' established crucial links with major corporations. Ferranti came in on the manufacturing side, W.H. Smith on sales and distribution, and National Semiconductor on service. Advance Technology, Jack's business, remains a seven-man band, albeit turning over tens of millions. As he said to me, 'We are fleet of foot. While others bury their profits in overheads, we develop new products.' Dangoor has now gone on to develop a new product range, while his notable, associated companies get on with the day-to-day business. It is a juggling act, a game as Michael Maccoby, who created the Corporate Gamesman, would say. The thing is that Jack is damn good at it!

FLEXIBLE COMMUNICATIONS

This fleet-footedness, and ability to respond or change tack quickly, is what characterizes the small enterprises. It can become a feature of the business's product line, as well as its style of operation. Alvin Toffler, in *The Third Wave*, has created the label 'prosumer' to describe such flexible interaction between producer and consumer. Anita Roddick, of Body Shop fame, put it this way:

> I've always enjoyed the momentum of the high street. You cannot stand still. There is an excitement and a buzz. And who else has a perfume bar where the customer can mix her own products? In fact, our shops are a mixture between a chemistry set and a toyshop!

This flexibility of approach goes even further, deeper into the whole Body Shop product line and style of operation. 'As far as the cosmetics industry is concerned', Anita told me, 'we have broken every rule in the book. We've never marketed hope. We've never packaged. We've never advertised. We're not controlled by design groups. And we're the only company who offer six sizes of one product, and a choice of mud, herbal or conventional shampoos.'

Both Advance Technology and Body Shop, in spite of their mushrooming turnovers, would still be classified as small and youthful businesses. Habitat/Mothercare, on the other hand, has entered a robust middle size and middle age. While it has established all the conventional organization structures, Priscilla Carluccio, who is head of product development for Habitat, still told me, 'I don't like hierarchies. I don't understand them. It's a way of protecting yourself from the outside world.' Tony Maynard, marketing director at Habitat, who shares some of Priscilla's concerns, put it this way: 'We need to develop sensitive and creative structures; retain that ability to react responsively as the need arises. In fact, the structure is evolving now. Inevitably change will result.'

As businesses mature, shedding the skin of the managed organization, they make a determined attempt to recover flexibility. In fact, the whole 'management of change' is a thrust in that direction. I find that most of my corporate clients today see their prime function as being in the so-called management of change.

An archetypal 'change-agent', for large companies, is the project manager. Vaci, a formidable engineer at ICI Paints, who was born in Greece and brought up in Australia, now heads the Motors Section's research and development. 'The project manager needs to be flexible,' he always tells me. 'I speak very differently to a research scientist as compared with the customer outside. I have to use the right approach to the right person. In Canada I have to think "Charlie" and in Germany "Karl".'

MANAGING CHANGE

Of course, the new communications technology is a superb tool that the major corporations use, in order to make their cumbersome structures more adaptive and responsive. Dr Rodney Armitage, who heads up the management services function at ICI's headquarters, has a beautiful way of putting it across: 'My picture of the future is of a pattern of communications, a set of random joints across a broad mesh. They join and then they disappear.'

Of course, Rank Xerox in Great Britain have now institutionalized flexibility into their much-publicized 'networking' mode. Phil Judkins, the coarchitect of the company's organizational change, is an intriguing character. He commutes from a Yorkshire town to London, where he becomes part of the business establishment. Yet he continues to wear his crumpled suit and to drive his Land-Rover, with a pile of radar equipment permanently in the back. Phil is an archaeologist, an electronics engineer and a personnel specialist, who heads up Rank Xerox International's Personnel and Resources function in London. He is a true chameleon, being one thing with me, another in his local community, and something else again with his colleagues.

Rank Xerox have produced a number of in-company booklets describing the difference between the 'networking' and the 'continuity' modes. Whereas networkers can work any place, and communicate in from their work stations equipped with personal computer and modem, the continuity people need to reside in a fixed and central abode. Whereas networkers get paid for specific work assignments, according to their output, the continuity people get fixed salaries. Though there are only a hundred or so official networkers on the payroll at the present time, working from an average of one to two days a week for the company, they are a growing influence. Moreover, as part of the 'offshore association', Xanadu, they join hands with those ex-employees who have set up their own businesses.

Of course, twenty years before networkers were conceived, Steve Shirley created FPL which has since become F, for Flexible, International. Steve, who craved for flexibility herself, as a wife, mother and computer programmer in the early days, has created a whole organization that is centred upon flexibility. 'Our working mothers can choose what time they work,' their publicity manager told me. 'They fit their job around their life. If your personal circumstances change, the company will always try to meet it by providing alternative work opportunities.' Of course, F is very unusual in having institutionalized flexibility. That is, in fact, what has made it unique. Most small businesses that excel are just naturally fleet of foot. As they grow larger, they have to create deliberate project-based and *ad hoc* structures in order to build in a means of responding rapidly to change. Finally, as exemplified by Rank Xerox, a whole new breed of networkers is introduced, to legitimize flexibility in patterns of work, as well as patterns of response to markets and technologies. Both F International and Rank Xerox have helped us to rethink the whole question of employment.

FLAIR/AUTONOMY/ENTERPRISE

ENTREPRENEURIAL FLAIR

Flexibility is not the same as enterprise, though the two have 'fleet-footedness' in common. For long we have lamented the waning of 'the spirit of enterprise' in Great Britain. Of course, all too few politicians recognize where that spirit actually comes from.

I can clearly remember Joe. Joe was Caribbean, a smooth talker and a sharp shooter. During his twenty-three years, prior to my having met him, he had hardly ever had more than two pennies to rub together. When we bumped into each other Joe was intent on getting in on the drinks dispenser market. This is the way he put it. 'I've got a goal, to build a business. It's achieving something. It just happens to be drinks dispensers. It's something I can do now. There's a market for it. I'm willing to take the risk. Ain't got much to lose. It's hit or bust.' In fact, on this occasion, Joe went bust. But he has now got involved with selling saunas, for the time being more successfully.

Another friend, Tad, is a Pole, who studied fish farming and decided there was more money in other things. Besides, his father, originally a professional man, had fled from Poland and had become a manual worker in this country. Tad was determined to prove himself, to regain his family's pride, to assert their real worth. When I met him he was considering getting into the computer accessories market. 'My goal is to make £1000 a week. But my problem is that I want to offer a wide range, and yet I don't have the money to carry the stock.' As a sober professional, I explained to Tad, at the time, that he was taking a high-risk approach. He could build up more slowly. This was his response. 'I can't afford a low-risk approach. I want to go it alone. I have to go in deep.' That is entrepreneurship for you. Tad is one of these aliens who are willing to have a go. Where would Britain's economic base be without such people, all foreign, displaced, insecure, entrepreneurial?

Iona Eichner, who runs Interlingua's Far Eastern office, is another person who displays much confidence, for good reason. 'The three of us older kids spent a year in French and then in German schools. We gained a kind of exposure as a result. I find the differences between people exciting rather than frightening. I know I will always fall on my feet.'

Iona loved the period she spent in Hong Kong, though she is now based in Singapore. 'We bought out this translations company in 1979. It was above a night club. "Bottoms Up" it was called, with pictures of bottoms in various parts of the window. I loved the business. I slapped it into shape, multiplying the profit five times in a couple of years.'

AUTONOMY AND ENTREPRENEURSHIP

Entrepreneurship is not restricted to new beginnings or to small businesses like Interlingua. There is a place for it in the larger company. Racal Electronics is a good case in point. Its chairman, Ernie Harrison, encourages what Peters and Waterman call 'autonomy and entrepreneurship'. There is a somewhat different flavour to it, though, as we shall see. It's not quite the same thing as starting a totally new business from scratch.

Mike Eyre, the research director of Information Technology Development, is what I call an 'enabler'. He is enabling a group of youngsters, being himself a technical man of some twenty years' experience, to create a new Racal venture. 'When I joined', Mike told me, 'there was a desk, a filing cabinet, and nothing else. Pete, our marketing director, and I sat there and looked across the desk at the empty spaces. Our highest priority was to attract entrepreneurs and creative innovators with the right technical background. The people who have joined us want to change the world. We've got a challenge.' These young technical 'change-agents' are hungry, psychologically, but not physically. Mike has placed a lot of emphasis on creating a physical and social environment which encourages autonomy on the one hand, but provides a community feeling on the other.

SPIRIT OF ENTERPRISE

Of course, once we reach up to the mature corporation, entrepreneurship goes through yet another metamorphosis. Peter Parker put it particularly starkly to me when describing his terms of office in British Rail.

At British Rail I was hugely exposed. It's like living in a piranha bowl! Bringing the reality of the marketplace into the political context of a nationalized industry is like creating a New Testament. Sometimes, of course, you have to fight, and by jingo if you do, you do. My approach is to take consultation as far as I can, and then, if you have to, it's war. I used to tell the politicians that if they wanted to take over negotiations, they could, but as long as I was in the driving seat, they couldn't tell me what to do.

So, as the business evolves and grows in size and scope, entrepreneurship is gradually transformed. The hunger for survival and achievement, in a very concrete and physical sense, is replaced by an urge to display initiative, exercise autonomy, and achieve psychological more than financial success. As we then gravitate towards a British Rail we are talking of the creation of 'a New Testament', in order to develop a new spirit of entreprise. That 'spirit' has to stretch across a much wider band of space and time than is the case for the individual entrepreneur. It has less gut feel to it, and more in the way of subtle influence.

SIMPLE FORM/LOOSE-TIGHT/COMPLEX

SIMPLE FORM, LEAN STAFF

Subtlety is indeed the name of the game when it comes to organization structure. In the early stage of a business's life it is improvised, and even, as Michael Eichner said of his parents, 'seat of the pants' or instinctive. Essentially, what is required in an excellent organization is a structure which is crisp and spare, unencumbered by hierarchy or complexity. Financial controls should be few and simple, but well specified. Delegation will inevitably be limited, but, in its limited context, it should be clear cut.

LOOSE-TIGHT PROPERTIES

As the organization develops, then the 'simultaneous loose-tight' properties need to come into play. Although, for example, Sinclair Research now has a properly constituted headquarters and management team, the loose-tight balance remains all-important. The director of overseas sales, Charles Cotton, put it very well. 'In each of our overseas operations', he said, 'we shall do our best to engender a situation where there's a little bit of Sinclair magic in each. They'll be mirror images of ourselves, not a blur of people in a complicated organization chart.'

Bob Latin runs the information technology section of STC's research department. Bob is not only a technologist with some vision, but he also thinks very actively about matters organizational. The way he maintains a loose-tight balance is by imposing an individualized business discipline.

> My division is run like a business, with a difference. All my people are encouraged to see themselves as a commercial entity. In other words, their personal security must ultimately depend on their marketability, and not upon their status in the organization. They need to see themselves, individually, like a multifunctional division, or like a product with high reliability.

In a more conventional sense Habitat/Mothercare's organization epitomizes that balance between centralization and decentralization. Ian Peacock, its financial director, both reflects and also supplements Terence Conran's own views on organization:

> Philosophically, I always think small. The more independent the better. It makes for *esprit de corps* and a sense of togetherness. It attracts better people and helps maximize profits. So we push authority as far as we can down the line, provided all remains consistent with overall group strategy and policy.

Once we move from the Habitat/Mothercares of this world towards the very large and mature corporations then we have a further shift, even a transformation. The modern corporation is indeed a very complex phenomenon, and it needs a structure that can reflect it. I have to say that I have not yet met a corporate leader who has attempted to create one.

COMPLEX STRUCTURE

One such leader who has at least begun to get to grips with the problem is Sir Adrian Cadbury, chairman of Cadbury Schweppes. He is a firm believer in 'sticking to the knitting', but has given much thought to the point of corporate structure in an evolving society. 'You need flexibility', he says, 'in responding to the heightened desire of "individuals" to live their own kind of life.' John Harvey-Jones expresses a similar viewpoint, but the implications of both are yet to be resolved. For neither has put forward a model of individuals' personalities to work on.

Let me emphasize, though, that when a company develops from youth to adulthood to maturity, its organizational attributes need to be progressively transformed. Starting off with a simple form and lean staff, and subsequently developing loose-tight properties, it then needs to assume even more complex form. The four major case studies should help us appreciate this.

INTUITION/DESIGN/EVOLUTION

The discussion I had with Adrian Cadbury, and have had since with innumerable students, mentors and clients, revolves around corporate evolution. In the early days of a company's life, of course, we don't refer to evolution, but to growth and development. All too few of us understand what business development actually involves. One of my business partners, Ken Jenkins, is an exception to the rule.

PERSONAL SENSITIVITY AND INTUITION

Ken was in middle to senior management with Shell before he decided, on turning fifty, to go out on his own. He started out in warehousing and distribution, and has since branched out into the engineering industry. Most of his interests are in the area of environmental engineering, and the companies with which he is involved do business all over the world. He still operates, in a sense, as a one-man band, an enabler, a genuine business developer. 'I take buildings, products, companies and people, all of whose potential is not being realized, and help them fulfil it. I'm a builder rather than an entrepreneur, I'm a capitalizer, not a capitalist. I recombine assets rather than strip them. I realize potential rather than exploit it. I'm in the building business, though it's not buildings I construct.'

Ken is an engineer by training, a manager through experience, and a gentleman in his approach. 'Financial analysis is okay, and I'm pretty good at it, but it must form part of a greater whole.

Take the three people I met last night. One was going bankrupt with the bank foreclosing on his house, and the others just didn't know what to do with themselves. But they do have a flooring company which is full of potential. Nothing will happen without me. To start with, I'll instil some confidence by putting up some of my money. Then I'll draw out a plan; lay some foundations. That's how I begin to produce a new situation out of an old one. I can bring something out, and let it grow. Perhaps it's the gardener in me.'

Ken is part of a growing number of enablers, in business and in the community, who, in the mature phase of their lives and having personally evolved, are in a good position to help new and small businesses do the same. Ken also said:

> Lark Engineering is descaling products. Quality Environments, the record company in which I'm involved, is improving environments. My property company is engaged in small-scale renovation. Turnpike Services conserves and rechannels merchandise, through warehousing and distribution. New Work Ventures, in which you and I are involved, enables people and companies to create new ventures. There's a theme there somewhere, don't you think?

DESIGN AND WHOLENESS

Building up businesses is an invaluable and poorly articulated activity. Conventional wisdom focuses on information, training and consultancy and not on construction. Knowledge of how to develop people, products and enterprises, in an integrated way, is rare indeed. In that sense, designers are a very much underutilized resource. For they are so often able to appreciate not only how to realize potential but also how things come together as a whole. John Stephenson, Habitat/Mothercare's design and marketing director, is a very good example. He conveyed his role to me like this:

> I have a hackneyed phrase. The merchandise is the message. I have a laid-back approach to marketing and design. I mustn't

get in the way of the merchandise. Or, to put it another way, design, merchandising and promotion must be seen as a whole.

So enhancing the product is what really counts, obtaining harmony of performance between what Oliver Gregory, head of design at Habitat/Mothercare, calls 'the stars of the show' – that is, the products – and the surrounding players – that is, the functions of business. 'My role is to connect it all,' Rob Margetts, research director of ICI's Agricultural Division, told me, 'Technology, customers, organization. I have to harness the full potential of these separate parts in order to develop the whole.'

Although designers are usually associated with physical things, their way of thinking can extend towards people and businesses, as Mary Quant indicated to me:

> All my designs relate to each other in endless variation. It's the way I think, moving diagonally, circling or curving. It's a female approach, although I notice a lot of successful men have it. That's the way our company works, allowing people to cross over diagonally, from one position to another, as the opportunity arises, ensuring a pattern of integrated development.

One of the successful men Mary may have been alluding to is Fred Eichner, chess player and cofounder of Interlingua.

> A game of chess, like many games including business, is a game of construction. To capture a queen you advance your pieces, but you have to anticipate your opponent's move. It's a slow and gradual process, but when it succeeds, it is a process of great beauty.

In the early days of business then, there is a distinctive 'building' function involved, which a few people, like Ken Jenkins, have articulated. As the business grows into a Habitat/Mothercare or a Mary Quant, organization design becomes necessary and desirable, especially if the principles of harmony and synergy are heeded. Corporate evolution is one more step beyond that.

Bob Malpas, chairman of New Ventures and board member in British Petroleum, is someone who has a particular grasp of such evolution. Bob is an engineer and ex-ICI man who also has a powerful grasp of conceptual issues. 'People in high places', Bob told me, 'can see across the whole company, its businesses, its functions and territories. We can, with this privileged helicopter view, pollenize and catalyse the glimmerings of vision that occur in diverse quarters.' Bob has in fact appointed Don Braden as head of his Ventures Research Unit to discover, and prospectively harness, the potential of those industries which will rise to great heights in the next fifty years. 'Unless you lead people', Bob told me, 'towards the perception that technology is a major tool to create new options for the future, the fruits of research cannot ripen. My role is to identify, with others, where glimmers of vision lie, articulate them, and then put weight behind them.'

At Bob Malpas's level, and within a company the size of BP, the words 'catalyst' or 'enabler' appear inadequate. Even organization design is too limited. For what is involved is the entire evolution of the corporation, technically, commercially and socially. This social aspect is more Peter Parker's concern than Malpas's, albeit in a different context. 'No enterprise is an island,' Parker proclaimed vehemently. 'You can't make a feast of economic recovery while 364 million people are unemployed. You've got to be socially sensitive and individually responsive.'

CREATIVITY/INNOVATION/RENEWAL

Finally, we come to that most fundamental and yet rare set of characteristics: creation activity, in the pioneering enterprise; innovation, in the managed organization; and renewal, in the developing corporation.

CREATIVE ACTIVITY

When I cast my mind over creative business activity, in a pioneering sense, I think of Mary Quant. She told me how, twenty years ago, 'for the first time, the young grasped the opportunity to get together, and to start businesses for their peers. We made every mistake, businesswise, in the book. But we went from one coffee bar to two or three. They became centres for architects, painters, tarts, con men! Our next step was to expand into all sorts of different product areas, to persuade people to make their products in different ways.'

We now know the result – the cosmetics, the dresses, the bed linen that Mary Quant has since designed. 'My eye', she says, 'just keeps finding new combinations. I love to juxtapose the bold with the delicate, the old with the new.' That sort of personal creativity is shared by Fred Eichner, Clive Sinclair, Zandra Rhodes and a select band of business pioneers who are suitably inspired. Terence Conran has been another, but in his case he advanced from creative design of his own furniture products to managed innovation within his company.

MANAGED INNOVATION

Managed innovation at Habitat/Mothercare takes place through its prolific design group. Oliver Gregory, head of design, told me, 'We understand the prime motive almost instinctively. If you think of the great innovators, they had unwavering direction. They produced style, an image. They had integrity, simplicity, dedication and attention to detail.'

The management of innovation is a subject much studied, from idea generation to project implementation, from vision to action, from creative invention to product championing and project control. Mike Eyre, research director at Racal's Information Technology Development, and a computer scientist of considerable experience, told me, 'In the early days you invent something. Gene Andahl was such an "architect", of the IBM 360. You need determination and imagination. Most people will tell you that you're wrong. After that comes the intermediate design task. You have decided you want to build a cathedral in Gothic style, seating seven hundred, at location X, painted sun yellow outside! Then you bring in the engineers and programmers and get on with implementation.'

CORPORATE RENEWAL

John Gardner, secretary of state for health and welfare in Kennedy's period of presidency, wrote a fascinating book entitled *Self-Renewal*. In it, he lamented the fact that innovation was so narrowly and technologically conceived. Composers and statesmen could be as innovative as scientists, not to mention business leaders!

In the spring of 1983, John Harvey-Jones was interviewed by the editor of *ICI Magazine*. The resulting article was entitled 'Metamorphosis'. In it ICI's chairman said, 'The industrial problem is that a company has to renew itself. The world is littered with the remains of once private and powerful companies that are now just names. . . . They failed to make sure they were continuously renewing themselves . . .'

Renewal, metamorphosis and transformation take things a step further than does evolution. It involves radical change, a quantum leap. John Dessauer, who was research director at Xerox Corporation, declared the innovator to be a revolutionary. Management's challenge was to handle such revolution. It involves, on the one hand, a return to the roots of the corporation's being and, on the other, the intervention of a 'rascal intelligence' that causes unpredictable leaps into a new level of integration between the business and its environment. In ten to fifteen years we may see Sinclair's electric cars in that light. ICI, by the turn of the century, may have transcended the chemical industry and landed somewhere else. Already, it has transformed itself from an 'imperial' into an 'international' business.

We have come all the way from individual activity to social evolution. In between and including the two are the characteristics of businesses that excel. Each of seven characteristics are represented, but transformed, as we move through the three main stages of business development. So 'hard work' (small business) turns into 'hands-on' (managed organization), turns into physical and human 'energy' (corporation). Similarly 'closeness to the customer', and indeed to the employee, turns into a coherent 'culture' and then into a 'community of interests'. 'Fleet-footedness' becomes 'flexible communications', becomes 'learning and information systems'. Entrepreneurial flair turns into 'autonomy and entrepreneurship', and then the 'spirit of enterprise'. An improvised structure becomes a 'simple form' and then a complex structure. Hunch and intuition turns into 'design for wholeness' before turning into conscious, 'evolutionary development'. Personal creativity becomes managed innovation which turns into corporate transformation or renewal.

So much, then, for the general characteristics of excellence, at each phase of a business's development. For the individual features underlying excellent performance in a particular country – in this case Britain – we need to turn towards our roots and towards the soil in which British business is rooted.

4. The Foundations of Excellence

The phases of business development are general. Roots are particular. For Peters and Waterman, such roots are to be found within the myths and rituals, and the shared values of the corporation. I take a somewhat different stand. For me, the deepest and most substantial roots lie firstly within the person – the business's creator, secondly within the product or service he creates and, thirdly, within the whole society of which he or it is a part. As a business matures, so the roots should spread from one to the other, remaining and developing the source, the origin, the true identity of the business.

PERSONAL IDENTITY

Many people starting up in business fail to reach down to the source of their inspiration. Brian was one person who didn't fail. He was a systems analyst in his fifties who wanted to branch out on his own, but initially lacked the courage and conviction. Eventually I helped him to reach down to the roots of his own personal motivation.

> When I was a child, just after the war, I used to amble through the streets of London, all bombed out and rubble. People were destitute. Businessmen were stillborn. Things seemed out of control. All that science which had gone into the war effort – what could we do with it now? I had to do something with it, to construct, to benefit, to solve, to harness technology.

Brian went on to set up in computer consultancy, with new conviction, but without the depth of imagination that Mary Quant had.

Mary Quant is one of the most magnetic personalities I have ever met. Her insight and gentleness draw you into her imaginative world:

> As a child, I didn't like stiffness or artificiality. I didn't want to grow up. I wanted people around me to move, run, dance. The image came to me first when I was eight. A tap dancer with a bullet haircut, wearing black tights, black shirt, black patent leather shoes and white socks. This black-and-white image branded my mind. That was it. It stuck with me for ever.

Now women all over the world buy the cosmetics, clothing, bed linen, wallpaper and stationery that have become the branch products of that root image. 'What I'm doing now', Mary assured me, 'I dreamt about as a child.'

As we have seen, Interlingua's roots, like Mary Quant's, also reach down to its founder's early childhood and social background.

CULTURAL IDENTITY

Once an organization grows to a certain size, it becomes very concerned with its 'culture'. It needs to root its seed idea in something beyond an individual personality. Terence Conran achieved just that when he progressed from Conran, the furniture designer and manufacturer, to Habitat. Through its collective and individual products, it has become totally distinctive, in a form that can be separated from its founder. 'The Habitat look', as Sir Terence has said, 'has gathered an increasing number of converts, as their eye becomes educated to appreciate simple and imaginative furnishing. Now, not only in furnishing, but also in toys and clothing, we are making good design accessible to everyone.'

Another company which has recently developed a distinctive and revitalized image in Britain is Rank Xerox International.

Hamish Orr Ewing, its chairman, has not only played an active part in public life but has also underpinned his company's recent moves into 'networking' by declaring:

- we must be adaptive rather than rigid
- we must enhance individual contributions
- we must enhance creativity
- we must be organic and involve people

In fact Orr Ewing, who has broad-minded views on business organization, has gone further.

We must, in Britain, rejoice in our individualism rather than attempt, and fail, by listening to the siren song of some other expert in Japan. If we are to compete, we must do so in a way that builds upon our cultural history and our psychology.

This brings me to the last, and most fundamental consideration of roots, at least insofar as Great Britain is concerned. For one of my main concerns has been to uncover deeply embedded roots of excellence in British, if not also in European, soil. After reading a number of economic and social histories of this country, I have come to the conclusion that four such roots are particularly in evidence: a creativity in the arts and science, a spirit of tolerance, individual eccentricity and a pursuit of quality. The four excellent companies which draw markedly on each of these roots are, respectively, Habitat/Mothercare, ICI, Sinclair Research and F International.

THE UNIVERSAL IDENTITY

Let me start with Conran, creativity and Habitat. Not surprisingly, Conran has spread his wings from manufacturing into retailing, and from Britain across to Europe, America and Japan. By now, as marketing director of Habitat (UK), Tony Maynard, puts it, 'We feel that we're part of a major, influential change in the human environment.'

So Conran has evolved a universal identity that is rooted in the creative pursuits of the whole of European civilization. Although Habitat/Mothercare is a relatively young group, it draws on a long-standing tradition. Over the past thirty years, Terence Conran has kept closely in touch, not only with the principles and practices of design, but also with the social and economic evolution of this country.

Tony Maynard's statement should, in fact, characterize our major corporations rather than the small and middle-sized company. As we develop from an individual's personal vision to a strong product identity, to something else beyond, we begin to confront the power and influence of the mighty corporations. Yet this originating source, or 'universe corporate', is something other than political or even economic power *per se*. How then do we characterize it?

Bob Malpas, research director at BP, gives us a clue. 'We must', he told me, 'become better explorers. For example, there is much to be done yet to convert difficult hydrocarbons, such as methane and heavy oils, into usable liquids such as gasoline and gas oil.' The vision of exploration, which stretches from the South Pole to outer space, has a power and a ring to it that extends beyond oil, automobiles or even biotechnology. It is rooted in man's distant past and in his foreseeable future. It is a recurring theme in all the great mythology, ranging from Icarus flying to the sun, to Orpheus in the underworld. It is an urge that possessed the founders of ICI, Alfred Nobel and Ludwig Mond, when they crossed the known scientific and technological frontiers of their day. In ICI's case, their inspiration virtually gave birth to a whole industry in this country.

THE CREATIVE GROUND

The 'corporate universe' arises from, not only the individual and his product or service, but also the whole community in which the business's foundations have been laid. The particularly British ground is what I now want to explore. The four areas in our soil that I have found to be particularly rich in nutrients are:

- creative enterprise
- a love of recreation
- a cult of individualism
- tolerance for diversity

Bernard Nossiter, an American journalist on the *Washington Post*, was one of the few people who wrote a book in the seventies which praised the United Kingdom rather than dismissing it. Nossiter, echoing prevailing opinion at the time – if not still today – wrote that 'Britons, to the dismay of most textbook writers, prefer tea breaks and long executive lunches, slower assembly lines and longer week ends to strenuous effort to realize higher incomes.' However, he then went on: 'This does not apply to all Britons, to countless craftsmen and artists, writers, film makers, those who work in the theatre, paint pictures, toil in the laboratories, or direct great department stores – those for whom work is a joyful, creative form of expression.'

Funnily enough, if we go back into pre-history, we find that Britons' love of metals, as well as of craftwork, goes back to the Celts and the Saxons. No wonder the most common name in Great Britain is Smith! In fact, Walt Rostow, the American economic historian, has attributed the Industrial Revolution to our combined industrial and artistic heritage. He claims that it was 'the organized creativity of the human mind', most pronounced in the Britain of the seventeenth and eighteenth centuries, that made all the difference. First there was the philosophical impact of Newton's new synthesis. 'Men were given a new sense of power and confidence, that there was a new order to be found.' But, second, and equally important, was the two-way linkage between scientists and toolmakers, on the one hand, and the lack of specialization, on the other. Physicists and chemists, such as Franklin and Priestley, were in intimate contact with the leading figures in British industry, like James Watt and Josiah Wedgwood.

The division between the arts and the sciences in the Victorian era was also less clear cut than many see it today. The great engineers, like Brunel, were creating veritable works of 'art' without ever realizing it, in the form of railway tunnels, magnificent bridges and other engineering works. When Charles Babbage, the father of modern computing, linked up with mathematician Ada Lovelace, the mother of contemporary computer programming, he found himself working alongside the poet Byron's daughter!

Businessmen and politicians in this country are preoccupied with our failure to exploit our natural inventiveness. There is a long history of inventors and inventions, from Babbage and computing, to Gabor and holography, to Crick, the discoverer of DNA and biotechnology, whose British inventions have been exploited abroad, primarily in America. We all know about the high proportion of Nobel prize winners in the sciences that are British. But we quickly go on to lament how little we have profited, commercially, from them.

All too often, in our orgy of self-criticism, we ignore the fact that if you consider creative activity across the board – science and technology, art and design, theatre and music, film and television, humour and entertainment, leisure software and interactive video – the picture becomes a much rosier one. In fact, having gone through a lean era in the past one hundred years, we are now finding that British design, in fashion, in furnishing, in art and sculpture, in advertising and in graphics, in leisure software if not hardware, is now leading the world. Interestingly enough, Terence Conran, probably the leading figure in the revitalization of industrial design, enjoyed organic chemistry as much as craft subjects at school. Design links the arts and the sciences, product and market, technology and business. It is for that reason that I have selected Conran's Habitat/Mothercare, to uncover the roots of creativity.

RECREATIONAL GROUND

While companies like BP and ICI have recently decided to consolidate their image as explorers and pathfinders, Clive Sinclair has probably captured the public imagination in Great Britain more than anyone else in this respect. However, perhaps it is not so much as an explorer that he has captivated our hearts and minds, but as something quite different.

Tony Tyler, editor of *Big 'K'*, the computer magazine for youngsters, and himself an eccentric, put it this way:

Industry doesn't have a good name among youngsters. In that sense Sinclair is a maverick. He is not seen as part of the establishment. He is perceived as being in a class of his own. The British teenager's adeptness in computing is almost entirely due to him. One and a half million kids bought the Spectrum.

He undercuts, he goes his own route. Sinclair's a bit like a Freddie Laker or a Richard Branson; except he's more of a comic book character, the cold genius with a hugely domed forehead!

Sinclair is a self-made man, not only in a business sense, but because he educated himself too. Although something of a technical genius, he still has that air of the gifted amateur about him.

Britain has been condemned more often than praised for holding on to the tradition of the gifted amateur. Students go off to Oxbridge, study classics, and then enter the hurly-burly of the City. Yet it is a tradition that this country would do well not to lose. To give you a flavour of the type, let me introduce you to William Caxton, who created a printing revolution in 1474. 'Caxton', according to the economic and social historian G.S. Trevelyan, 'was an early and prominent example of a well-known modern type, the individualistic Englishman following out his own hobbies. As a successful merchant he made enough money during thirty years to devote his later life to the literary pursuits he loved. Caxton began by translating French books into English. While so engaged he fell in love with the mystery of printing with movable types.' Thereafter, Caxton created the country's first printing press and, in the last fourteen years of his life, 'did much, as translator, printer and publisher, to lay the foundations of literary English'.

Many, many Britons have followed in Caxton's footsteps. Hobbies, leisure and recreation take place outside of obligatory work, but well within pleasurable occupations. Again, Bernard Nossiter sums things up very nicely. Commenting on the supposed preference that the British have for leisure over work, he argues: 'The preference for leisure over goods applies chiefly to those labouring over routine or arduous tasks. This work cannot, does not enlarge personality; quite the contrary, it diminishes it. They work because they must, to earn enough to support themselves and their families.' Nossiter then maintains that people engaged in non-routine, challenging and meaningful activity, be it called 'leisure' or 'work', do get deeply involved. I call this sort of activity, in the home, the factory, the community, or the office, 'recreation'.

GROUNDS FOR INDIVIDUALITY

Though Sinclair is very much an individual, his organization has not been designed to cater specifically for the individuality of his employees. In many ways it is still run as a small business, with the innovator and entrepreneur at the centre, and a small group of managers around him. F International, by contrast, prides itself on its F-lexibility. Its basic reason for being is to enable women to shape their work around their lives, rather than vice versa.

Great Britain is a mecca for the individual. Whereas the Americans, like the Japanese, are extremely good at teamwork, the British like to do their own thing. Individuality and entrepreneurship do not necessarily go together. For the latter demands a kind of commitment that is often antithetical to the freelance, freewheeling, free spirit. In fact, no less an establishment source than the Conservative Office in 1949, in prescribing 'The Right Road for Britain', came up with the following lofty sentiments:

> Man is a spiritual creature adventuring on an immortal destiny, and science, politics and economics are good or bad so far as they help or hinder the individual soul on its eternal journey.

This may all sound rather far-fetched, but the roots of individuality do stretch a long way back. In the fourteenth century the feudal manor and the hierarchical structure of English society were already beginning to break down. The English village was gradually transformed from a community of serfs to a society of free men. Of course, many of the serfs won this freedom at the price of divorce from the soil. Ironically, it could be argued today that factory and mine workers are winning their freedom from physical labour at the price of a divorce from employment.

In the fifteenth and sixteenth centuries, cottage industry and the guild system flourished. Yet, in the two centuries thereafter, with the rise of merchant capitalism, a new individualism emerged. It had something to do with the breakdown of feudalism, and the rise of individual freedom, but capitalism had even more to do with a new kind of emerging self-interest. Individual, free enterprise was born, but, as Trevelyan puts it:

A rampant individualism, inspired by no idea beyond quick monetary returns, set up a cheap and nasty model of modern industrial life. Man acquired formidable tools for refashioning his life before he had given the least thought to the question of what sort of life it might be well for him to fashion.

Free enterprise has almost always had a double edge to it in Great Britain, although personal freedom, at least for the last hundred years, has been dearly cherished. This is nowhere more clearly in evidence than in the Englishman's relationship to his garden. British vegetable gardens are the most highly cultivated of any agricultural areas in the world. Gardens are a place of refuge, and an outlet through which the individual expresses his personality.

GROUNDS FOR TOLERANCE

Sinclair's business, in organization if not in sales turnover, is still a small one. F International and Habitat/Mothercare have developed, organizationally, to a level of greater complexity. But when we come to ICI we take a further leap, qualitatively as well as quantitatively. For a mature and multinational manufacturing enterprise needs particularly strong roots, or foundations, in order to survive. If you ask senior management at ICI, they would argue that it is their 'seam of technology' which comprises their roots, and underlying British inventiveness which is their nourishment. For me, the roots of ICI's excellence lie in its tolerance for diversity, and fortunately, although sometimes we may be led to believe quite the opposite, Great Britain has a long-standing tradition in tolerating diversity. In my opinion, the company will develop successfully into the twenty-first century, providing it can accommodate a very wide diversity of technologies, individuals and nationalities.

Out of the very marginality, diversity and spirit of tolerance within Britain emerges an international society and economy. Britain should be better placed than most, certainly better than the Americans or Japanese, to develop the multinational enterprises that are so characteristic of our day and age. Our cultural heritage, even geographical positioning, our international language, and the City of London, all point in the same direction.

Sadly, my own experience has led me to believe that often the Roman or Norman in us – the rule of law, and the imposition of uniformity – overshadows our Celtic or Viking spirit of creativity and enterprise. ICI, within its overall spirit of tolerance, still has maddening examples of stultifying bureaucracy. The same applies to every university within which I have worked. This imposed uniformity goes all too often against the natural grain. The British are by no means as disciplined organizationally as the Germans, the Swedes, the Swiss, the Japanese or even the Americans, although we do occasionally come across a company like Marks and Spencer which proves to be the exception rather than the rule.

The challenge for British business, and especially for the maturer companies, is to give full expression to our diverse heritage, and to outgrow the uniformity of the managed organization. There is no better staging ground, upon which this conflict between uniformity and diversity can be worked out, than ICI. Started by a Swedish entrepreneur and a German innovator, it was then spurred on by a power-hungry Scotsman, Harry McGowan, into an era of unprecedented expansion. Upon McGowan's retirement it entered a long period of managed uniformity. Today, with its charismatic new chairman, it is reemerging, to spearhead a new form of tolerance for technological, personal, social and cultural diversity.

The roots of a tree, or business, lie closest to the soil, or the environment. In the smaller business, those roots may be widely spread, but not yet deeply set. So the pioneer's identity will comprise much of the roots' substance. That is the case with Sinclair. His personal inspiration has combined with the fertile recreational soil in this country, and the bedrock of electronic technology, to produce Sinclair Research. In Steve Shirley's case, however, the company's roots are already more deeply set, as is also the case for Conran. So the individualistic and creative environment is exercising a great influence on the emerging cultural identity.

Finally, in ICI's case, the fertile soil, the grounds for diversity – chemically, economically, socially – exercise a profound influence on the composition of the roots. They create a large part of the corporate universe, the business's cosmopolitan reason for being. But let us investigate further, starting with Sinclair.

5. Sinclair Research

Education of an Entrepreneur

1950–57   Sinclair pursued, as a schoolboy, his electronics hobbies. Left school to follow his own path.

1962   Sinclair Radionics was born, to produce radio kits.

1962–80   The company grew to four hundred people, and eventually ran into financial difficulties.

1979   The National Enterprise Board stepped in, and decided to pursue the electronic instruments field.

1979   Clive established Sinclair Research, to pursue the home computing field.

Birth and Growth of Sinclair Research

1980   The world's cheapest computer, the ZX80, was launched.

1981   The new and improved ZX81 came on the market.

1982   The Spectrum, designed to be a major extension of Sinclair's computer range, was launched.

1983   The flat-screen TV – the first one with a single chip for circuitry – was introduced.

Loosely Controlled Expansion of the Company

1983   A loose management structure was established.

1984   The Quantum Leap was launched – only a partial success.

1984   The £4 million advertising campaign was initiated.

1985   Sinclair's first electric car was manufactured and sold, initially at least, intermittently.

Managerial Consolidation

1985   Downturn in the personal computer market.

1985   Robert Maxwell takes over the management of the company, appointing a new chief executive.
1985   Sinclair becomes life president, taking over R and D, and withdrawing from active management.
1985   Maxwell backs down and Sinclair seeks alternative form of consolidation.

Sinclair Research: a Pioneering Enterprise

TOLERANT GROUNDS

Sinclair Research is our first excellent company. Though still a small business in form, at least until June 1985, it has made an enormous impact in Great Britain. Sinclair has become something of a legend, a hero in the classical sense, who has undergone innumerable trials and tribulations along his magnificent journey.

Now his company has been taken over by Robert Maxwell. The reasoning behind the takeover was provided by the *Financial Times* (18 June):

> Sinclair Research was until recently a remarkable success story. In 1980 it became the first company in the world to launch a computer which cost less than £100 – at that time an exceptional price. Since then, it has sold over 5m computers worldwide. The company's problems stem from the weakening of the British home computer market which still accounted for a majority of its sales.

As I followed the temporary demise of the home computer market I was, at first, filled with despair. What would happen to our folk hero? When Robert Maxwell took over the ownership of the company, that is, 85 per cent of the shares, I wondered where this would all lead. At first I thought that, invigorated by foreign blood, Sinclair was entering fertile British grounds, from which the roots of excellence of all the companies in this book have sprung. But it was not to be. In August 1985 Maxwell pulled out, ostensibly because operation. Whether he will eventually succeed or fail is open to question, but his story is still worth telling. If the British public and, in particular, the British community do not find a way of accomodating his style of operation, Britain will not have a very bright future. If, as the months go by, Sinclair does not maintain his development, root and branch, we need to ask ourselves not only what went wrong but what we could in Britain have done to help.

INDIVIDUALITY AND ECCENTRICITY

It's this English thing, the historical eccentricity, that produces originality and more. That's why Britain is a leader in games software. It's culturally rich.

Tony Tyler, editor of *Big 'K'*

In a matter of five years, Clive Sinclair has become a household name. Representing the spirit of eccentricity and recreation, he has won over thousands of young converts in his native land through the excitement generated by his product. Moreover, because of his creative genius and farsightedness, he has had as much influence on the country's social and economic development as such larger characters as the chairmen of ICI or BP. Bearded and twinkle eyed, he is readily recognizable in the newspapers, and some look to him, in particular, to cure our 'economic ills'. Finally, in a corporate context, he is seen as very much the antithesis of organization man, and much more the representative of thousands of individual citizens, particularly those who are male and in their teens, and who love to play, to tinker and to 'recreate'.

THE AGE OF RECREATION

One and a half million kids bought the Spectrum. They know it like an old guitar. Their adeptness is due to Sinclair.

Nicky Xikluna, computer journalist

Sinclair Research is not a large company. True enough, it has grown very rapidly, from nothing to a turnover of £100 million in five

SINCLAIR
A PIONEERING ENTERPRISE

BRANCHES

BRANCHES

ENTREPRENEURIAL FLAIR
'Clive reads a research paper, applies the Sinclair cooking to it, and comes up with a product that sells.'

IMPROVISED FORM
'In each of our overseas subsidiaries, we'll engender a bit of Sinclair magic.'

MENTAL AGILITY
'Clive's a real time operator. The minute an idea pops in his head he takes it further.'

HUNCH and INTUITION
'Clive's real strength is that he is able to sense there will be a market for 'X' million, often without justification.'

PERSONAL CONTACTS
'We avoid doing business with people we don't like.'

HARD WORK
'Clive works incredibly hard, but not in a conventional sense.'

CREATIVITY and INVENTIVENESS
'Clive's at his happiest when he's inventing and being creative.'

PIONEERING ENTERPRISE
Sinclair Research

CENTRAL

CORE

PERSONAL IDENTITY
'Sinclair is a maverick. He's not seen as part of the establishment. He's like a comic book character. The cold genius with a hugely domed forehead.'

'We're not as technocratic as the Americans, nor as stylish as the Italians. We're a bridge between the two. As a result we've taken to the Micro.'
DIVERSITY

GROUNDS for BEING

'One and a half million kids bought the Spectrum. They know it like an old guitar.'
RECREATION

'The kids are jumping ahead. They have the urge to create.'
CREATIVITY

'It's this English thing, the historical eccentricity, that produces originality and more.'
INDIVIDUALITY

ROOTS

ROOTS

71

years. But it is still a midget in comparison with the ICIs and even the Habitat/Mothercares of this world. Sinclair's significance as far as *The Roots of Excellence* is concerned lies in attributes that reach far deeper than pure economic performance.

I have referred to 'recreation' as representative of the best in both work and leisure; also to the innate tendency of British people to prefer 'leisure' over goods. I put leisure in quotation marks because I am referring to active recreation, as opposed to the passive frittering away of time. Leisure, therefore, stands in opposition to boring, degrading or apathetic activity, but encompasses creative, joyful and fulfilling work.

Fifty years ago, John Maynard Keynes, perhaps Britain's greatest economist, predicted the part that leisure might play in our society:

We are being afflicted with a new disease of which some readers may not yet have heard the name, but of which they will hear a great deal in the years to come – namely technological unemployment. This means unemployment due to our discovery of means of economizing the use of labour outrunning the pace at which we find new uses for labour. . . . All this means in the long run that mankind is solving its economic problem. . . . I draw the conclusion that, assuming no important wars and no important increase in population, the economic problem may be solved, or be at least within sight of solution, within a hundred years. This means that the economic problem is not – if we look into the future – the permanent problem of the human race. . . .

Will this be a benefit? If one believes at all in the real values of life, the prospect at least opens up the possibility of benefit. Yet I think with dread of the readjustment of the habits and instincts of the ordinary man, bred into him for countless generations, which he may be asked to discard within a few decades. . . .

For many ages to come the old Adam will be so strong in us that everybody will need to do some work if he is to be contented. . . .

When the accumulation of wealth is no longer of high social

importance, there will be great changes in the code of morals. We shall be able to rid ourselves of many of the pseudo-moral principles which have hag-ridden us for two hundred years, by which we have exalted some of the most distasteful of human qualities into the position of the highest virtues. We shall be able to afford to dare to assess the money motive at its true value.

From *Economic Possibilities for our Grandchildren* (1931)

Much more recently I came across a description of an interview given by Isaac Asimov. Asimov, the extraordinarily prolific science and science fiction writer, was giving his views on the future of education:

I feel that once people begin to educate themselves, by way of computerization, they will make missionaries of themselves. Every person who educates himself is not only a student, but also a potential teacher, and an intellectual missionary. There may be in this world a kind of explosion of creativity, as people try to make sure that their own interests are as widespread as possible; perhaps we might call it 'intellectual imperialism'. In a sense, the whole earth is likely to become a university. As to the actual physical structure that now supports the universities – perhaps we will have an upsurge of lecture halls and exhibition halls. Just as one particular use of a structure declines, another will arise. It is hard to look into the future and see it clearly.

Asimov then goes on to reflect upon the world of his dreams:

There was a time in British history, for instance, when the few aristocrats who had landed estates could rely on their world being run by their tenants and servants; they themselves could be dilettantes. My dream is of seeing the earth like that, when it is not unfortunate human beings of the lower classes who run it, but where computerized robots produce the necessary goods, where the population is carefully controlled, and where human beings are then, one and all, intellectual aristocrats, who can count on having the world run, leaving them to be creative. I'm not sure that this is in the least bit possible, but it is my dream.

Finally, he elaborates on his initial vision:

> The kind of world I would like to see is one in which the world's industry is lifted, to the largest extent possible, off the surface of the earth and put into space. We could then have what many people dream of — a pastoral world, free of those dark satanic mills. Yet they would be sited just a few thousand miles up, and we could still benefit from them, while they spew their pollution into outer space from which everything would be swept away into the outer solar wind. Also I would like to see our microscopic forms of life, that are forming the carbohydrates and fats and proteins for us to eat, in large vats out in space where they can get all the energy of the sun, and where they can be purified and treated and sent back to earth as food.
>
> I would like to see people living in space, and having laboratories and observatories out in space. Perhaps earth itself will become the wilderness area, a pleasant place, a garden spot where people can go for vacations, where they can investigate earth's ancient history, where they can see a large, incredibly complex ecology working out. Earth will be no longer the leading edge. It is out in space, in an expanding spatial civilization, which will be the leading edge. Earth will have achieved the retirement it so richly deserves.

From *Futures* (August 1974)

What Sinclair Research is doing needs to be seen within the broad perspective that Asimov provides. For we are witnessing nothing short of an educational and cultural revolution, which a purely economic analysis overlooks.

THE SINCLAIR RESEARCH CORE

PIONEERING ENTERPRISE

Sinclair Research is a pioneering enterprise. It is pioneering in that it has only existed for five years, and Clive Sinclair is still the man at the centre of it all. His personal identity and the company's identity are inextricably interwoven. Sinclair's personal inventiveness, market intuition and personal contacts still play a major part in the company's survival and development. Although a core management team has recently been established, it reflects Sinclair's style rather than imposing a strong structure on him.

But Sinclair Research is a pioneering enterprise with a difference. It has to be, in order to grow to £100 million in sales in five years. The difference is reflected in the marriage of interest between Sinclair and five other parties. First, there is the love affair between him and his customers; mainly, but by no means exclusively, teenagers. Sinclair has truly entered the British tinkering spirit, and so enabled a vast number of small-scale businesses to develop alongside him, providing software and peripherals for his deliberately unfinished products. Secondly, there are the independent entrepreneurs, like David Potter of Psion, who provides much of the software for Sinclair, and Richard Hease, who used to be a major distributor before he went bankrupt. Thirdly, and very importantly, the magazine publishers and the retail outlets, like W.H. Smith, play a major and intimate part in marketing his product. Fourthly, and very significantly, major subcontractors like Timex and Thorn EMI are the manufacturers. Finally, there is Dixon's chief executive himself, and his management muscle.

So Sinclair Research, as a pioneering enterprise with a difference, is driven by a technological entrepreneur with powerful technical and commercial ambitions, but is supported by a whole infrastructure of both 'big' and 'little' people. Sinclair's customers, suppliers, distributors and subcontractors are part of an enterprising community, each one supporting the other.

Sinclair's 'trunk route' lies through this technical, economic and social network, rather than up and down any formal hierarchy. Let us now investigate his business branches.

BRANCH ACTIVITIES

Clive's at his happiest when he's inventing and being creative.
Nigel Searle, managing director of Sinclair Research

CREATIVITY AND INVENTIVENESS

Inevitably, the Sinclair story must start with the man himself. For more than any of our other case histories, even including Habitat/Mothercare, this is a story that revolves around a single individual.

My interest in electronics started at school. I was rather lost in the normal course of school events, and took up a personal interest in the subject. Actually, mathematics came first, as far as the curriculum was concerned. I pursued electronics in my spare time.

I chose not to go on to university because I'd got very tired of academic subjects at school. What I wanted to study wasn't what school wanted to teach me. So I decided I'd rather learn on my own, and follow the path that I naturally chose. Besides, at the time, there weren't any universities specializing in electronics, possibly with one exception. In any case, even if there had been, I was very much wanting to get out into the world and to explore a freer sort of society than school, or even university, provides.

So I became a technical journalist for four years, having left school at seventeen. That took me through to 1962, when I founded my own company, Sinclair Electronics. The first products we produced were radio and amplifier kits, sold by mail order. By 1967, when company turnover had reached £100,000, and the product range included hi-fi systems, I moved to Cambridge. Continued expansion took me to St Ives, in Cornwall, five years later.

In 1972 I launched the 'Executive', the world's first truly pocket calculator. The initial selling price was a then-revolutionary £79! We won several design awards, £2.5 million worth of export revenue, and number one position in the UK calculator market. From 1973 onwards, we invested heavily in R and D for other products, notably digital watches, pocket television and scientific instruments.

Up until 1976 what had now become 'Sinclair Electronics' had enjoyed fifteen years of strong turnover and profit growth. In that year we ran into trouble, as we got into difficulties with chip supplies for our digital watch. As a result we had insufficient internal funds for the final stages of the pocket TV project, and the National Enterprise Board agreed to make a capital injection. The world's first two-inch pocket TV was launched in 1977, together with major additions to our other product ranges. In the instrument field we introduced three new digital millimeters, becoming one of the world's two largest producers in volume terms.

But by 1979, the NEB and myself parted company over future direction. They saw the future in the instrument field, and I believed it lay in consumer electronics. So we divided our interests, and I established Sinclair Research in the consumer electronics field. Sinclair Electronics has continued trading in the instrument field, under a different name.

In February 1980, the new company launched the Sinclair ZX80 personal computer. It was the first computer, worldwide, to sell for less than £100. At the launch, I predicted that its availability would dramatically expand the personal computer market both in the UK and overseas. More than 100,000 were eventually sold, over 60 per cent for export, before production ceased in August 1981.

At that stage, as is the case now, people were not quite sure what to do with their personal computers, but they still wanted to get a feel for them. It's a bit like the old story of 'what good's a baby?'. The personal computer, even now, is very much like that. We know that a child's going to grow up to be something, and there's great excitement in that, a sense of possibility that we don't have – we can't see where it's going. With personal computers I feel just the same thing. We don't attempt to sell them on the basis that you've got to have one. We sell them because they're entertaining and educational things to have. They also enable us to learn about computers, which are affecting our lives after all, more and more.

What I do believe is that the machines that'll follow – we don't know yet what they'll be, but we can have a bit of a glimmering – are going to be invaluable. Not too far in the future we will be able to put a machine into the home that is, in a real sense, intelligent, that can be a general factotum, an adviser, or a mentor.

In March 1981, we introduced the more advanced ZX81, then priced at only £69.95. It has since come down in price by almost half. By the end of 1983 it had sold over a million units worldwide, in more than fifty countries. The further advanced Sinclair Spectrum, designed for a wide range of home and educational applications, was launched a year later. That, in turn, has sold over a million, and has now evolved to become the centre of a comprehensive system. A number of computer peripherals have been developed to enhance its data storage and expansion capacities. Finally, in September 1983, after six years and £4 million development, we launched the flat-screen pocket TV. It now sells for £79.95, by mail order only.

Most recently, in February 1984, we introduced the Quantum Leap. Designed for the serious home, business or educational user, it represents a genuine quantum leap in computing performance, and at £339 costs far less than a comparable machine. I see it as a further step in my plans to create a comprehensive computer range, applicable to a wide variety of markets and users. We are also collaborating with ICL to develop an ultra low-cost, integrated terminal/digital work station.

What I'd like to see, in due course, is a computer which has some sort of personality so that you can go round to it in the morning and talk to it. Maybe it has some sort of face that appears, I don't know, and you can say, 'I'm not feeling well', and it says, 'Well, what's the trouble?' So it can actually act as a doctor, as long as there isn't a severe problem. This kind of possibility excites me enormously. We will never be able to meet the demand for doctors; they are overworked as it is, and the population is continuing to age. So if we can replace at least part of it with a machine, the benefit will be very great.

There is an enormous amount of invention, and gadgetry, that serves no real purpose, and I'm very concerned that we don't produce that. We try to seek a need and meet it. In the case of our machines it's the young people who take to them, particularly. The fourteen-year-olds are quite extraordinary. Programming used to be thought of as a sort of arcane matter. Now it's become the province of children who are superb at it.

Yet, interestingly enough, the other group who have taken to home computing are retired people.

The concept of it just having to be a young mind is, in fact, quite wrong. Perhaps, it's a mind that is free of the burdens of everyday life. The forty-year-old is absorbed in his job all the time, but not the fourteen- or sixty-four-year-old. It's very useful that the retired have found a new interest in life. But it's so important for all of us to keep in touch with the computer revolution.

We've spoken, probably, for the whole of this century, about a coming revolution, and about the end of work and so on. Finally, it has actually happened, because it suddenly has become cheaper to have a machine to do a mental task than for a man to do it. At the moment we're talking of low-level mental activity, but it will increase enormously. Just as men's muscles were replaced in the first industrial revolution, men's minds will be replaced in this second one.

The enormous benefit to society lies, firstly, in removing the vast satanic mills, and the huge conglomerations of people working in close proximity. I personally find such conglomerations frightening and demoralizing. If we do work together, it should be in relatively modest numbers, in sensible sorts of social groupings. But, of course, there won't be many people employed in manufacturing industry as a whole. It will be very slight compared with the numbers today.

That's the sort of change that happened to agriculture. In the beginning of the eighteenth century, we had 70 per cent of the people employed in the land. Now there are literally 2 or 3 per cent. Exactly the same will happen in manufacturing industry. Indeed, ever since the war it has been happening, in that we've just about halved the numbers employed in manufacturing.

The thing is, though, that we're not going to enjoy the sort of society we're creating, unless we can educate people to have a taste for living. There will no longer be the situation where people go to the factory, produce the goods, and come home and fall asleep. For their life to have any richness people will have to develop tastes for the arts, for literature, for poetry, so that in later life they can appreciate the world they live in. That is one of the reasons I have moved, in partnership with Patrick Browne, into publishing. Sinclair Browne only publishes books which progressively approach the problems of contemporary society, either through fiction or non-fiction.

The emphasis in education will have to change, therefore, from inculcating knowledge, pure and simple, to inculcating desires for living, for art, for sport, for all sorts of activities. I foresee a return to full employment, but of a different kind, somewhere in the nineties. We don't have as many teachers, people in medicine, and all sorts of other professional and skilled people as we should. Our hours of work will probably decline, but there will be work to be done, by both people and machines.

Computers today are superhuman in their ability to handle numbers, but still infantile in their ability to handle ideas and concepts. But there's a new generation of machines coming along which will be quite different. The fifth generation. The human brain's got something like 10,000 million cells, and each of these is a pretty complex device in its own right. So there's literally billions of components in a human brain. Now a computer, wonderful as it may seem, has thousands, almost millions of times fewer components. But there is now an explosion going on in the complexity of the machines we can make. By the turn of the century we should be able to make a machine as complex as the human brain.

People have not recognized what an extraordinary change this is going to produce. Within the not-too-distant future we may not be the most intelligent species on earth. The consequences could be marvellous, but we must stop to consider them. We could have a Periclean Athens where the machines replaced the slaves the Greeks had, and we could all be living lives of great interest and so on. But it won't happen unless we plan for it. It's also worth bearing in mind that if any one nation acquires the ability to make these machines ahead of the rest of the world, it would have a quite unbelievable advantage.

Those of us working in the area are opening Pandora's box. What will come out we don't know, but it excites me very much, and I'd like to be among the leaders. Responsibility for the ultimate outcome lies with those of us developing the technology, and if I didn't believe it was a beneficial prospect, I wouldn't be working on it. But we must consider how to control the development, to prevent the making of a Frankenstein. And we also have to grapple with philosophical problems.

First of all, we know that we're conscious by analogy, but we will never know whether a machine is conscious. Secondly, we do know that a computer can be programmed to exercise imagination. Imagination is some sort of process of random thoughts being generated in the mind and the conscious or subconscious selecting, and allying some, and blocking others. The machine can do the same thing. So a machine only becomes different from a human being, if we believe in a soul. It boils down to a religious matter. If human beings have souls, then clearly machines won't and there will always be a fundamental difference. If you don't believe humans have souls, then machines can do anything and everything a human does. I don't believe we have souls and so personally I believe that we are essentially machines.

There is no purpose then other than to enjoy our lives. I enjoy mine by being an inventor, not an entrepreneur or a prophet, but an inventor. What one must realize is that an inventor is not just someone who comes up with ideas. Most people have ideas. The difference between the average person and the inventor is that the inventor for some reason has the urge to see his ideas through to fruition. And the difference between the successful and the unsuccessful inventor is that the successful one not only sees them to fruition, but he creates the products people end up wanting.

There's a plethora of ideas. They're all around us. We, because we're known to be an inventive company, get thousands thrown at us all the time by people thinking: 'Ah! There they are, they'll love this idea, and they'll pick it up and run with it.' But of course we don't. The inventor has to do it himself. I have to do it myself. And if there's one thing I would like to create in my lifetime, it is artificial intelligence. I would love to live to see it. I would be very disappointed to miss that.

The Roots of Excellence

Clive Sinclair is a very complex man, as all inventive geniuses are. His public image is that of a rather cold, austere, even 'soulless' character. Yet at work, according to David Potter, founder of Psion, he is playful, expressive and full of emotion, and his pursuit of physical fitness is well publicized. So he is a man with not only brains, but also muscle and heart. His technological vision is extraordinary, although his social and psychological vision is basic and instinctive, rather than explicitly developed.

HUNCH AND INTUITION

Clive's real strength is that he is able to sense there will be a market for 'X' million, often without justification.

David Southward, Sinclair Research director

Sinclair, above all else, is a man of his time, in his place. To me he is the archetypal English eccentric. The British nation is in his soul, even though he denies that he has one! Somehow, he is completely in touch with the national psyche. As tinkerer, as hobbyist, as introvert, as individualist, he represents the 'best of British' and is thus able to draw it out of others. David Potter has told me that Sinclair has, above all else, extraordinary market intuition. Because intuitive feelings are notoriously difficult to verbalize, I invited someone other than Sinclair to describe what Sinclair might feel about the environment in which we are now living and to characterize the way it has been evolving. Tony Tyler, editor of *Big 'K'* and a student of pop culture, has succeeded beyond expectation:

I have my own vision, though it's still evolving. We have a talent in this country for leisure, and for creative activity, and the new medium of computers is a channel for both.

How did an anarchic guy like myself, you may well ask, come to computers? I love writing, painting and music. And I came to realize that the computer allows me to exercise all my talents, at one and the same time. It's a synthesis machine.

The home computer boom, in this country, has followed the rock 'n' roll era, directly. The same sorts of kids who are buying

computers, today, were playing guitars twenty years ago. My
target market, for the magazine, is the young people with a
sense of humour, a sense of appositeness, and an awareness of
'fitness', i.e., what fits. It's a case of Pete Townsend versus
Elvis Presley. The one was a lead guitarist and the other a
thickie singer. What lead guitarists got out of their music
yesterday, they're getting out of computers today. It's a mixture
of macho prowess, the joy of doing a painting, the creativity of
making music, the pleasure of creativity.

Rock 'n' roll has died. Parents who were concerned about
their kids playing guitar are now worried about them staying
indoors and playing computer games. And it's not a class thing.
The fact that W.H. Smith is selling home computers must
indicate that they have appeal across the board. I get badly spelt
letters on crumpled bits of lined paper. It's just like the rock
business, classless.

The Brits are rather good when it comes to pop culture. They
have a sense of style and a technical suss. They're unlike both
the Americans and the continental Europeans. We form a
bridge between those two cultures. The American revolution
was not a populist one, and the French was. Our revolution was
industrial. We're not afraid of technology, yet we are artistic.
So we're not as technocratic as the Americans, and not as
stylish as the French or Italians, but a bridge between the two.
As a result we're good at software, and we've taken to the
microcomputer.

What we're best at is recreational software. We're a bit lazy,
as a nation. That dilutes the Prussian work ethic. We say to
ourselves, 'Hang on, why am I doing this?' We're quite enthusiastic for things that really interest us. Sinclair, and his
enthusiasts, are a model in that respect.

In actual fact, there are two types of software designer.
There's the fearfully masculine type who produces
spread-sheets, data-base programs and the like. They're also
the types who work on the hardware, like the people who made
the lead pencils for artists to use. These types are not the ones
who are able to make the computer user-friendly. They're too
caught up with the mathematics to get inside the minds of

others. The other type is the fun-loving, artistic programmer, who creates games for the leisure market.

We're moving towards an era where 80 per cent of our population will have no so-called 'work'. So constructive use of our leisure time is all-important. There is intrinsic value in games. After all, in the early days of the Beatles John Lennon's parents were probably saying, 'It's all very well playing the guitar, but how are you going to earn a living?' There are kids who have never done anything at school. They become prime candidates for delinquency. If they are good at computer games, that gives them a basis for self-respect.

Games software is advancing in degrees of sophistication far greater than business software. After all, improvements to the first Wordstar package have been basic variations on a theme. Spread-sheets today are only a modest advance on the first Visicalc program developed four years ago. They've merely been polishing the stone since. In computer games there's a new concept every week. Five to ten per cent of the games which come through to us involve totally new concepts. Some Adventure games may take a year for the player to finish. It's like long-distance duelling via a cathode ray tube and keyboard. It sucks you in. It's almost like a drug. You can get immersed in it, like the finest novel. It's a novel on the screen, a moving picture and musical experience that is truly interactive. It's a synthesis of novel, music and art.

In fact, I object to the word 'game'. It's muddy. It could mean a war game, games people play (psychologically speaking), or a game of hockey. Also, the word has a connotation of frivolity and time-wasting. A computer game need be none of these things. And some young thug, who turns out to have fantastic jet fighter reflexes, may reveal a whole set of undiscovered talents in the process of playing 'Space Invaders'.

The real product of the future, of course, is the software. When everyone has a computer, it's the software that will have infinite possibilities. Sinclair opened up the whole market here, but the future lies with software. When I say software, of course, you have to realize that there's a big difference between people writing basic programs and those writing in machine code. The first involves the well-known linear thought patterns, the flow charts. The second involves some mystical symbiosis between man and machine. It's like the painter choosing a colour, or the musician choosing a note. It's like fiction which goes much deeper than documented fact. You have to probe the hidden depths of computer memory.

You don't need teachers. All you need is a computer and good software. We have a young boy, aged fifteen, who has written the most brilliant articles for us about machine code for the Sinclair Spectrum. He has written three of the bestselling programs for the machine. When he leaves school he'll be making £50,000 a year. But, for the moment he's stopped writing in because he's busy with his 'O' levels!

The fact that he and most of the other young people interested in computers are boys is a distortion. It's because the boring, analytical types have done a hijack. At the same time, half a dozen of the magazines are edited by females. Our star reporter is a girl aged twenty-two. We encouraged her, you see. We didn't put her off. So in three months flat she became computerate.

In harnessing the British market of hobbyists, of tinkerers, of individualists and of eccentrics, Sinclair has tapped an incredibly rich vein. Now Sinclair Research is gearing itself up to tap similar markets in other parts of the world. All of this represents good psychology, as well as profitable business. There is nothing like profiting yourself, by fulfilling the needs of others.

As little as I like the term, I am reminded, at this point, of Toffler's 'prosumer'. In his book *The Third Wave*, he explains:

Until the Industrial Revolution, the vast bulk of all the food, goods and services produced by the human race was consumed by the producers themselves. . . . The Industrial Revolution ripped apart this underlying unity. . . . The two halves of life that industrialization split apart were production and consumption. . . . Today we are begininng to see a progressive blurring of the line that separates producer from consumer. We see the rising significance of the 'prosumer'.

Toffler then goes on to describe such examples of 'prosuming' towards the twenty-first century:

Instead of a dress pattern, for example, tomorrow's prosumer might well buy a cassette with a program on it that will drive a 'smart' electronic sewing machine . . . it may also become possible to program specifications into the automanufacturing process via computer and telephone.

Toffler thus pictures a generation brought up on part-time paid work as the norm, eager to use their own hands, equipped with many cheap minitechnologies in the home. In fact in Britain, via the Sinclair revolution, this is already happening. A nation of 'Smiths', of tinkerers, of gardeners, of do-it-yourselfers, is waking up to the prosuming challenge and opportunity. Self-service is turning into self-sufficiency, self-satisfaction and self-development.

It is a positive eye-opener to read the computer magazines on the newsagents' bookshelves. Not only are there over sixty of these magazines – half a dozen devoted exclusively to Sinclair's products – but their shape and form is fascinating. They are truly interactive. Some 2000 young people in this country have become software designers for leisure, for pleasure, for profit, and for communication. Hundreds of peripherals manufacturers have set up as small companies, to provide add-ons, to the 'underdeveloped' Sinclair product. In fact, the product has been deliberately, I believe, unfinished to give full vent to the nation's tinkering and inquisitive spirit. The consumers have become producers and vice versa.

This interdependence is also visible in the dealings between hardware manufacturers and software houses. In Sinclair's case this has been especially true in their relationship with Psion, who produced the business software for the Quantum Leap (QL).

Psion are currently one of the major software houses in this country. The reason for Psion's early concentration on software development was David Potter's growing recognition of the worldwide shortage of quality programs for the rapidly expanding microcomputer marketplace. Although some of the demand was being met by a new 'cottage' industry of independent software engineers, most of whom sold their product through small ads in specialist and hobby magazines, he realized the consumer would require far more comprehensive, easy-to-use and 'bug'-free packages.

However, by identifying the better-quality products already available and making marketing agreements with their originators, Potter was able to quickly expand his own business in a number of countries. At that point there was no time or resource to develop Psion's own products, but with the introduction of the Sinclair ZX81 – the first internationally marketed 'volume' home computer – he chose to Psion-brand certain 'hobbyist' programs and sell them to Sinclair distributors around the world, quickly gaining high penetration. And although Psion also created products for other makes of micro, it recognized that Sinclair had identified a prime market opportunity which it was to dominate heavily in volume terms, particularly with the introduction of the Spectrum. So Psion continued to work closely with Sinclair, and as a result of this association was instrumental in setting industry software prices.

By early 1983 Psion had sold one million software cassettes, and such was the acceleration in demand that by September of the same year, 500,000 units were sold in a four-week period alone. Now Psion has sold its three-millionth piece! And a single product, Flight Simulation, for the ZX81 and Spectrum, sold over half a million units. Psion has ridden very successfully on the back of Sinclair, or, as Potter might argue, vice versa!

ALL IS NOT LEISURE

Of course, Sinclair Research has not restricted itself to the leisure market, but this is the business that comes naturally to it. Within 'leisure' I am including education and business games. The QL is intended for recreational, educational and business purposes.

If we look at wider developments in microcomputing, we find the underlying technology is being pushed relentlessly forward all the time: powerful microprocessors, progressively larger memory chips, 256K RAMs, for example, are producing a lot of 'enabling' microelectronics. A lot of the push is coming from the semiconductor houses, producing components without any specific idea of what they will actually do. Instead, they're making components with a wide range of potential. This relentless technical curiosity is therefore pulling us along. For £100, every six months, you can put in a box a more and more powerful collection of electronics. It really is extraordinary. Today you can be sitting and playing with a £9.99 chess program on a £100 Sinclair. Twenty years ago a chess program was the ultimate challenge for any computer. So, extrapolating ten years on . . .

As Richard Cutting, director of Sinclair's Metalab, has said:

> We have a fantastic number of propositions put to us, but we confine ourselves to items which have mass market potential. Nowadays most homes have a TV, and a lot have a video recorder. Many now also have a computer for £100 or £200 which can do some interesting things. But if you had one you could talk to, and get access to encyclopaedic knowledge – legal, medical or technical – it requires no leap of the imagination to see how you could have such a thing in your home. By the end of the decade we shall be seeing this kind of facility.

> In summary, the computer revolution, here, in America, in Europe and Japan, is much bigger than many of us think. What the man in the street sees is just the tip of the iceberg. The effect of microelectronics is huge and diverse. We can see the microcomputers, and bits and pieces of electronics in our TV sets. But the market is growing massively, at 40 to 50 per cent a year. We're talking of a market running to excess of $10 billion this year. And there's so much more to come.

> Microelectronics will be taking over the control systems of everything, whether finished products or factory processes, whether capital or consumer goods. Think of all the controls, for example, built into a motor car. The mechanical devices activating the spark plugs, the mixture of petrol, and the electrical side. We will be doing away with a tremendous amount of metal. That's just one example. The same applies to a myriad of products. Then there are the products which don't yet exist, like

information centres in the home. . . .

Finally, it would be a mistake to confine Sinclair's thinking to computers. His interest in the applications of technology extends far beyond. We have seen the first offering of the Sinclair Vehicle Project. That conforms to the same mass market formula. He has also sold, via mail order, several thousand of his flat-screened televisions already. There are a lot of other areas. . . .

IMPROVISED ORGANIZATION

Sinclair is one of those inventors who is instinctively in touch with the marketplace. His approach is to 'suck it and see' rather than to do advance market research of an analytical kind. As a result he sometimes does come unstuck, but providing the love affair between himself and the British public lasts, his market instinct should hold him in good stead.

Nigel Searle, managing director of Sinclair Research, describes the evolution of the more conventional side of the Sinclair operation very well.

I work harder in an environment where someone else is setting the objectives. In other words, I enjoy a somewhat unconventional working environment, in which innovation plays a large part, but I'm not the one to do the innovating. I hate being regimented. You might say, in fact, that I'm a mercenary in that I'm willing to sell my time and my ability to serve a cause that isn't my own. The thing is that working for Sinclair Research enables me to become involved in much larger stakes than I could, working for myself. That's why I'm here now.

The usual problem for an inventor and entrepreneur is, once his company begins to grow large, he doesn't want to be bothered with the day-to-day detail. Clive is happiest when he is inventing and being creative. He's not an organizer and a manager, but a great inspirer and motivator of his researchers. The minute he comes across something interesting in a magazine and an idea pops up in his head, he rings someone up, to take it further. He works very hard, but not in a conventional sense;

most of his social meetings are with people with whom he can discuss ideas.

Over the past couple of years, as the business has rapidly grown, we've become less concerned with product innovation, relatively speaking, and more with marketing. We define our business now as conceiving, developing and marketing new products in the consumer electronics field. And I think I have had an influence in making the transition away from almost 100 per cent dependence on product innovation.

The transition hasn't, in any way, been dramatic. It has meant the recruitment of people with different sorts of skills. We used to take on mainly engineering graduates. We now have graduates with a marketing and accounts background. Of course, we're still only one hundred people, in a business turning over more than £50 million. On the other hand, two and a half years ago, when we were twenty people, everyone reported to Clive. I wouldn't have operated any differently at that stage. But now it's a different scale of operation, and I don't think Clive would have enjoyed working in a conventionally structured environment.

The way I see it now is that if I were MD of a company with thousands of investors, I'd be charged with the responsibility of running the business, in a generally efficient and effective manner. But the situation here is different. Clive owns 85 per cent of the shares. It would be pointless to run the company in a way which conflicts with his objectives. Therefore, one either agrees with his principles or not. I happen to agree with them. We see a virtue in subcontracting, and in minimizing the number of employees. That keeps up the quality of personnel. Then, neither of us believes in hanging around the corridors of power, licking people's boots. We believe in minimum government interference, certainly in our line of business. Thirdly, we don't want to do things that others can do better, bearing in mind our scarce management resources. The time may come where we may need more control, but we're a long way from it now. Besides, I don't see ourselves growing into a company with a thousand people at headquarters. Very soon we'd begin to break down into manageable and semiautonomous cells. We have some embryonic business units already, like the one concerned with the pocket television.

We have a large number of people, then, concerned with the coordination of our subcontractors. We have two major manufacturers of our computers, Timex and Thorn EMI, and a host of suppliers of peripheral products. For example, our printer, who supplies our manuals, does tremendous business with us. All told, a Sinclair product will be made up of products from 20 to 25 suppliers.

In a normal organization, some supplies of components are assembled in house. But the only putting together we do is a packaging operation. The cables, the power supplies, the software manuals, the cassettes, as well as the computers themselves, are all manufactured outside. I have a production director to interface with all the outside factory managers. What it means is that our time and effort, on the manufacturing side, is involved in getting the right relationship with the right people. We try and set up a situation where if we make profits they do, and vice versa. We like them to share in the risks. This means that there must be considerable trust between us.

Also with our customers, there's an open and honest relationship. Sometimes you might even accuse us of being naive. We avoid doing business with people if we don't like them. It's a principle of Clive's I've stuck to. Even when we could make money on something, if we don't like the people, we drop it.

His major influence on the business is in the area of future product concepts. There are a number of projects being undertaken in the company now which wouldn't exist if not for him. Because he has ideas, faith in them, and the ambition to make them succeed, he inspires other people. The electric car project started within Sinclair Research, and was then taken outside. Because myself and others here feel that personal computers is our business, we would never have embarked on such an enterprise. But Clive thinks that two successes are better than one. We have two groups here, the technical and the nontechnical. The technical side is structured very informally, whereas the management is structured more conventionally and hierarchically. One of my jobs is to construct bridges between the two, although the whole ethos, amongst senior management here, is to avoid thinking in a restricted, functional way. Clive has direct contact with several senior technical people, but less with non-technical management.

In order for ideas to develop till they contribute as a product, one person must work at it, as a product champion. Sometimes this person is inspired by Clive, but not always. Ultimately there has to be one person who is personally committed. The size of the team is not important. The groups of people virtually allocate themselves, working on projects they have chosen to develop. A number of new products are now being developed, far more numerous than the current offerings.

SMALL AND VULNERABLE

As we can see, Sinclair Research subcontracts manufacturing and distribution out, almost completely, so that it remains primarily a research and development operation, and secondarily a selling operation. They do what they, as a company, and Britain, as a nation, are best at. Sinclair has avoided getting involved in large-scale organization which cuts across the British grain. However, it does make for a certain vulnerability, and requires great skill in managing across organizational boundaries. It also makes him vulnerable to circumstances beyond his control, like a downturn in the market. In fact 1985 has been a very difficult period for all emerging computer companies. They have had to face the trauma of 'growing up' from pioneering enterprises towards managed organizations. *The Times* (18 June) had this to say:

> Robert Maxwell's takeover of Sinclair Research with a £12 million rescue deal must be the final proof that the days when technical experts could both research and develop products and run the companies themselves are over.
>
> Sinclair Research still has to appoint a managing director and is likely to follow other home computer companies which have replaced their technical whizz-kids of the 1970s with managers experienced in selling such unrelated products as soft drinks, shaving equipment and hi-fi. The new UK managing directors

of Atari and Commodore are both marketing men aiming to sell computers to wealthy customers.

Sinclair have now brought in Bill Jeffrey as chief executive to bolster their management. They have truly begun to enter the second stage of a business's development.

ENTREPRENEURS AT THE CENTRE

Clive reads a research paper, applies the Sinclair cooking to it, and comes up with a product that sells.

Richard Cutting, director of Metalab

Sinclair is not only an inventor, but also an entrepreneur. Nigel Searle, on the other hand, sees himself as an 'entrepreneurial manager', in style and outlook. Nigel is surrounded by a small group of people who have a similar approach in the areas of production-cum-research and marketing. The person who has been with Sinclair Radionics and Sinclair Research for the longest period of time is David Southward.

David teamed up with Clive after he had been involved with other new technology-based businesses in his own right. He is a mechanical engineer by training, as well as being entrepreneurial in outlook.

My overall role is to look after the more mechanically based activities attached to Sinclair Research – things like magnetic recorders, printers and keyboards. All electronics is mechanical engineering, in the end. We're working with fractions of a micron. What makes us at Sinclair unique, is that we go for the numbers game. I don't think there is any company which has grown, in a self-financed way, faster than we have. We've nudged, always, a million pounds per employee, and we're now a hundred people.

As mass producers, we've also gone the subcontracting route, so we don't do the manufacturing ourselves. It all stems from the bad experience we had at Sinclair Radionics, where we were manufacturing the product, and employing four hundred people.

When you manufacture yourselves, and you're not careful, you camouflage the true cost of your products. But when you sub-contract, you know the real cost of what you buy in. At the same time, because we go for large-scale manufacture, we can have a small organization! Supposing there are four hundred parts in a Spectrum computer, whether you're making one or a million, the amount of work you do is virtually identical. In fact, the subcontractors we've got could be considered part of the company. Timex in Dundee, for example, is totally dependent on us. But we retain an arm's length relationship. And we stay small, with one hundred people. Perhaps, in time, there'll be a whole set of one-hundred-man companies, interlocked one with the other.

Although Clive only comes here once a week, and is busy with many outside interests, he has installed a unique R and D philosophy amongst us. If you come out with a new product, you know that it has a limited life. Its life is dictated by some event over which you have little control. Somebody else comes out with a product twice as good at half the price. So if you can bring forward the launch date by even a day, you're effectively increasing your turnover by perhaps £100,000. The incentive to save time is therefore extremely high. If we have to send a taxi to get a widget to Exeter fast, we think nothing of it. It's an attitude of mind. We're not desperately organized. In fact we're distinctly disorganized. One of the differences between us and Timex is that they're organized. They have systems for everything.

It's our belief in the numbers game, and this push towards the same target, that keeps us going. We don't go to a place with full working drawings. We throw something at our suppliers and say make 100,000 a month. The supplier then has to make up the precise drawings himself.

Clive himself is very creative, of course, and always looking for new avenues. And because we're a dynamic company we can afford to attract good people. I'm not sure whether the innovation part isn't overemphasized. We take risks. At the time nobody thought that the ZX80 would have sold. It was so functionally primitive. It wasn't as good as a calculator at calculating, and there wasn't any software to turn it into a games machine. But people were prepared to buy it because they wanted to learn how a computer works. And it's led to an explosion of people producing add-on units. . . .

The picture we get from Southward is of a strange amalgam of mass production and 'small is beautiful'. As Sinclair goes for the numbers game, he is able to have components mass produced, at low cost. But, because he subcontracts the manufacturing out, he is able to keep the numbers of his own staff down. So both big and small retain their respective forms of 'beauty' under the Sinclair umbrella. Southward goes on:

The worst possible sort of case was Cambridge Instruments. That was the exact reverse situation from Sinclair. We were selling instruments, from £50,000 to £100,000 each, and encompassing a wide range. We'd sell just a few a year, and yet customers would expect to receive them in a short space of time. You can imagine the stocks we therefore had to carry, of parts, and the financial implications. I see that kind of approach as providing one of the principal reasons for the dominance of the Japanese. Our great crime in Britain is that a company like GEC has dropped out of the consumer field. They have gone for a small number of expensive installations. What we and the Japanese have done is to say that there is a world market for, say, videotape recorders. You then make a million a year. In flat tubes, we could have manufactured a thousand a month, but the cost per unit would have been enormous.

Quality is not in the Rolls-Royce, it's in the Ford Fiesta. You've got to mass produce the Fiesta, so you cannot afford to give a product individual attention. That means the quality of the engineering has to be very much higher. In this country we don't sufficiently realize it. A few years ago, Sinclair was the biggest user, in the UK, of printed circuit boards, and that was when our turnover was only £27 million a year. That's crazy!

RESEARCH AND DEVELOPMENT

Interestingly enough, it is the 'numbers game' and the bias towards action, rather than the ingenuity and bias towards innovation, that is greatly magnified, and commented on, in the organization. Richard Cutting, director of Metalab, puts it this way:

> Prior to last July 1983, we could hardly identify a research centre. But, by this stage, Clive wanted to establish one, and to pull a group of people together. So I was brought in, to do just that. And because of the extreme commercial orientation of the company, the work going on is very goal oriented. It goes beyond R and D to production engineering, start-up, and hand-holding at the launch stage. One sees the whole spectrum of business activity here, except for the actual production which is contracted out.
>
> Our top priority is absolute adherence to the commercial prospects for the resulting product. It features absolutely and basically: the ZZ product whose target manufacturing cost is so much, and whose selected features are this and that. Every decision along the way is made against that context, at a given price. All this is very necessary if we are to practise the Sinclair principle of offering large numbers at affordable prices. The development of the ZX80 was a phenomenal story. Four short years ago virtually nobody knew what a computer was. Then, with the onset of the ZX80, at £100, followed by the ZX81, at £39, an enormous number of people got their hands on a computer. Sinclair has enabled millions of people to gain hands-on experience. As a result, our position is extraordinary. Our market share in the UK, in physical units, is 40–45 per cent, which is overwhelming compared with other industries. Acorn and Commodore are down to one quarter of that level.

SALES

The high-volume, low-cost approach at the research and production end, is supported by the strategy that Charles Cotton, manager for overseas business, has adopted:

I have found of all the British companies, that Sinclair was the most Japanese in its business philosophy. Shoot for high volume at low costs. At the same time, their technology was providing unique products which were also attractive from an industrial design point of view. It fitted with all the things I'd learnt, in corporate planning, about getting down the experience curves. Sinclair had learnt, initially through getting things wrong, so that he was now able to get things right. And the company was making a product that had worldwide relevance. They weren't in the fashion business, but were making something of long-term utility. Moreover, Nigel Searle was prepared to talk absolutely frankly about everything. He threw everything out, in order to get feedback. It was a style of management I welcomed.

Since Sinclair Research was founded, in July 1979, Bill Sinclair (Sir Clive's father) had done a good job in recruiting agents in some forty different markets. But a lot of them were one-man operations, and business was getting bigger and bigger. Many of them were hobbyists who had been associated with Clive in the days of watches, radios and hi-fis.

I have every expectation that the other European markets will become as big as the UK. My task is to decide on the kind of organization we require to market overseas, in order to secure the sales. One of the characteristics of high-growth businesses is that the cash demands to fuel the growth are huge. A lot of our agents weren't attuned to this themselves and wanted to remain small businesses. So the question was, could we encourage some of our skilled distributors to find the capital, and others to recognize that they would be outgrown? It took me time to get to grips with this new context. I had been used to flat-growth situations. Meanwhile, I decided that in those countries where business is likely to be as big as in the UK, the sales operation should be run like it is here. That involved France, Germany and Italy.

The company's management must be seen to be competent. Clive is not a monolith, and he's not the sole source of new products. Over the next two to three years the distribution of our sales will switch. My aim is that only 20 per cent of our business will come from the UK. That means sales of £300 million overseas. It is important for Sinclair Research to be perceived as an aggressively international company. We must build on Sinclair's individual competences.

Clive has a rare ability to combine his unique grasp of electronics technology with skill in spotting consumer applications. Technology is always a means to an end, a saleable product. He sees ourselves in the high-volume, mass market, and therefore not niche dependent. He is also able to come up with the most economical and elegant solutions to technical problems.

Take this circuit board here. The Apple II equivalent would be three times the size. For one of our chips, that you see here, another machine would need tens of components. The other real contribution Clive has made is to employ the highest standards of industrial design. He is very concerned about image, and the surroundings of his product. So we are all desperately keen to retain the Sinclair magic.

That's the advantage of being small. In each of our overseas operations, in Europe and abroad, we shall do our best to engender a situation where there's a little bit of Sinclair magic in each. They'll be mirror images of ourselves, not a blur of people in a complicated organization chart. It's like lots of Sinclair nuclei. This will be made possible by keeping the numbers small, by defining what essential activities are, and by ensuring that inessential ones are done elsewhere. Central to our purposes is our product and the selling of it. Support services such as market research, PR and consultancy can be bought in. In the final analysis, we must 'stick to our knitting'. We don't touch the product: we don't manufacture it; we don't warehouse it; we don't distribute it.

Charles Cotton has brought life to the Sinclair magic. The imagery he provides of 'lots of Sinclair nuclei overseas' is very powerful. Cotton also highlights the technology/market coupling which is so much a feature of the Sinclair approach to innovation. In the final analysis, he reiterates, Sinclair must stick to the corporate mission. The production of computer software, and the distribution of Sinclair products, has been left to others.

ENTREPRENEURS AT THE PERIPHERY

In the same way as the computer's performance is enhanced by 'peripherals', so the performance of Sinclair's entrepreneurial management has been enhanced by independent, and interdependent, entrepreneurs at the periphery. In fact the computer industry exhibits, at one and the same time, features of the pioneering and the mature company. Independent entrepreneurship goes hand in hand with interdependent associations. Nowhere is this more clearly expressed than in the relationship between hardware and software production. So let me allow David Potter, the founder of Psion and close associate of Clive Sinclair, to tell his tale.

SOFTWARE ENTREPRENEUR

I decided to set up a business. I saw what was going on in California, in microelectronics. The most difficult decision of my life was to give up my tenured position at London University. I started Psion in a one-roomed office on the Edgware Road. At the time there weren't any markets, like now. It was dominated by hobbyists and lots of kits were being produced. On the software side a whole cottage industry was developing.

When I started off I had some facilities from the bank, so I had access to £100,000 altogether. When you start modestly, as I did, you have to sell rapidly. I examined the market, and saw that people were producing things which could be marketed much more widely. So I entered into marketing agreements with manufacturers and distributors. I picked Sinclair as a big player. I didn't concentrate on plenty of others who had fallen by the wayside. These decisions proved well founded. It rapidly came to a stage when we were selling so much product that Sinclair came to us. We entered into an agreement to produce software, which we create and manufacture and they distribute. They came to us to discuss new hardware, and if they have a software requirement, they seek our cooperation.

RETAILING ENTREPRENEUR

The relationship between Sinclair and Psion is not unlike that between the company and its distributors, both independent and retail. The first of the retail chains to sell the Sinclair product was W.H. Smith. John Rowland, its merchandise controller in the computer field, has been primarily responsible for forging the links between his company and Sinclair's.

We have been selling newspapers and magazines, books and stationery for many years; records had been introduced only in the 1960s. The idea grew up that if we could sell records, then we could also sell record players and cassette recorders. So we did, and that marked the beginnings of electronic leisure.

W.H. Smith are always looking for new opportunities. They took me on to implement the new venture into leisure electronics. Later on we were asking ourselves what big new markets we could move into. We identified two areas: video software and computing. That was at Christmas, 1979.

Video had a spectacular growth, but initially there were problems with the software. One was the price, which was too high. We thought the answer to this would be rental, but this was not profitable.

The other market opportunity was in home computers. Remember: in 1979 there wasn't a market. There were pocket calculators, Atari games, and the Commodore PET – the only home computer.

Having written reports on the home computer market, I was told by the company to go out and do it. The approach was 'let's experiment'. So we obtained some special fittings and wrote on them 'Computer Know-How'. We bought a supply of computer magazines – at that time, all imported from America – and ordered a few PET computers – the only computers then which people might have considered using at home. (In 1979 there were just four magazines on our standard lists and 17 computer books. Today there are 68 magazines and about 680 books.)

The first 'Computer Know-How' section – set up as a pilot scheme – was put into our large Brent Cross store. It was exciting. The staff looked at it, but appeared to be apprehensive. The customers – who were hobbyists – loved it: they were grabbing the magazines and books while they were still in the packing cases!

Following this success we looked around for a home computer; the only one was the Sinclair ZX80. It was fragile – but a computer at £100; who could ignore it? We wrote to Clive Sinclair, who was very interested. He said, 'I don't think the ZX80 is what you're looking for, but I've got something new coming up.'

We discussed with our managing director the possibility of merchandising computers. We were prepared to take the risk if he thought it was justified. He did, so we told Clive Sinclair he could have an exclusive deal.

Clive Sinclair knows exactly what he wants to achieve. I got on well with him, and I worked very closely with him and his team on the project. As for my own team, while we have to fit into the company as a whole, we are almost completely autonomous.

We put the ZX into our stores on 24 September 1981 – and it's been selling well ever since! Originally we were going to sell it in only twenty-four branches. However, when we were ready it was already September, so we decided to put the ZX into one hundred branches. Three hundred and fifty staff were trained in three weeks; they learned by using the equipment and by writing programs.

The project was a great success. More computers went into more and more branches, and we must have sold 300,000 over three years.

Our market penetration in computer sales is 10 per cent. We can see one and a half million machines being sold in 1984; our share will probably increase by 15 per cent. But later on things could get more difficult. There's a lot of glitter around, based on the American experience. But we have to play our own game.

PUBLISHING ENTREPRENEUR

Richard Hease has played a major part in the birth and phenomenal growth of computer publications. Like David Potter and John

Rowland, he could almost be considered part of the Sinclair team, and like so many characters in our entrepreneurial play, his roots have penetrated foreign soils:

My mother is a schoolteacher and my father ran a garage. She is Belgian and he is English. My first experience of business was working in my mother's family brewing business in Belgium. From my father I learnt about the mistakes I shouldn't make. My mother still teaches today. She has written books on the education of immigrant children.

I started out in life as a journalist on a local paper. I then moved on into advertising, marketing and PR. As a journalist I acquired an enquiring mind. I first got into business through my wife, who was a florist. We set up one shop and then another. When we eventually sold out she had fifty people working for her. I used the money to set up my first business.

In 1977 I launched *Which Computer?* That was the first of the proper computer magazines. The only ones around at the time were weekly trade magazines. The professionals and business people were being bombarded with information, but there was nothing to help them sort it out. So *Which Computer?* proved pretty successful. We went on to launch twenty further publications, including books and newsletters, in the computing field. Typical magazines were *Practical Computing* and *Educational Computing*. Meanwhile, there was a change in the way computer users perceived magazines. The opportunity arose to launch 'user' magazines, which we did for IBM, Sinclair and DEC. My ambition, at that stage, was to recognize business opportunities, and to exploit them.

People tend to think in isolation. Magazines are a starting point. You can package them in different forms. My infrastructure was the computer industry. I operated on gut feel. I watched the market trends. I had the foresight to see patterns changing. I've always known how to package information.

In the course of 1982, we'd met Clive Sinclair. He had asked us to produce Mensa's newsletter. I agreed, and then spoke to him about developing a modem for the ZX81. We were sitting in his flat one day and he was telling me that the ZX81 was dead. I said to him, 'Your problem is you don't have it distributed widely enough.' I said, 'Give me the machines and I'll distribute them.' We scribbled down terms there and then. In the industry one's word is one's bond. Bob, my partner, had previously set up a distribution system for another manufacturer, so he knew what to do.

We stored the first delivery of 2000 machines all over Bob's house. But gradually the business developed. We talked to the buyers of multiples, and organized a lorry. It was like those early days when we asked W.H. Smith to take our first computer magazine, back in 1978.

We became the exclusive hardware distributor for Spectrum. The business was phenomenal. There was a time when Clive was giving us £4 million credit. Then Rothschilds, the bankers, took a stake in Sinclair, and told him he couldn't do that sort of thing. We appointed Arthur Anderson as our auditors, around that time. Our company by then had fifty people. I knew I had to find proper financing for the business. So we amalgamated as the Prism group, and went for outside finance. Our turnover, up until 1982, had gone up from £1 to £2 to £3 million. By 1983 it was up to £10 million, and by 1984 it had jumped to £32. So I went to the bank and also sold 10 per cent of our equity, on a private placement.

In the meantime we had entered into a joint venture with an American publisher. He'd linked up with the Chinese. I felt Sinclair could do well in China. I went over in August of 1983. We set up a deal to make Sinclairs in China, a tripartite one between Sinclair, ourselves and the Chinese. It will soon be on stream. It all happened through contacts, and it was a marvellous opportunity to spend two weeks there.

That brings us up to 1984. I have a company that has a £32 million turnover. I'm aiming for a stock market listing in sixteen months' time. Then we can start acquiring companies and develop into a private British Technology Group, then we can exploit other people's ideas and market them worldwide. That's the way things are evolving.

In January 1985, Prism went into liquidation. The launch of Hease's Wren computer had backfired. Prism had overreached itself.

Like Richard Hease, Sinclair's position is always vulnerable. The personal computer market is an extremely volatile one, as companies like Commodore, Atari, Osborne and Acorn have demonstrated. To be in it is like riding a tiger. Risk-taking abounds. Unpredictability rules. Sinclair is often accused of leaping before he looks, and of taking uncalculated risks. But he is still there, and my prediction is that, in some shape or form, he always will be. The time might come when Sinclair's entrepreneurial cells split and reform in some totally fresh combination. The Maxwell takeover and the subsequent dissolution are already seeing to that. But he is too far ingrained within the British psyche to fade into oblivion.

MENTAL AGILITY

Clive's a real time operator. The minute an idea pops in his head he takes it further.

Richard Cutting, director of Metalab

An accurate picture of Sinclair Research cannot be formed merely by focusing on its inside operations. Its entrepreneurial activity spills over any conventional boundaries, to embrace David Potter of Psion, John Rowland at W.H. Smith and other such people. Entrepreneurs and entrepreneurial managers form a close-knit communications network. This personal network is extended through printed, as well as electronic communications.

The nerve centre of the whole operation, the nodal point in the communications between producer and user, supplier and distributor, manufacturer and retailer, is in fact the computer magazine. In that sense Richard Hease played a very important part in the evolution of Sinclair's business. Magazines such as *Sinclair User*, *ZX Computing*, *Sinclair Answers*, and now *QL User*, are important characters in the Sinclair story. Yet they have emerged independently, spontaneously and profitably, without any direction or control from Sinclair himself. Like the User clubs, which also have their important part to play in the company's success and evolution, the magazines, the hardware, the software, and the users, form one spontaneously happy band.

SOFT TOUCH

Empathy, enthusiasm, encouragement and engagement are all qualities associated with the Sinclair phenomenon. The British public have been amazingly tolerant of any problems or shortcomings in the Sinclair product because of the extent to which they have become involved with the whole enterprise. Ironically, this has happened irrespective of the degree of charm, charisma or warmth that Sinclair, as a public figure, may exude. As far as the general public is concerned, it is his product, his performance, his success and his implicit empathy with consumers that has won them over. In addition, there is a quality within the field of personal computing that has been in Sinclair's favour. For, intermingled with the high technology, and the analytical programmer's mind, is, as Tony Tyler has said, a soft touch of romance and fantasy, of mythology and fairy tale.

For some strange reason the soft cultural touch has become particularly prevalent in the world of high technology, at least in some instances. I was made less aware of it in Sinclair Research than in Psion. The following are David Potter's thoughts:

If you're a company producing a mainframe, or NASA putting a man on the moon, you need a complex and vertical structure. But the structure that is right for us is a string of pearls. It's beautiful, it works well, and people work well inside it. Psion is the string, the whole work of art.

A vertical structure, after all, can be totally destructive. Big can get really ugly. But with our kind of culture and values and dynamic, we can be incredibly effective. Small is beautiful here. There's an *esprit de corps* second to none. I've never experienced anything like it. But what happens as we grow? We don't want to develop into that corporate thing, a cog in a large corporate wheel. So I've arranged the organization horizontally rather than vertically. Each part is a separate entity. The important thing is for each entity to have its separate culture and drive. Racal is like that.

Everything we put out must add to the quality image of Psion. That is reinforced by our strong culture. The sense of vigour and drive here is incredible. The way people work is unbelievable. We don't have a clock in the place. Nobody is measured in that sense. There are people working here every weekend. Nobody is ever told to do this or that. The reality is that our engineers, our creative people, feel that they are at the forefront of things. An engineer doesn't get his reward through financial means. He gets it by creating the best and most interesting products of the future. If he's surrounded by others like him he's in seventh heaven.

What about my own rewards? Nurturing, creating and growing an enterprise where people get a lot of fulfilment, which is very successful and which, in some vague way, helps the country to prosper. There should be many more companies like us. There are tremendous opportunities in the industry. At one level you've got the macho thing, to be the best and the greatest. We certainly want to be at the forefront. We must be. We must be able to compete with anyone. At the other level, there is the nurturing and developing of our people. The crux of everything, in our business, is people. And it's not only engineers. We now employ, for example, computer graphics people who you might say are developing a new art form.

Psion is at a stage where I still have substantial effect, but I don't produce the software any more. I can't even make final decisions for the copy of our brochure. How do we achieve something so beautiful as our latest brochure? It's by creating a style and an atmosphere, by getting in the sorts of people we do, and by continuously expressing our views. It's people, it's style, it's atmosphere. We're unique in never having had one person leave on the software side. That's in four years.

David Potter's words, and Psion's atmosphere, undoubtedly will make a lot of managers sit up and think. If not a youth culture, what similarly vibrant culture is being set up in your company, you might well ask?

Certainly, the world of personal computing does have its own enchantment, especially on the recreational side. A wealth of imagery, story-telling and adventure has been brought into computer games. While I, personally, was all too inclined to dismiss them, I was first brought to my senses by John Rowland at W.H.

Smith. He revealed to me that the situation is much more complex than I'd originally envisaged. In tracing his own software path he indicated that games are going through an evolutionary development, from arcade shoot-ups to complex strategy formulations.

In the beginning, I didn't have the software to buy. So I followed the children around the fairs, seeing what they liked. Our orders were placed on that basis – the most important thing is 'the buzz in the playground'. But, as with the record industry, the top ten in software are always changing.

If you have to categorize the products, there are three varieties: arcade/shoot-up, adventure and strategy games. Now, in fact, people are looking to get more out of their software. Three years ago there used to be the bat and paddle stuff; then there were the things you shot down. Now you still shoot things down, but you have to refurbish your resources. Games are not so reactive any more – they are more interactive. And some of them are now extremely sophisticated, especially the Spectrum games.

There are something like 2000 programmers, each with their wares to sell. It's like a pyramid, with a few big software houses at the top and all the others down below. Some of the software designers are brilliant.

In fact, within the personal computer industry, two cultures have formed. Firstly, the rational, analytic culture has found primary expression in the business software – the spread-sheets, the data bases, and the forecasting models. In this area, the British software houses have competed well with the Americans but without great distinction. Secondly, the intuitive, imaginative culture has found expression in recreational software – the arcade, the adventure and strategy games – where, in fact, this country leads the world. Sinclair has always been intimately linked with the leisure market, the young and adventurous kids, and their tinkering parents. He has never been close to the establishment, whether through schools, universities or business. It is questionable whether he will ever make real contact with such bodies, despite repeated attempts in this country, and recently in

France, and whether he would not be better off staying with the leisure and the recreation market, thus capturing the imagination of young kids and older hobbyists, tinkerers and game players all over Europe and America.

Finally, one of the main reasons I see for the failure of such diversifications as the C5 electronic car is the lack of such a coherent corporate strategy within Sinclair Research.

HARD WORK

> Clive works incredibly hard, but not in a conventional sense.
> David Southward, Sinclair Research director

Clive Sinclair has almost as much of a reputation for running marathons as he has for producing electronic gadgetry. The company's focus on speed of reaction and on quantity of product is undoubtedly an extension of Sinclair's physical energy and behavioural orientation. It is an attribute – the speed if not the running – which has been picked up collectively by his management team. And it is Sinclair's physical product, at the end of the day, that really counts.

Sinclair's physical product is both an expression and a culmination of his whole being. One man has become the nucleus of an entire industry. Sinclair Research is merely part of a much wider social and economic phenomenon. Its significance, culturally and educationally, has no bounds. In fact, as Isaac Asimov has suggested, a new structure and dynamic for education has been born. In its time it will overtake conventional schooling, and provide the scope for individualized learning that Sinclair missed as a young boy. His personal frustrations have been reoriented and redeployed to dynamic effect.

Sinclair has brought his inventive genius, his market intuition, his propensity to take risks, his yearning for freedom, and his urge to make an immediate impact, to bear upon the world. Not only has his management team received these energies, but through their organizational prowess, they have enabled Sinclair to build up an enduring business entity. While his inventive genius has remained self-contained, his entrepreneurial and active energies have not only been received, but have also been further magnified by independent, associated entrepreneurs. Not even Sinclair is an island, and without Potter, Hease and Rowland, Sinclair Research would have had very little impact of its own. Most important of all, though, in the whole Sinclair story, has been the part played by the British public, for they have received and responded to what he has provided. In fact, the degree of mutual understanding that exists between Sinclair Research and its customers is exemplary. The creative, anarchic, playful and individualistic urge within the British people can be developed much further. To the extent that we can picture Sinclair at the nucleus of a much larger organism, so we can conceive of the enormity of the potential for growth. Innumerable entrepreneurial cells are waiting to be formed and reformed, out of the mixture of Sinclair magic and the public interest. The climate is right. Both the supply side, enabling technologies, and the demand side, recreational opportunities, are growing in leaps and bounds. The nerve centre of the whole operation – the printed aural, visual and electronic media – is growing apace, and this country has a particularly good reputation for its newspaper, magazine and television journalism.

Most importantly, young people have taken to the personal computer, in this country, like ducks to water. And yet, in some perverse way, while this pool of young talent is spreading with the Sinclair revolution, there is a continuing call for 'educated' technologists. Educationally we are still living in the past, waiting for our schools and colleges to deliver the goods when we should be focusing our attention on the 'mechanics institutes' of the twentieth century. In other words, it is from the computer user clubs and from the thousands of young software engineers and peripherals manufacturers, who have spontaneously risen to the surface, that we should be drawing our skilled personnel. We should become, visibly and demonstrably, the recreational software and hardware capital of the world. This would enable us to draw on our strengths, and market their economic and cultural outcomes overseas, as we have done in the theatre, in television, in music, in publishing, and in activity holidays. Through the full exploitation of educational technology, we should be able not only to profit economically, as a nation, but to reform these very institutions which have inhibited our progress.

Clive Sinclair, who comprises the nucleus of that evolving organism – which we might call Sinclair Inc. – had to leave the establishment, in order to reform it. Such a reformation could become like its illustrious predecessor, if we succeed in magnifying Sinclair's efforts, and in aligning them with Britain's true potential. What would result is not a religious reformation, but an educational and commercial one, drawing on Sinclair's nonconformist roots in both respects. In spurning conventional management and instruction Sinclair has released the most constructive form of English eccentricity. For he has transcended, rather than merely reacted against, conventional wisdom. He has developed a higher form of order, a true recreation. His inventive genius, his improvised organization, entrepreneurial flair, flexible communications, closeness to a particular kind of customer and bias for action all form part of a whole evolving organism. To the extent that each and every one of us tunes in to Sinclair's revolution, a significant part of our future will work, through re-creation.

Ironically, though very much the individualist, Sinclair has not created an organization that explicitly caters for individual self-expression. Rather, that is part and parcel of his product. In other words, the originator's blueprint is reflected in the fruits of his business tree, but not in its organizational core. It has been left to Steve Shirley, founder of F International, to create an organization that builds work around individuals' lifestyles.

6. F International

1933	Steve Shirley was born Vera Stephanie Buchthal in Dortmund, West Germany.
1938	Evacuated from Germany.
1939	Brought to England by Quakers.
1951	Took a job at the Post Office Research Station.
1951	Became acquainted, at evening classes, with the first computers.
1955	Obtained a BSc. in mathematics.
1959	Married Derek Shirley, a Post Office engineer.
1959	Became a computer programmer and designer with ICL's precursor.

Pioneering Days 'FPL'

1962	Went out on her own and formed her own company, Freelance Programmers.
1963	Her son was born, mentally handicapped.
1964	Freelance Programmers was incorporated as FPL.
1964	FPL began to build up a panel of homeworkers.
1966	Profit-sharing scheme established.
1968	Took on a partner to share the burden of the business.
1970	The recession hit. The partner left, taking a chunk of precious business.
1973	The company was back in profit.

Expansion and Consolidation 'F International'

1974	F International was formed.
1975	A Danish subsidiary was created.
1976	F International opened up in Holland.
1978	The company went into America.

1978   The UK was divided up into regions.
1979   Steve became a vice-president of the British Computer
        Society.
1981   Alison Newell became managing director, UK.
1981–84 Turnover went up from £3m to £6m.
1984   Cindy Morelli appointed managing director, overseas.

F International – A Managed Organization

FLEXIBILITY AND ROOTS

For many skilled people homeworking provides a freedom and
flexibility in line with their needs. . . . Our people have the will
and wish to work from here, and to organize themselves as
such. Work is varied. Discipline is inborn.

Rosie Symons, promotions manager

THE PURSUIT OF FREEDOM

The pursuit of individual freedom has been a central theme in the
development of Great Britain, if not Western civilization as a
whole. All too often I have been struck by the inconsistency
between the freedom we exercise in our lives as a whole, and the
constraints we face within established organizations.

Steve Shirley, in creating F, for Flexibility, International, has
brought freedom and individuality into the mainstream of organizational life. What she has done, in essence, is to enable people in
general, and women in particular, to fit their jobs around their
individual lives.

F INTERNATIONAL
A MANAGED ORGANIZATION

BRANCHES   **BRANCHES**

AUTONOMY and ENTREPRENEURSHIP
'We've created an environment in which to give people opportunities.'

LOOSE-TIGHT PROPERTIES
'F International's flexible working methodology depends on tight project control.'

FLEXIBLE PATTERNS of WORK
'Flexibility is the key factor, especially for working mothers.'

DESIGN for WHOLENESS
'The twinning of technical excellence with a recognition of employees as whole people is essential to 'F's philosophy.'

PRODUCTIVITY THROUGH PEOPLE
'I'll sometimes buy an original painting, and take it into an office. The homely touch.'

CORPORATE MISSION
'One woman's inability to work in an office environment has turned into hundreds of women's opportunity to work in a non-office environment'.

HANDS ON
'People feel they ought to be busy.'

CENTRAL

MANAGED ORGANIZATION
F International

CULTURAL IDENTITY
'Our people fit their jobs around their lives'.

CORE

GROUNDS for BEING

'There is a need for non-conformity... the faultless repetition of a computer programme is an attack on creativity.'
CREATIVITY

'For many skilled people home-working provides a freedom and flexibility in line with their needs.'
FREEDOM

'Lady Lovelace, Lord Byron's daughter, was the world's first computer programmer.'
RECREATION

Steve Shirley, born a Jewess, fled from Nazi Germany, to be brought up in Britain by Quakers.
DIVERSITY

ROOTS   **ROOTS**

F FOR FLEXIBILITY

F International has drawn on the old traditions of the cottage industry, and brought them into a modern, electronic light. This required someone with an understanding of both tradition and modernity. Steve Shirley has drawn on the stream of consciousness of her own Jewish background, her English upbringing, and combined them with the developing computer technology of her day. Equally important was her identification with feminine accomplishments in household management, which she extrapolated into project management. Steve drew on the true roots, or origins of excellence, by reaching back towards her ethnic (family), genetic (female) and innate (mathematic) potential. She has transformed the world around her by painting her picture on a canvas large enough to include any others with shared roots and potential.

Having transformed the world around her, Steve has now decided to take a back-seat role in the development of her original company. In the last few years, in particular, a corporate identity has been formed apart from the company's originator. The very term 'F', for flexibility, is a symbol for this separate identity. A culture and structure of flexibility has been built into the company's working style, and project management system. Its roots have now spread beyond the pioneer's own identity towards those of a wider corporate constituency; that is, people simultaneously developing a home and a career.

THE F CORE

F International has now become a *managed organization*, and the structure of its major, UK operation, is outlined opposite.

The international group has separate Scandinavian, and Benelux subsidiaries, each with its own managing director. Similarly, there are four UK regions, each with its own regional management. A simultaneously loose-tight structure of control pervades.

Yet F is a managed organization with a difference. That difference is spelt out in its recruitment advertising (see opposite).

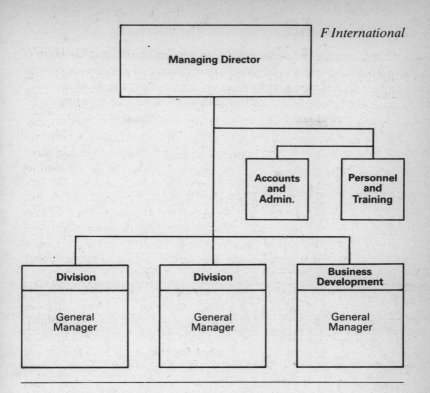

F International

Managing Director

Accounts and Admin.

Personnel and Training

Division / General Manager

Division / General Manager

Business Development / General Manager

Fitting your life round your job?

Home vs Career

Many people today are reluctant to surrender career options for family responsibilities, but find it difficult to maintain a conventional job while running a home. Or maybe you're just tired of wasting time travelling to work every day.

A Different Style of Work

Our company is one of the most successful, independent software and systems houses in the UK. We are also renowned as the pioneers of a new way of working which enables computer professionals to work flexible hours from a home base.

115

We are currently looking for personnel in this area with recent experience of general programming and data processing, who are able to commit themselves to a minimum of twenty hours per week working from home on specific projects.

In return we can offer you flexible working structure, opportunities for professional and personal development, local work with real career opportunities, fair rewards and all the benefits associated with working for a large, well-established and expanding company.

In fitting the job around people's lives, the management structure has to take combined account of home and work. So, although the hierarchical management structure appears clear cut, it has to bend accordingly. Flexible work patterns include not only 'flexitime' but also flexible work locations and contracts of employment, self-employment, or variations in between.

BRANCH ACTIVITIES

HARD WORK/HANDS ON

Factory work, or work on a construction site, carries with it an image of hard labour. But what about housework? Women, and increasingly men nowadays – who have taken to ironing, hoovering, dishwashing or scrubbing the bath – know what I mean. The rate of productivity at F International is tremendous. As managing director, Alison Newell, says, 'It's the working mother bit. People feel they ought to be busy. When you've done a day's work you still have got to listen to the children's worries.' So physically, if not also mentally and emotionally, work never stops. The memory of Steve Shirley rushing about the place – from computer to family to client – is still contained within F's corporate psyche. It is resuscitated every time she arrives, suddenly and unexpectedly but genially, at someone's front door. She is imminent. She is also gregarious.

The pioneer's inclination to work hard is therefore still in-grained within the organization. What F has not yet done is to extend its 'energy' frontiers to incorporate the health and fitness revolution which has entered our lives, and particularly those of women.

UNITING HOME AND WORK

F was born out of a social mission to unite home and work. Steve only got into computing because it seemed a good idea at the time. She has created opportunities for women to make a whole out of two parts – family and work. When you have a mission in life you have no choice but to fulfil it. In the preamble to the company's new charter, we read:

> F International is a group of companies which have sprung from seeing an opportunity in a problem: one woman's inability to work in an office has turned into hundreds of people's opportunity to work in a non-office environment.

At the age of five, Steve Shirley was brought out of Germany by the Quakers and adopted by a family in England. Having no blood family around her at the time, you might say she was destined to create an extended family of her own thirty years later. In the early sixties Steve had acquired a husband, a child and a lot of expertise in computing. At the age of twenty-nine, 'now retired with a young baby', as she put it, she discovered that computer programming, since it needs only a desk, a head, and paper and pencil, is a job that can be done at home between feeding the baby and washing nappies. So she decided, in 1962, to interest other 'retired' pro-grammers, such as her, to join up on a freelance basis.

More than thirty years later, when I went to visit Brian Mills, the UK company chairman at 'The Bury' office in Buckingham-shire, I took along my eight-year-old son. While Brian and I talked, my young boy and his nine-year-old girl friend entertained themselves in the boardroom, writing messages to each other on the whiteboard.

The acceptance of family responsibilities alongside work is

absolute. Office meetings, among F personnel themselves, are seldom held before 10.30, to allow time for children to be taken to school, and 'When one of us says we're taking the day off because it's our children's sports day, everyone immediately understands.'

The premises at 'The Bury', where board meetings are held, are like a well-kept home. In fact warmth and hospitality are the pervading features of the corporate culture there. It was often difficult to distinguish the work environment from a homely atmosphere, and vice versa. Yet, because of the inevitable disruptions of time and place, caused by juxtaposing home and work, F has developed an absolute 'cult of efficiency'. The promptness of return calls, of replies to letters, and of appointments made is remarkable. The staff have deliberately had to compensate for the difficulties of communicating across multiple workplaces. And the noticeable feature is not the proliferation of technology, but sheer down-to-earth practical reliability.

Along with the efficiency and the practicality goes a certain style. As Steve told me, 'One of our drivers made an interesting comment the other day. We have a company pin, so we can be recognized, but he said he could tell us apart even without looking for it. It's something about the briefcase, the smartness.'

The company also has its bulletins, its newsletter, its service awards, and its anniversaries. But in addition to these there are special homely touches. 'We send flowers or potted plants for certain occasions. I'll send our MD, Alison, a card when she returns from abroad, saying something like "Thank God you got back safely!" I'll sometimes buy an original painting, and take it into an office, to set the tone. It all goes towards creating a homely atmosphere.'

It is interesting to compare and contrast F with other software houses, for there is something very distinctive about the programming culture at large. Brian Mills, the current UK chairman, who used to run a competing company, CMG, put it like this:

When I first came into this industry machine capacity was scarce, estimating was poor, and programmers were esoteric animals. In the sixties it was the 'in' thing. I have worked with teams of programmers for forty-eight hours at a stretch. Nights were nothing. It breeds a commando, crack regiment. People with IQs in the 160s. and they were doing it all for the clerks and accountants. It was in an era when people were saying that we British were lazy. Yet they were working their guts out for people they didn't even identify with. The key to being a programmer is obsessive perfectionism. Both my partners were bloody good programmers. One would stay up all night balancing his household accounts, the other hung his suits in order of the date of purchase.

Also, in a service organization like ours, the people and the product are inseparable. At CMG we created a hothouse environment. We were constantly pushing people to the limits of their capabilities. If you don't perpetually create new challenges for them, you're lost. But there are differences between CMG and F International. Women don't see their work status as their whole being.

The other thing about programmers is that unlike, say, accountants, they're doing something esoteric. Like the foreign legionnaires, their loyalty is to each other. They don't feel they belong to their company. They belong to computing and to themselves. Again, with women it's a little different, because there's always something else in their lives.

But both men and women do like to have a leader. Steve is a charismatic, emotive leader. At the same time, she has a curious humility.

What F has not yet managed to do, successfully, is to create an integrated 'community of interest', including customers as well as freelancers and employees, which shares a root vision apart from the one contained within Steve's own psyche.

FLEXIBILITY IN CAREER DEVELOPMENT

Flexibility is the key factor, especially for working mothers. This means they fit their jobs around their lives.

Alison Newell, managing director

The F culture is distinctive, but not overwhelmingly so. The homely atmosphere, the cult of efficiency and the charisma of its founder are apparent. But, above all, it is the F-lexibility that stands out in more ways than one.

In the first place, there is the F-reedom which transcends F-lexibility. From an early age Steve Shirley campaigned for changes in the laws on suicide and birth control. She had experienced, at a very young age, what tyranny could do to people. Understandably, freedom is an obsession of hers. But there is no freedom in a community without discipline. Tom Lloyd, in his book *Dinosaur & Co.* (1984), which incorporated Steve Shirley amongst its high-tech entrepreneurs, put it in this way:

> Working women who wish to become mothers face a cruel choice – either give up work at what will often be a crucial stage in their career, or stay on and pay someone else to enjoy the pleasure of raising their children. The story of F International is, to a large extent, the story of one woman's rejection of that choice.
>
> The existence and prosperity of a company like F is also corroboration of a kind for my thesis – that rapid technological change has consequences that extend far beyond the technology itself – the pace of change represents a major upheaval in the system of production and puts a high premium on flexibility.

As can be seen from the following case studies, F has a very flexible approach to career development. First, Alison Newell, the managing director:

> I disliked school intensely. I didn't like the structure and the environment. It was structure for the sake of it, and it didn't meet the students' needs. So I left a year early, once I'd got my mediocre 'A' levels. I went to the College of Technology, at Aston University, and started a degree course in physics, chemistry and maths. It was a bit daft, as I hadn't done chemistry at 'A' level. So, after a year of higher education, I left, having no clear idea of what I wanted to do.
>
> I was looking for something that would really interest me, something which would capture my interest, that I hadn't yet found. My father was a hot-metal printer, and, at an early age, I

helped him set up the type in galleys. I set up the panels for adverts in telephone boxes, and got paid for what I produced. That gave me a good and early insight into business. I found it all very interesting, and went on to work for Legal & General.

I worked there for three years, and was promoted to chief programmer. But I wasn't terribly enamoured with the structured environment within the insurance industry. It was so traditionally status conscious, with its multilevel canteens! I was paid 95 per cent of the normal rate, being a woman. But I was extremely anxious to continue my career, and therefore needed to balance the two sides of my life.

After I had my first child I saw an advert, from FPL (as F International was then called), for a marketing executive. I had discussed with my employer the possibility of a part-time job, and they offered me a four-day week. But that wasn't what I wanted. I wanted to play a large part in the bringing up of my child, and a nine-to-five working day would inhibit that. So I joined FPL.

The brief I had was very loose. It was going to be selling, building up the southeast. The strongest customer base, at the time, was still in and around Buckinghamshire, north of London. This was 1974. I loved the job from day one. I had immense freedom. It was all up to me. There was nothing stopping me. It was up to me to make a success.

I succeeded from the beginning. We were just entering a boom time for data processing. I found that it was easy to sell, right from the start. Firstly, I could trust the quality of our product and, secondly, I had a very practical approach. Some of the companies, at the time, weren't sure how to go about things. The selling at FPL led on to project development, which also became my responsibility. It was a period of hectic growth. I stayed with the projects I sold. I then became the overall manager for the southern region. That was in 1979. I was appointed to the board, as technical director, and in 1981 I became managing director.

Next, Rosie Symons, PR manager:

I left Kodak in 1972, when my daughter was born. While looking after my baby, I soon found out that there was time for lots of other things. Through my professional training and personal drive I'd built up a self-discipline which enabled me to have time on my hands. I was a bit of a workaholic.

I very quickly became relaxed in my role as mother, and, rather than look around for more domestic jobs, it occurred to me that I could do something useful. I had a good three or four hours every day to spare. Babies can be demanding, but it's up to you. One tends to be drawn into the maternal world, and nothing else. I wanted more than that.

When my daughter Melanie was three months old, I saw an ad in the local paper for a secretary to the personnel manager of FPL, to work from home. It suited me perfectly and I got the job. In 1972 F International had 150 people on its books. The job involved processing applications, and general liaising with staff, regarding availability for projects. As the flow of applicants increased I needed an assistant. My next door neighbour, with a baby the same age as mine, took on the job, which was very convenient for both of us. I stayed on till 1975, when I was expecting my second baby. At the time, the company was starting to centralize the personnel function (together with other key business management positions) to the extent that it required a full-time, office-based person. That was impossible for me, so I opted out, saying that I wanted to return if and when a suitable niche came up.

However, I had also decided that I did not want to be solely a 'mum at home', and Steve Shirley who lived nearby used to give me special research projects and secretarial work. In addition I took on *ad hoc* assignments for the company's documentation manager. So you can see that if your personal circumstances change, the company will always try to meet it by creating alternative work opportunities – in this instance, support roles for me. I did that for a year, by when I was itching to get my teeth into a proper job. At that time the PR manager was looking for a PA, again to work from home. By then one of my children was at school, and I wanted to be more than a secretary. I wanted a job that required initiative. So after a while I told my manager I wanted to become more involved, and she was more than willing. I became her deputy. Everyone in F

International is given the opportunity to review their job description through management reappraisal.

In 1979, the PR manager left, and I was asked to take over. As it happened, we were in the throes of moving house at the time, and my ninety-three-year-old grandfather was coming to live with us. He was going blind, had suffered a heart attack and needed a lot of care. I panicked. How would I cope? I told the personnel manager. As far as I'm concerned my family always comes first. I can always pick up on my career. So she said I could slide into the job gradually, taking as much time as I needed to settle our 'new' addition into the family home.

People can come from anywhere and go everywhere, subject to innate ability and interest. The company has a firm policy of promotion from within, and there is many a diagonal path to development. As a result there is a strong orientation towards training on the technical side, as well as in sales and management.

As far as the technical 'panel' of freelances are concerned, they are required to have four years' background in computing. It is where they go from there that makes F for freedom, flexibility, freelance or female, so distinctive. In an article in *Software Management* (November 1982) a journalist imagined what it would be like looking at the business world through a Martian's eyes.

You take a sample of humans, split them into two halves called sexes, and use one group – the males – to fill all senior and managerial posts requiring high creativity, initiative and intelligence. Naturally, the other half – the females – will then provide a much higher proportion of those qualities than what is left of the male half, as the Martian might see it. Then, if you handicap the female half so as to ensure that only the truly determined and highly motivated ones get a chance to be considered for these posts, you get a marvellous natural selection barrier. Facing handicaps, provided you have the character to overcome them, is a great builder of character.

FLEXIBLE, PROJECT-BASED MANAGEMENT

The handicap that women and single-parent men within F International have faced is that of managing a dual career with a difference – running a workplace and a home – and in overcoming that hurdle they have developed both the specific qualities and the general strength of character required to manage diverse, temporary and flexible assignments. This, in fact, is the second key that has opened many a client's door – F International's excellence in project management.

The task of the well-organized person at home is precisely analogous to that of the project manager. Consider all the powers of organization required for the smooth running of a house being transferred into the conventional, and preferably project-based, workplace. No wonder Rosie Symons, the PR manager, puts it this way:

> At the core of our success is our method of staffing and our approach to management. Our people have the will and wish to work from home, and organize themselves as such. The work is also varied, precisely analysed and estimated. Tasks are defined and costed. They know what's expected of them. They also can't slip. Discipline is inborn. Flexibility is the key factor – especially for our working mothers. It means they can also choose what time they work, when they know they won't be distracted from the demands of children. They fit their job around their life.

VERSATILE COMMUNICATIONS

Journalists and academics have heralded our era of telecommuting, where information rather than people will commute to work. F International have got on with homeworking, with the minimum of technological fuss. It has been the flexibility of attitude rather than the flexibility of the technology which has enabled the organization, and its business, to work. Steve Shirley said this to me:

> Communications are highly dependent on telephone and postal services and on a few key people, executive secretaries mainly, remaining relatively still while the rest of the organization re-

volves around them. Infrequent but regular meetings bring together project teams, sales people and estimators in a web of contacts. These are particularly important to efficient functioning as face-to-face contacts are relatively unusual.

There have been experiments with visionphones. There have been experiments with teleconferencing. There is a current investigation into Micronet which uses people's personal TV sets (assets on which F International might capitalize), so as to operate a crude, wide area network.

In practice, the organization uses telex, telephone (with answering equipment to cross social and international time differences) and, most recently, telecopiers. While operating facsimile equipment is still much like watching grass grow, F International gets enormous value from being able to transmit scribbled notes to distant colleagues. Technical bulletins and newsletters help spread professional and personal information through the network; these are circulated by post and courier services, as are a multiplicity of papers, files and memoranda, cassettes and occasionally floppy discs.

While some tasks have been defined as needing a high level of commitment, this is generally avoided and so part-time, home-based workers can hold very senior positions. The organization provides career opportunities, not just work, to its homeworkers and is continually defining and redefining itself, taking its form by matching members' needs and market requirements. In this matching process, the organizational structure achieved is minimal and working procedures are more important to effective functioning than are fixed, official relationships.

Freelancers are designated as 'panel', being attached to a regional or national office or, occasionally, with corporate or group association.

A characteristic of the workforce is that most people have deliberately considered whether or not to work and retain the responsibility and enthusiasm generated by their choice to do so. Panel members are particularly independent in this sense and regularly adjust and monitor the overall balance in their lives. But it needs someone, in the first place, to get the work in for the panel members to do.

So in their system of project management, as well as in the approach they have taken to career development, flexibility has become the company norm. At the present time, though, this is more characteristic of their working methods than of their use of communications technology. Emerging developments in electronic networking have only been taken on board, to date, in an experimental and tentative form.

AUTONOMY AND ENTREPRENEURSHIP

We've created an environment in which to give people opportunities.

Alison Newell

An Environment of Opportunity

Freedom of choice is one thing. Entrepreneurship is another. In fact, the entrepreneur brings a degree of single-minded commitment into business that often stands in the way of freedom. F International has never had an easy relationship with entrepreneurial activity. In the early days, when Steve Shirley was on her own, her entrepreneurial impulse was strong, but never dominant.

In the period up to the early seventies the company struggled, at times desperately, to keep its head above water. The period since then, and particularly in the last five years, has seen an accelerating increase in turnover and operating profit.

Yet the entrepreneurial cut and thrust remains somewhat in the background. At the moment Steve is concentrating her efforts on creating new overseas business. But it is seen by some core personnel as peripheral to the mainstream business. Alison Newell sees herself as a risk-taker, but immediately she acknowledges it, she alludes to the environment for opportunity she is creating for others. The 'enormous lift' she gets out of having done a great job seems as much to do with quality *per se*, as with recognition for achievement.

There was a period in the company's history when entrepreneurism had a relatively free rein, in between the days of pioneering and rational management. Steve had stepped back

F International Workforce

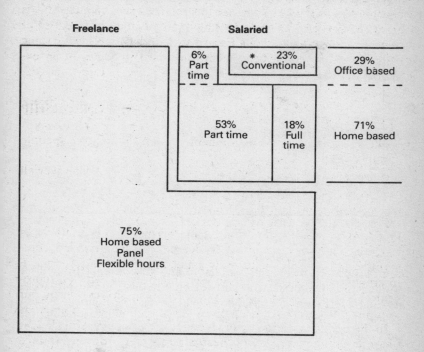

Freelance

Salaried

6% Part time

* 23% Conventional

29% Office based

53% Part time

18% Full time

71% Home based

75%
Home based
Panel
Flexible hours

89.75% part time or flexitime
10.25% full time
*5.75% Office based and full time and salaried
        i.e., conventional employees

(Asterisk refers to diagram)

Graduate disciplines	%
Computer science and maths	6
Engineering	5
Scientific	14
Arts	71
Others	4
	100

F International Revenue

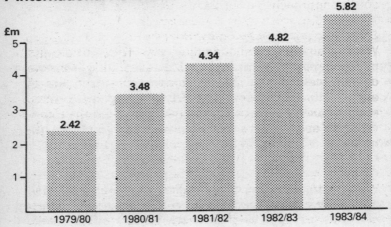

from a position of overall leadership and several entrepreneurial women took up the central and regional helms. The results were mixed. It left ambivalent feelings. The seven UK regions, as well as the three international subsidiaries, do still have some autonomy, but the degree of autonomy is now limited.

In many ways, the company's view of entrepreneurship is reflected in its charter. Quantity of profit is subordinate to quality of product, and of personal lifestyle. It is visibly a means to an end, and economic returns have to be judged alongside psychological rewards.

Corporate Charter

Professional Excellence
Our long-term aim is to improve our professional abilities so as to maintain a quality product for our clients. It is also our aim to develop fully our pro-

fessional potential as people and to develop our organization in a way which reflects our own individuality and special approach.

Economic and Psychological Reward

We also aim to realize and enjoy fully the economic and psychological rewards of our efforts resulting from the development of the unique competitive advantage of our structure and capabilities. We aim to achieve profits, reward our employees commensurately with their contribution and provide an attractive return to our shareholders.

Growth

We aim to grow our organization to its full potential, nationally and internationally. We aim to grow at least as rapidly as the software industry as a whole as we take our place in it in order to maintain our own position as an attractive employer and a competitive supplier.

F International, in summary, does not have the cut and thrust that characterizes some aggressive and male-dominated companies. Whether that is a loss is open to question. I myself formed the impression that there is not enough of an entrepreneurial tradition to draw on. This may be one of the remaining weaknesses of an organization dominated by women, who, so far, have not had as much exposure to aggressive entrepreneurship as their male counterparts. The time may well be approaching when more men need to be drawn into the company, although, naturally, this would require a reappraisal of its underlying ethos.

LOOSE-TIGHT ORGANIZATION

F International's flexible working methodology depends on tight project control.

Steve Shirley

The 'Humanware' Business

F International is two businesses rolled up into one. That is its problem and its opportunity. It is a bespoke software house. It is also in the business of personnel recruitment and development. In a way, the company's joint business is 'humanware'. As a software house it is somewhat distinctive, but not especially so; as a personnel business it is very distinctive, but not commercially so. In other words, the company generates its profits out of computer services, and its social kudos out of personnel services. Well, that is not entirely true. For in a service business it is difficult to divorce product from people. Because F has succeeded in recruiting and developing quality personnel in a business where their supply is scarce, it has secured a certain competitive edge. The question is, has this edge been exploited to the full? Is its business concept fully developed?

I find it useful to start with an analogy from Habitat/ Mothercare. Conran initially became involved with furniture manufacture, and subsequently with retailing. Similarly, Steve Shirley started off in computer programming and graduated into computing services. The distinctive feature of Conran's activity was product design. The distinguishing feature of the F activity was 'work design'. Conran has since expanded from furnishing into clothing and publishing, with product – as well as interior, graphic and fashion – design at the core.

What, then, is distinctive about F International's work design? There is certainly nothing unusual in the organization as a whole, except for the high proportion of women in management. As far as its 'product line' is concerned, it does have the advantage of being independent of any hardware supplier, but that again is not unique in the industry.

Product Line

As a generalist systems house F International is not allied to any hardware supplier and is therefore familiar with a wide variety of manufacturers' hardware, including Amdahl, Burroughs, Control Data, DEC, Ferranti, GEC, Hewlett-Packard, Honeywell, IBM, ICL, Intel, Motorola, NCR, Nixdorf, Philips, Prime, Tandem, Texas Instruments, Univac, Wang, Zilog and many others. F International has implemented numerous applications on mainframes, minicomputers and microcomputers for both centralized and distributed systems in on-line and batch mode.

Software experience covers not only most applications languages but also much systems software including TP monitors such as CICS, EN-VIRON/1 and Shadow, and Database packages such as IMS, DD/1 IDMS RAMIS and System 2000, IMAGE and TOTAL, and ADABAS. Hardware and software evaluation is undertaken both for dedicated and general applications, and for industrial processing techniques.

F International Brochure

When I analysed the company's specific services I discovered that some were industry based (e.g., manufacturing, insurance), some were hardware based (e.g., IBM, DEC), some were process oriented (e.g., program development and training), and some were product oriented (e.g., documentation and data base). There was no obvious underlying theme.

THE CONCEPT OF WORK DESIGN

Where there is an underlying theme, however, is in the approach to 'work design', stretching back from selection and recruitment, to staff development, ultimately reaching project management. Project managemsent is in fact a natural extension of the flexible structure of work design that has its roots in the pattern of household activity. The question that remains is to what extent, and at what stage, if any, will the company exploit the full potential of the concept?

The Roots of Excellence

Interestingly enough, those engaged with information technology see it as a meand to accommodate individual variety and flexibility. Hence the advent of 'bespoke production', flexible manafacturing systems, and home-based work stations. How much more powerful might 'work designs' be which accommodate individual variety? To explore this concept a little further we need to look at the way the company, the industry and society are evolving.

Work Design

F international is an independent computer systems house with a countrywide workforce comprising 800-plus highly skilled information processing technicians. Founded in 1962, the company has gained international recognition within many major market sectors.

Computer consultancy, business and scientific analysis, systems design, programming, installation and maintenance of software, and training are amongst the complete range of software services provided to industry and government. The company operates in geographic regions with regional managers responsible for all work undertaken from the initial proposal to the implementation and acceptance. F International's unique flexible working methodolgy depends upon full project control technoques including estimating, auditing and performance recording. Personnel are accepted into the orgainzation with a minimum of four years' experience in the industry and statistics within the group show an average of over ten years' experience each.

F International Brochure

DESIGN FOR WHOLENESS

The twinning of technical excellence with a recognition of employees as whole people is essential to F's philosophy.

Steve Shirley

FROM COTTAGE INDUSTRY TO ELECTRONIC COTTAGE

In the earlier part of this book I revealed the common patterns in the evolution of physical, economic and social organisms. There is a time to pioneer, a time to expand and a time to develop. These phases correspond with the new enterprise, the managed organization, and what I have called the 'enabling company'.[1]

In the beginning there was Steve, Shirley, Freelance Programmers, and a few customers – large companies with mainframe computers. The product line was narrowly based and, for the first ten years, a few key individuals were crucial to the business. Steve, the pioneer, was at the centre of it all.

From the outset, FPL was very much aware of its social, as well as its economic significance. Steve was part of the flow of history, taking one step back to cottage industry, and two steps forward, into an era where both women and information technology were asserting themselves. Yet there must have been times, when overdrafts loomed large as the recession hit, that economic survival took precedence over all else.

FROM ENTREPRENEURISM TO STRATEGIC PLANNING

The seventies was a period of expansion, from a turnover of some £50,000 in 1969 to £2.5 million in 1979. A loose-knit regional organization was established run by a small number of entrepreneurial women. F had outgrown Steve's initial pioneering, but had not yet become a managed organization. Their first personnel manager, Jane Wilkinson, who was recruited in 1982, puts it like this:

[1] See my article on the enabling company in *New Patterns of Work*, ed. David Clutterbuck (Gower, 1984).

When I joined, a personnel function hardly existed. Alison became MD in 1981 and asked me, initially on a freelance basis, to help her define the organization structure and jobs. She wanted a change from the highly competitive, decentralized structure, which existed at the time. It had the best and worst features of an entrepreneurial company, one region competing with the other. Each region had developed its own structures and work procedures, and one hardly communicated with the other.

My aim was to get people talking to each other. Also, there was no training, other than of a technical kind. Alison, in fact, wanted me to develop a programme of management training which I have now instituted. Also, we weren't professional saleswomen. We combined selling with everything else. So we brought in a sales consultant, and now we have a dedicated sales team.

Along with the improved comunications, management training and professional salesmanship, Alison Newell devolved the system of strategic planning. Steve, in the meantime, was busy creating a proper board structure, both for the UK company and for the overseas interests, heavily involving non-executive directors. All of them have plenty of experience in business and computing. So what was previously an entrepreneurial company has now become a properly managed organization, albeit with a fair degree of territorial autonomy.

MANAGING INTERDEPENDENCE

The question is, where does the organization go from here? That may be a premature question, given that 'scientific management' has only existed throughout the company for two to three years. Steve Shirley has herself told me that the time has now come for F to learn how to manage innovation. While developing the overseas interests, she has been considering both franchising and new forms of multinational business. But the key to the next stage of its development lies, to my mind, with market forces.

The relationship that F International has with its customers is an intriguing one. Given that most of them are big organizations using mainframe systems, the image of David and Goliath immediately comes to mind. But that is a false image. A better image would come from ecology, through the symbiotic relationship in which many forms of plant and animal life are engaged. The company's closeness to the customer is intriguing on three counts. Firstly, F personnel may well 'live' on the client's premises for considerable periods of time. Secondly, they genuinely work together with the customer on projects. Thirdly, 80 per cent of F's custom is repeat business, so close associations are maintained and developed. It is as if the systems analysts, designers and programmers become 'imployed' by the big companies, without actually being employed.

This degree of interdependence marks, in fact, the third phase of an organization's development. It is, indeed, a particular characteristic of the 'development' or 'enabling company', as opposed to the independent business or holding company. It means that the business concern and its customers are intricately interwoven, one with the other. It is almost as if a new boundary needs to be drawn around the organization and its market environment:

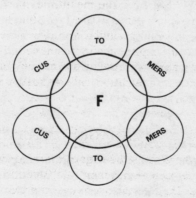

According to Alison Newell, the way that F's market has been evolving is like this. When computers were first installed, the financial area was the major user. But nowadays the computer has in some cases become the powerhouse of the whole company, including production, distribution and sales. So computer-related decisions are increasingly being made by company boards. The following is an extract from F International publicity material.

Interdependence between Company and Client

The intricate wiring systems of the new 146 aircraft were developed and maintained by F International in liaison with British Aerospace technologists.

Continuing several years' working association with the Plastics Division of ICI, in Welwyn Garden City, we were assigned to provide on-line engineering documentation, and the facility to monitor projects using costs and time display systems.

The development of a Pensions/Personnel System for Wiggins Teape, the paper manufacturer, involved close liaison with their computer technologists, and is one of many continuing assignments.

Documenting the Accounting Systems for Franklin Mint of London, gave us an insight into the world of fine books, stamps, porcelain and coins.

Whole new industries are now developing which can offer new technology-based services. At the same time, industry's perception of companies like F have changed. Using the services offered by a software house was once considered to be an admission of failure. Today it is a symbol of progress. It adds flexibility and reduces overheads. It also calls for a particular kind of relationship, one in which customer and supplier work together.

In the early days FPL's business was built around programming and systems design. Now it is increasingly called upon to be involved with systems analysis and commercial problem-solving. Programming, or so-called 'code generating', has been reduced from 75 per cent of turnover five years ago, to 40 per cent today.

In essence the function of the bespoke software house is

changing from one of supplying a service, to that of being a link organization. At the same time, F is both working with the computer users to develop their applications and being called upon by the hardware suppliers to sell their products. The software house is becoming the link between source and application via the systems that it builds.

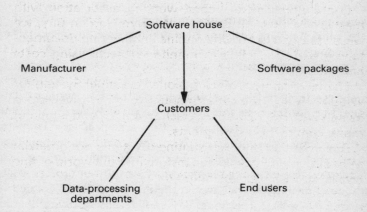

The Changing Interface

To that extent an ability to conceptualize a business, its systems and its components, together with skill in recognizing and building relationships, is becoming all-important. The function of catalyst, facilitator, bridge builder, which is already well known in the field of organization development, is now entering into systems building.

So the role of enabler, in the context of an enabling company, may well supplant that of the manager – in the context of a conventional organization. That is a challenge to which F International, with its background in organizational experimentation, should respond with no great difficulty.

CORPORATE MISSION

WORK AND FAMILY

And yet Steve's business is unfinished. The two previously alien concepts that she has forged together are 'work' and 'family'. As she explained to me:

> I'm in the process of developing a credo, a charter to cover the non-quantifiable aspects of our business. You need to be able to express those absolute qualities that are so important to business and to life. The twinning of technical excellence with a recognition of employees as whole people – writing programs or attending their children's sports days – is essential to our philosophy and structure.

People use their flexible employment contracts to accommodate their other life interests and they do so publicly with a freedom which is not often experienced in other organizations. They are also aware that few other corporations would allow part-time workers such responsible jobs, let alone part-timers working from home! Steve suggests in addition that the nature of project working may contribute to this image. People's activity is defined in terms of the work to be done, rather than any auxiliary characteristics of employment.

So far so good. The very existence of F International, its 800 panel members and 250 employed staff, is the fulfilment of a dream. But there are hurdles still to be overcome.

F International Charter

F International is a group of companies which have sprung from seeing an opportunity in a problem; one woman's inability to work in an office has turned into hundreds of people's opportunity to work in a non-office environment. Because of its unusual origin, F International has a clear sense of its mission, its strategy and its values.

Mission
F International's mission is to become a leader in the rapidly growing, and highly profitable, knowledge-intensive software industry. It aims to achieve this by exploiting, through modern telecommunications, the development of the unutilized intellectual energy of individuals and groups unable to work in a conventional office environment.

Strategy
F International's strategy is to maximize the value of its unusual asset base by establishing a competitive advantage over conventionally organized firms, and eventual imitators of its approach, through cost and quality competitiveness. This occurs by the development of a methodology which ensures quality and by establishing a company ethos which binds people who work largely independently and often alone.

Values
People are vital to any knowledge-intensive industry. The skills and loyalty of our employees are our only asset. Equally important is the knowledge which comes from the exchange of ideas with our clients and their personnel. It follows that human and ethical values play a pivotal role in the way in which a company like F International conducts itself.

In the first place, by not yet being involved in the personnel selection, recruitment and work design business, F is somewhat dependent on others for the fulfilment of its mission. Unlike Conran, for example, it has not marketed its unique design principles. Secondly, in wishing to delegate authority to the utmost, Steve Shirley has taken, in recent years, something of a back-seat role. It is therefore particularly important that her qualities as an innovator are suitably magnified. They will only be magnified to the extent that her presence, as a creative force, is exercised, received and formalized. As a result, Steve's interest in establishing a research function, as a formal entity, is well founded. The degree to which such a research function is technically, or socially based, may be the key to a next big step in F International's development. The company has already proved itself as a social and economic force in Britain, and in Europe and America. The question is, how can its widely based reputation as a social force, magnify its more narrowly based commitment as an economic one? How can the roots of its excellence, seeded through Steve Shirley's own background and vision, and grounded in the evolving state of our society, be deepened? Can it extend its symbiotic base, which it shares with the biggest and the best companies in the land? Can F International provide the social as well as the technical ingredients that so many of its clients lack, while these same clients return some of the economic as well as technical ingredients, which would bolster F's long-term growth? Can and should F do for our postindustrial society what Alfred Marks, Brook Street Bureau, Urwick Orr or John Humble did for our industrial one? These are all questions that the company will continue to ask, because its business is never finished.

7. Habitat/Mothercare

Pioneering Days

Designing and making furniture

1952   Terence Conran opened his first workshop in Bethnal Green.
1953   He opened a showroom in Piccadilly Arcade.

Creating new enterprises

1954   Conran and partner set up four soup kitchens.
1956   The Orrery Restaurant was established.
1956   Conran Fabrics was created.
1956   The first Conran Design Group was established.
1959   Conran Contracts was created.

From Entrepreneurship to Management

A continuing phase of entrepreneurism, on a larger scale

1962   Conran moved from two workshops into a proper furniture factory.
1964   The first Habitat was established in Fulham.
1964–68 Three more Habitats were opened.
1968   Habitat merged with Ryman.
1969   A mail order operation was established.
1970   The merger with Ryman was terminated.
1971   Conran Associates, a new design group, was created.
1971   The Neal Street Restaurant was opened.
1971–73 Twelve new Habitat stores were opened.
1973   Habitat in France was opened.
1973   The Conran Shop was created.
1974   Habitat established its own warehouse.
1976   Share ownership scheme introduced.
1977   Conran set up in the USA.

The Roots of Excellence

A period of consolidation and growth

1977   Chris Turner became Habitat's chief executive, with a brief to professionalize management.

1980   There were now 47 stores, in the UK, USA, France and Belgium.

From Professional Management to Integrated Development

A new era of public responsibility

1981   Habitat becomes a public company.

1981   The Conran Foundation sets up the Boilerhouse Project to further design in the UK.

An era of joint venturing opens

1982   Habitat moves into Japan and links with Seibu.

1982   Habitat merges with Mothercare.

1983   Acquisition and gradual resurrection of Heal's.

1983   Joint venture between Morgan Grenfell, Habitat/Mothercare, and Richard Shops.

1983   Joint venture between Conran and Octopus Books.

1983   Now is spawned, as a division of Mothercare UK.

1984   Group headquarters established in Heal's building.

1985   A Heal's/Habitat/Mothercare/Now complex is established.

The Operating Subsidiaries

Habitat UK (including The Conran Shop and Heal's – see below)

Modern furniture and home furnishings, around 40 per cent imported. Through 46 stores, not necessarily in prime locations, and by mail order. Targeted at younger B-C1's. Around 1700 full-time equivalent employees. Trading profits of £8.0 million on sales of £73.4 million. Net selling area around 600,000 sq. ft.

Heal's

General furniture and home furnishings through the principal store in Tottenham Court Road, London, and one branch in Guildford. Limited mail order, e.g., Christmas catalogue. Targeted at older, more affluent end of market. Losing money prior to acquisition in April 1983 on sales of around £10.0 million, but now totally revamped and beginning to make its mark.

Habitat France and Belgium

Modern furniture and home furnishings, more than 30 per cent imported. Through 24 stores, not necessarily in prime locations (including 3 Grand H superstores), and by mail order. Targeted at younger B-C1's (Grand H C1-C2's). Around 800 full-time equivalent employees. Profitable since 1977 with sales currently around £41.0 million. Net selling area around 430,000 sq. ft.

Conran's USA

Modern furniture and home furnishings, nearly 50 per cent imported. Through 10 stores, not necessarily in prime locations, and by mail order. Targeted at younger B-C1's. Around 400 full-time equivalent employees. Now securely into profit on sales of £21.5 million. Net selling area around 185,000 sq. ft.

Mothercare UK (including Now – see below)

Everything for the mother and her child up to ten, mainly of UK manufacture. Through 216 predominantly high street/shopping centre stores and by mail order. Mass market appeal. Around 2900 full-time equivalent employees. Most significant profit contributor – £25.6 million on sales of £185.4 million. Net selling area around 750,000 sq. ft.

Now

New concept in clothes retailing, introduced October 1983 in five UK test shops, targeted at the ten- to sixteen-year-olds of both sexes. Includes small, inexpensive, impulse purchases for traffic building. Results so far very encouraging and expansion in progress.

Mothercare Europe

Everything for the mother and her child up to ten, significantly of UK origin. Through 28 predominantly high street/shopping centre stores in seven countries and by mail order in certain of them. Mass market appeal. Around 300 full-time equivalent employees. Marginal trading results on sales of £15.1 million. Net selling area around 80,000 sq. ft.

Mothercare USA

Maternity wear and clothing for children up to six, almost exclusively of American origin. No hardware. Through 197 stores predominantly in non-prime shopping malls. No mail order. Around 900 full-time equivalent employees. Still in loss, but decreasing, on sales of £37.0 million. Net selling area around 260,000 sq. ft.

Conran Associates

Design consultancy with offices in London and Paris and a subsidiary, Conran Advertising, in London. Around 100 full-time equivalent employees. Useful contribution of around £0.5 million.

Richards

Women's wear with broad market appeal through 210 prime located UK stores. No mail order. Currently operated through joint venture company with ownership split 48 per cent Habitat/Mothercare, 48 per cent Morgan Grenfell, 4 per cent management. Currently unexciting trading results on sales of around £40 million while complete refurbishment and market reorientation under way.

Group Services

Group Design and Marketing
With offices in London and New York. Provides all design and marketing services required by retailing companies, including product design, fashion design, store design, packaging and graphics, advertising and point of sale, mail order catalogue design and photography.

Group Finance and Administration
Based at Group HQ in London. Coordinates throughout entire group provision and control of funds, tax planning, assessment of investment opportunities, monitoring of financial performance, maintenance of proper accounting and statutory records, provision of legal and corporate services, preservation of good relations with Stock Exchange, major banks, City institutions and various professional advisers and formulation of overall group policy in such other areas as executive personnel, property, data systems, and general administration.

Group Operations
Also based at Group HQ London. Coordinates group-wide understanding and execution of agreed trading strategies and formulae, consistency of store merchandising, layout and display, provision of required standards of customer service, monitoring of all aspects of operational performance and appropriate staff training and personnel policies.

Ian Peacock,
director of finance and administration,
1984

Habitat: a Designed Organization

We understand the prime motive, almost intuitively . . . a style, an image . . . integrity, simplicity, dedication, and an attention to detail.

> Oliver Gregory, design director

Of high arts . . . in this country there is abundance, and of mechanical invention. What remains to be done is to wed art with mechanical skill.

> Sir Henry Cole, Royal Society of Arts

CREATIVITY AND INNOVATION

Steve Shirley, and F International, have drawn on the individualistic streak within the British nation, and created the flexible structures to accommodate it. Sir Terence Conran has tapped the roots of art, craft and design, in Britain and in Europe, and has developed a new approach to retailing out of them. The path has not been an easy one, and there have been many struggles along the way.

Conran's struggles have been not so much with business monsters, but with monstrous taste and with offending ugliness. In creating Habitat, he established a newly designed era of retailing in its stead. He symbolizes the creative vigour that has featured so strongly in this nation's history. Conran has created a corporate culture and an overall style which are totally unique. It is through that culture that I want to introduce the Habitat/Mothercare story.

CORPORATE CULTURE

Habitat opened on 11 May 1964. . . . It was an essential part of trendy London and the swinging sixties.

> Bartie Phillips, author of *Conran: the Habitat Story* (1984)

Habitat/Mothercare
A DESIGNED ORGANIZATION

BRANCHES

BRANCHES

AUTONOMY and ENTREPRENEURSHIP
'Philosophically, we think small.'

LOOSE-TIGHT PROPERTIES
'We have had to ensure that creativity is allied to discipline'.

FLEXIBLE SYSTEMS
'It's still a very individual business and it breaks all the retailing rules.'

DESIGN for WHOLENESS
'Everyone is interested in everyone's job'.

TEAM WORK
'We seem to find, very quickly, loyal lieutenants and staff... We've got fused together into a team.

CORPORATE MISSION
'Well-designed products accessible to people of modest means.'

HANDS-ON, VALUE DRIVEN
'A burly figure in jeans climbed out of his Mercedes and made a beeline for a pot of paint.'

CULTURAL IDENTITY
Habitat/ Mothercare

CENTRAL

'We understand the prime motive almost intuitively... a style, an image... Integrity, simplicity dedication and an attention to detail.'

CORE

GROUNDS for BEING

'There must be a kind of religion of workmanship in England.
RECREATION

Habitat opened on 11 May 1964. It was an essential part of the swinging sixties.
SELF-EXPRESSION

'Of high arts... in this country there is an abundance... and of mechanical invention.
CREATIVITY

I loved the whole circular process from digging clay at one end to selling pots at the other.'
DIVERSITY

ROOTS

ROOTS

147

Before I came to write the Habitat/Mothercare story I had almost convinced myself of its central theme – 'design and evolution'. But when I came to review my interview material I discovered something else. The associated theme that announced itself, loud and clear, was that of 'culture'. In other words, it was the cultural or social fabric of the organization, its 'style', as the designers might say, which has proved all pervading. Aesthetic, dramatic and pragmatic, the culture is probably best captured not by a series of 'still pictures', but by a moving, 'theatrical play'.

Heal's, particularly in its early days, had a lot in common with Habitat's origins. Heal's has been the leading name in home furnishings for most of this century, and just recently Conran has taken it over, with the intention of renewing and revitalizing its image and merchandise. The reopening of Heal's, in May 1984, gave the Habitat/Mothercare group culture an opportunity to express itself.

RECREATION THROUGH TEAMWORK

Oliver Gregory, design director:

> I remember a year ago, walking through the Heal's building with our company secretary. His comment was: 'Have we actually bought it?' It really was in a shocking state. It had just grown, over the years, like 'Topsy'. Walking around it was a nightmare. It was a warren, and obviously much too large for the Heal's operation in 1983.
>
> The point of buying it was to construct the headquarters of the group, alongside four of the stores, in one unified centre. Over the years we had grown and dispersed into lots of different offices. The optimum space for each was worked out, which resulted in an expanded Habitat, and a Heal's reduced in size. Mothercare was positioned in the old Heal's contract showroom and Now in a disused loading bay.
>
> We kept the main entry, as a grand entrance, with a colourful centrepiece of a flowershop. The individual businesses remained separate. It would have been lovely to make it all like

one big department store, but logistics made it impossible. The problem was made worse by the antiquated features of the building. Nearly every opening had been protected by fire shutters, which crashed down at regular intervals.

Heal's was left exactly as it was, at least in terms of its exterior image. We retained the large bronze lettering and the fenestration. But inside it was a different story. We had to make enormous structural changes. Air conditioning the whole retail area redesign was an awesome job.

It was like a new child being born. Behind the scenes, countless technical things had to be made. The district surveyor paid us a visit, almost daily. The place was a mess of wet concrete, open trenches, drains and constant running water. We had no proper existing structural drawings for the building. So we were always finding pipes, wires and drains in unexpected places. Setting off the fire sprinklers, accidentally, seemed almost a daily occurrence.

From March 1984 onwards the design team moved into the building. Almost all of us were working on site, long hours, and rarely did we go home before ten at night. The builders, in fact, worked all through the night, in shifts.

In the build-up to the last month, prior to Habitat opening, there were six large trucks of Habitat merchandise arriving each day, to stock up the shop. We had a massive project review chart, which was up on my wall, from day one. It showed the projected build-up, including shop closing, refit, stock build-up, budget preparation, selection of builders, price setting, and so on. Our designers also showed what had to be done with every square foot of building space.

We had to work out, in advance, how much space each retailer would require, as a result of their projected sales and profits. It was up to the individual operating companies to decide that. Each of us has a budget, a time schedule, and uses for each. We had to design the thing, build it for an agreed price, and open it on the agreed day. But it was only in part a question of mechanics. All our work was infused with the family influence. To the young team of people who were going to work in the new Habitat store, it was a revelation. They all became part of this rolling thing that was going to happen. Everyone watched it happen, day by day, as they struggled to avoid the wet cement. It was very interesting to see their reaction. They never believed it was going to be finished. But it was just possible. I think a lot of theatrical producers feel that. It was just possible.

It just had to happen. It was blind faith. We were building staircases until two days before. We were painting until the doors opened, and in lots of cases we had to put up temporary finishes. And then, of course, the display people had to do their work in the last few days.

Terence Conran, chairman:

We knew we could do it, on time, but nobody else did. The thing is, we've done it so often before. We've trodden that knife edge again and again. And you know you have to make compromises. In the end you have to take control over yourself and your contractors not visibly, but knowingly. You succeed by sheer force of persuasion and determination. It's like asking Montgomery how he knew that he'd be able to land his troops. It's just force of personality, determination and team spirit. There are all sorts of problems you have to deal with, all the time, every day. But you have to keep reminding yourself that you're going to do it. You see, if you take it back twenty years, we physically built the first Habitat ourselves. We have a lifetime of experience behind us.

The store manager himself had no real reason to believe that we would be ready on time, but he brought with him thirty young men and women to work on it. They had no evidence that we would succeed. It seemed impossible. But they ignored the dust and the dirt, and got on with it. There were no histrionics, no drama, none of that English attitude, 'We can't do it'. An incredible atmosphere and team spirit built up. The manager wasn't a man of particularly high stature, but he built up a dynamic, well-oiled team of young people. They put up with tremendous hardship and bonded together, as if they were fighting a war. They will remember it for the rest of their lives.

Oliver Gregory:

And we didn't have to sit down and explain to each other how we might get things to work. Amongst those of us who had been working together for a long time it was instinctive. And the day after we opened, I was no longer interested. Emotionally, I was keyed up no more. We were on to the next show.

There is, in fact, an analogy with the theatre. A good show has its stars, appeals to the public, and makes good money. We have to open a shop with excellent merchandise, that appeals to our customers, and that makes us financially successful. The merchandise are the stars of course. We run alongside, providing the setting in which the stars will successfully perform. That's what it's all about.

Of course, the setting must be appealing. You can't fool people by a slick showing. The merchandise is all-important, but without an enthusiastic sponsor, who can present and talk about it, the event will fail. In other words, bad display and the merchandise won't sell.

The look of the shop, you might say, is like the music to a score, and the catalogue is like the programme. The catalogue gives the specific flavour, and the facts: the score provides the overall setting, and the delicate harmonies.

It's like professional theatre, and certainly not repertory. We're not here to give a slapdash performance, or to make a fast buck. In repertory, if the scenery doesn't arrive, it's quickly forgotten. We're here to stay. We can't afford to have many off days. We're going to have a very long run. And, in the end, the analogy breaks down. A person goes to the theatre and is transfixed by Olivier's Othello – his walk, his hands, the overall impression. But you remember it as theatre. Here our sofa is something of daily use. It gets old and tired with quality, like an old suede coat. We want our merchandise to be used with pleasure, and to last. We are here today, and won't be gone tomorrow.

THE ATTRIBUTES OF CULTURE

There are two unique features to the culture or key lines in the script. First and foremost, the products are the stars. As John

Stephenson, a board director, puts it, 'the merchandise is the message'. All else is merely setting for the stage play. And yet the setting is all-important. Without the musical score, the programmes and the scenery, the play would be threadbare, the story would lose its appeal. It is the physical layout, the colourful harmonies, the light and the sound, that provide the overall context for the product content. The whole effect is a sum of the parts, and more. The overall picture has integrity.

WHOLENESS

> Everyone working here has a special interest in what sells and what doesn't. One of our peculiarities is the way people are interested in each other's jobs. Every accountant is a frustrated designer. There is a wholeness about it.
>
> Chris Turner, chief executive of Habitat (UK)

> I enjoy being associated with the products. I relate to them. I remember once going into a Conran shop, and stroking the merchandise. I just love it.
>
> Alan Hughes, personnel director

Secondly, the story of birth and recreation is continually being retold. The opening of Habitat, on 11 May 1964, was both a symbolic event and also a physical reality. Every time a group of people come together to design a new interior, to lay wet cement on a new floor, to bring together a new combination of merchandise, the story is being relived, reinforced and renewed. The ritual of the opening ceremony and the routine of project planning and budgetary control, provide the reinforcement. The fresh geographical, commercial and aesthetic context as well as the changing product content stimulates renewal. At the same time the Conran look, 'as if seen through one pair of eyes', provides the continuity. The drama can unfold, full of suspense and surprise, but its roots lie deep and firm.

PRIME MOTIVE

Oliver Gregory, design director

> In designing an organization, you've got to be very sure of what you want to do, unwavering, but not hidebound. You must keep to that straight line, and get in a nucleus of excellent people. Then you build on that. We've formed and reformed. We've been very lucky. We seem to find, very quickly, loyal lieutenants and staff. We've got fused together into a team. We understand the prime motive, almost instinctively. If you think of the great innovators, like the Bauhaus, they had unwavering direction. They produced a style, an image. They had integrity, simplicity, dedication, and an attention to detail.

A CULTURE OF SUBCULTURES

As we shall see after investigating all branches of the company's activity, the culture is mulitfaceted. In other words, there is a genuine 'metaculture', substantially represented by Conran's own colourful personality, that acts as a 'holding company' for separate subcultures. These subcultures which are clearly visible include:

- a culture of *harmony*, of wholeness, of interdependence between functions, between people, between products, and between the organization and its environment

- a culture of *recreation*, where birth and death plays their natural part in the evolution of the company, and as the drama of personality and business unfolds

- a *family* spirit that pervades Habitat in particular, and is gradually pervading the entire group, whereby brothers and sisters combine together under common parenthood, with Conran himself as father and the design world itself as the mother

- a culture of *openness*, whereby an outsider like myself is welcomed, in the same way as the public at large, and in the same way as the Iraqi Selim Zilkha and the European Paul

Hamlyn have become – historically and currently – part of the Conran association

- a culture of *warmth and fire* where cut and thrust is allied with humour, and even love, so that 'grommets' and 'young grommet' become a dual symbol, of fiery authority and warm affection

- a culture of *action*, whereby, amidst the wet cement and display panels lies an immediate world of physical objects and activities

All this cultural richness was visible to me, looking in on senior management and the group merchandise, from the outside. At the same time I severely doubt whether the mainstream of the company's staff are aware of it. The sort of care that goes into the display of merchandise has not yet gone into the revelation of the organization's culture. The potential community of interest between the company and its customers, suppliers and employees, has only been partially tapped. Habitat/Mothercare, in that sense, has a very strong corporate image, but little coherence between its approach to merchandising and its approach to people.

In order to discover why this might be, and how significant its impact is, I needed to move on to the company's evolution, and, in particular, on to its current style of 'managed organization'.

THE HABITAT/MOTHERCARE CORE

FROM PIONEERING TO MANAGEMENT

Habitat/Mothercare is now a professionally managed organization, but it obviously did not start that way. Back in the fifties Conran was a furniture designer, who had his own small factory. Habitat was conceived of in the early sixties, because he had nowhere suitable to retail his products. In the sixties and seventies one Habitat after another opened up, but in the words of Habitat's UK managing director: 'Seven years ago Habitat was still very much a disorganized, entrepreneurially run group of shops. It was run by people more interested in design philosophy than in retailing.'

Those were the pioneering days, when, as Conran himself admitted, he knew virtually nothing about retailing. It was a time of joy, of adventure, of tremendous group spirit, and immense hard work. But professional management didn't come till later. Chris Turner, the chief exeutive, told me:

My brief, in 1977, was to make things run more professionally. I was to lend my strengths to the back room. I spent a lot of my initial time trying to organize the warehousing, the computing, the stock control and the personnel, in order to get some system and logic into the whole thing. I built up a larger team of professionals, comprising experts in each field, although nearly all of them had grown up in Habitat. When I had taken over, the management committee was a hotchpotch. Now we have a buyer, a merchandiser, a warehouse manager, a market director, as well as a much more professional personnel function. We also have a director of systems, and a retail director to concentrate on running the shops. Recently I also appointed a property director. Each man is an expert in his own right. That's how Habitat has been turned from a group of shops to a chainstore run by professionals.

It may sound as if, in the process of professionalization, Habitat has lost its character. But we tried to ensure that individuality would not be lost. One of our strengths, in a sense, has been our 'amateur enthusiasm'. So we tried to breed our own experts. Our warehousing director used to run a shop. Our personnel director came up from the stores. So none of them have the attitude 'I don't care about the shops'.

So Habitat evolved to a new phase of development. Yet in moving from a pioneering phase to a stage of professional management, the spirit and individuality were not lost. The new phase transcended, rather than replaced, the old one. Alan Hughes, as personnel director, reinforces the point:

When I first took on this job, Chris asked me to do two things: to raise the efficiency, and the status of the personnel and training functions. While the organization was in its early stages the personnel function was *ad hoc*. What it's really about now is policy, formalizing things, fairness, conditions of employment, and trying to create an atmosphere where people can be respected as individuals. It's a tremendous advantage, though, that the company has such a strongly defined identity. There's no them and us. We all eat at the same tables. And it's all Christian names.

The development of marketing is part of the same story. Although it has now become an established entity, it remains small, and subordinate to the wider design and marketing function. As Tony Maynard, marketing director, stresses:

At Habitat you had a bunch of talented designers, and awful briefing. All of the thinking had been communicated face to face in meetings without much record. This was OK when few people were involved, but the game had changed and I had to do something about it. That was in 1981.

Yet, I have to say, the short line of communication did fire my imagination. There was a feeling that everything wasn't weighed up in figures: 'Yes, I know what the figures say, but do you *feel* that's the right thing to do?' Terence would often say. You couldn't measure everything through immediate results or awareness surveys. My opportunity to contribute was far greater than it had been in my previous employ. There was no manual of procedures. To start with, there was just me, and my empty desk! But by now, a whole marketing strategy has evolved. We gradually outgrew the small company outlook when, in hard times, marketing would be the first tap that you would turn off. That's changed now, fundamentally. The results were there. Whereas in the mid-seventies there were 450,000 catalogues selling at 45p, we now sell 850,000 at double the price. The introduction of direct response advertising, moreover, made people realize that, with the right approach, you could build up a consistent brand image. Since then we haven't looked back. The marketing function remains small, but well established.

THE EVOLUTION OF MOTHERCARE

Mothercare's evolution has been different. Its founders, Selim Zilkha and Barney Goodman, made a very thorough study, particularly of Marks and Spencer, before they started out. There was an existing blueprint which they applied. They also invested very heavily in computerized systems from the outset. It was pioneering with a difference. It was as if birth and adolescence were collapsed into one. It might have led them to brilliant success; or to disaster. Mothercare became like a precocious child, a bit bored with life, almost too sophisticated for its own good, but a brilliant starter – as Kevyn Jones, one of the board directors, has said:

> Mothercare, as a product-market concept, developed in stages – from a specialist store for the mother to be and her infant child up to age three and then five, and then ten. The concept he developed, and the systems he installed, were unique. Selim Zilkha, the founder, was brilliant. He must have been one of the first retailers to computerize on a significant scale. But even more important than data are people. We invested heavily in training.

So Mothercare, through Zilkha, was born with a burst of brilliance, and a more than usual dose of financial support and professional back-up. The company was never allowed to enjoy, or to suffer, the exhilaration of youthful exuberance. People 'grew up' very quickly, and very systematically:

> Our training was, and is, centrally controlled and locally administered. We start people off with programmed learning, and they go on to learn about their departments thoroughly. Once they graduate into becoming junior management trainees, they have projects to work on. They are then put through a further training exercise to review their knowledge. The next stage is departmental management, and, thereafter, assistant store manager.

From the start, Barney Goodman took responsibility for people, as well as property, while Selim looked after merchandising and systems. Marketing was shared between them, and ultimately fell between two stools. Kevyn Jones said:

> Towards the end of the seventies, after our operation had expanded enormously, Barney Goodman went to live in America. At that point marketing became an entirely secondary part of our business. We drew too much on history, looking backwards rather than forwards. We lacked imagination in our choice of merchandise, and price reduction became the major part of our sales drive. That was a mistake. We had a fabulous year in 1979/1980, but then we began to go downhill.

It is true that Mothercare drew too much on history, albeit an abbreviated one. Their history failed to incorporate the spontaneity of childhood. It is also interesting that a mother's business was started by two fathers, so that a genuine union of masculine aggression and analysis, with feminine sensitivity and intuition, was perhaps hampered. For more reasons than one, therefore, the child protégé of the seventies (Mothercare) had to be taken under the wing of the better integrated adult of the eighties (Habitat). It is to Zilkha's great credit that he recognized his own emerging weakness, and Conran's corresponding strengths.

Conran brought in a complete change of style, not only in merchandising, but also in management. Whereas Mothercare brought with it all the strengths, and the weaknesses, of a business professionally managed from the centre, Habitat was still an amalgam of entrepreneurial and managerial cultures. It was the designer's mentality which continued to bridge the gap between the two.

Interestingly enough, while I was in the process of writing my book, something very significant happened to the Habitat/Mothercare group. Kevyn Jones was appointed to the main board, as operations controller for the whole. The pendulum had rightly swung a little once again, from Habitat-led design to Mothercare-led systems. Conran, forever one to seek the balance, had spotted the need, in the group as a whole, for better operational control. In that sense, Tony Maynard's words to me were more than prophetic:

> It is inevitable that, as the organization gets bigger, one needs procedures, so that the standards can become acceptable. It's how such systems are employed that counts. Mothercare, of course, have come through a different metamorphosis. Looking five years ahead, we will have evolved in method, and Mothercare will have evolved creatively. There has got to be the installation of a greater sense of routine at Habitat. But we would hope there would never be a group, steamroller approach – or a movement away from a company of caring individuals to the limb of an eyeless giant.

HABITAT/MOTHERCARE BRANCHES

> We've created, and stand by, our case in the high streets . . . well-designed products accessible to people of modest means.
>
> Terence Conran

THE BIRTH OF INDUSTRIAL DESIGN

Terence Conran and his family have led colourful lives, and created businesses small and large. It is the nature and extent of Conran's business that forms the substance of this particular story. For Habitat/Mothercare represents nothing less than a design-led revolution in retailing. The roots of his revolution run deep.

In 1919, with the formation of the Bauhaus School in Germany, arts and crafts were formally amalgamated for the first time within one school of design. The function and discipline of industrial design was first born. Thereafter, students of the Bauhaus emigrated to countries throughout Western Europe and North America, but ironically bypassed Britain. Design, in this country, was supposedly left to languish behind Italy, Germany, France and the United States of America. It seems to me ironic that this should have been the case; given Britain's rich heritage of Celtic arts and crafts, strong tinkering spirit, and legacy of Victorian engineers. But it was apparently so.

In 1946, Conran was still a teenager. He was fortunate to have attended a school with a strong creative bias, and he had an inspired man, Don Potter, to teach him craft subjects. They worked with metal, wood and clay, and Conran acquired a great desire to make artefacts. He set himself up with a workshop at home and built his own pottery kiln. He also did a lot of welding, and, in order to make the activity viable, he had to sell his wares to friends and relations and to a local toy shop. Conran himself says:

> One memory that stands out is of a typical English pottery in Farnham. They made terra cotta flower and chimney pots. It was a completely self-contained unit. They dug the clay themselves, made the pots, and then sold them on the spot, from a builders merchant's yard. They even made use of the local farmer's wasted pea sticks for firing the kiln. I used to cycle seventeen miles there and seventeen miles back to be part of this compact and fascinating business. I remember working at a foot pedal wheel, making little flower pots. A penny for five. Funnily enough I enjoyed doing one, repetitively, after another.
>
> I loved the whole circular process, from digging at one end to selling at the other. It was a wonderful example of self-sufficiency.

So, in Conran's youth, the seeds were sown. The union of man and nature, art and science, design and business, was there for him to see. Conran, like Sinclair, is at one with his country. Both use technical ingenuity and sociological imagination to link the tinkering spirit with self-sufficiency. Whereas Sinclair is closer to science and mathematics, Conran is closer to art and nature. Yet, at the point of industrial design, they both meet.

It was Conran's combined interest in things artistic and botanical that led him on to studying textile design.

> I was apparently good at recognizing, understanding, and detailing relationships in artefacts, in plants, and in chemistry. So I took a course at the Central School of Arts and Crafts in London, in textile design.
>
> I became very interested, immediately, in the process of

screen printing. I found the historical aspect fascinating. I used to go off to the Victoria and Albert Museum. I also worked in the evenings for one of my tutors. He used to produce Matisse panels. Each would fetch a million dollars today, but those times were still very austere. To find cloth we had to go down to Petticoat Lane and search around for it.

After about eighteen months at Central School I began to get itchy feet. I had become friendly with the sculptor, Eduardo Paolozzi. We shared a workshop in Bethnal Green. He taught me form and I taught him practical skills. At that stage I was really beginning to get interested in making furniture for myself. There was nothing on the market that I liked. So I started making things for myself and for friends. I had a particular style.

The fact that there was nothing 'likeable' on the market had its historic origins. If we go back to the Industrial Revolution, we find that the maker began to be separated from the customer. In many cases, too, the maker was also separated from the final product. He saw only a part of the whole. He became the tail of the elephant that was blind to the rest of its body. In between maker and customer appeared a host of middlemen. They counted figures until only figures counted. So began the collapse of standards that spurred the English revolt against manufacturing, with John Ruskin and William Morris at its head. Taste was supposedly relegated to the world of decorative arts, so that manufactured artefacts became, by definition, tasteless. In 1919 Walter Gropius set out to change all that. But neither the manufacturers nor the retailers in postwar Britain were touched by his thinking.

After college, Conran found himself working for an architect who was doing work for the 1949 Festival Exhibition. He even did the interior design for a flying boat:

There was terrific enthusiasm at the exhibition. The designers thought that the new world had come. But the energy began to dry up, as the exhibition wore on. Industry failed to seize the opportunity.

A DESIGN HERITAGE TO DRAW ON

Nevertheless, Conran continued with his furniture and textile designs. And he had to think more seriously about selling. That image of self-sufficiency was lurking in the background, and, more importantly, he was beginning a crusade.

> I started to consider, in greater depth, design philosophy and its importance to industry and society. I was convinced that design added to the quality of life. And everything made is designed. I felt very deeply that well-designed artefacts should be made available to people at a mass level. So I continually asked myself, how can I get out of this backwater, and touch the real world?

The Conran crusade was not a lone battle. He did have a heritage to draw on.

In his book entitled *In Good Shape – Style in Industrial Products 1900 to 1960*, Stephen Bayley has pulled together design principles and practices that reflect the Bauhaus tradition. Bayley, who is director of the Conran Foundation, believes that industrial design is the art of the twentieth century. He presents the views of *The Times* art critic, Arthur Clutton Brock, in 1916:

> Good design and workmanship produce beauty in all objects of use. That is the common sense of the matter. But human beings never attain to common sense unless they aim at something beyond it. There must be a kind of religion of workmanship, if workmanship is to be good. What we need most in England now is this religion: and we need a condition of things, a relation of all the parties concerned, in which it will be possible to do good work for the sake of it.

Ironically, it is only now, in the 1980s, that these words are genuinely being heeded in Britain, and being supported by an ever more design-conscious establishment.

A more eloquent statement of Brock's rationale, and one which is shared by both Conran and Bayley, is that of Walter Teague, the American automobile designer. Teague had significant influence over the world's greatest industry in the forties and fifties.

As a thing becomes perfectly adapted to the purpose for which it is made, and so approaches its ultimate form, it also advances in that power to please us, which we call beauty. Use is the primary source of form. The function of a thing is its reason for existence, its justification and its end. It is a sort of life urge thrusting through a thing and determining its development. It is only by realizing its destiny, and revealing that destiny with candour and exactness, that a thing acquires significance and validity of form. This means much more than utility, or even efficiency. It means the kind of perfected order we find in natural organisms, bound together in such precise rhythms that no part can be changed without wounding the whole.

LEARNING BY DOING

Conran faced up to the frustration, in the fifties, of sharing the sorts of ideals that Teague espoused, but of not having the means of bringing them about in this country. He was still producing his distinctive style of furniture in basements, and transporting pieces to customers by Underground. Very gradually, he accumulated some capital by renovating the buildings he moved into, and then selling them off. Still desperately short of money, he hit on the idea of a café-cum-soup kitchen with a psychiatrist friend, and they soon created a chain of four. When Conran sold out he accumulated still more cash. He started up a textiles conversion business and got involved with shopfitting and design. That brought in still more money. Then came a quantum leap, when he moved from two inefficient little factories in London to a new site in Norfolk. For the first time, in 1962, he produced a range of domestic furniture, and sold it to eighty different retailers round the country. The quality of display was terrible. The furniture shops looked like great stagnant pools filled with brown lumps of scum! Conran felt he had to do something about it:

So we tried to open a prototype shop, ourselves, embodying various principles. Above all, it had to look busy. We developed it with 50 per cent furniture and 50 per cent other household goods, like kitchen utensils, lighting and floor cover-

163

ings. We also knew that our customers would be young, so we incorporated a toy department. The shop opened with lots of publicity, though we'd had no experience in retailing. We made every mistake under the sun. But we had enough energy and life to ride over the problems. At the time, the new-look clothes shops were just opening. There were lots of Italian restaurants. There was the beginning of a feeling of change, and our shop fitted perfectly into this. Of course the other retailers insisted that it was one thing for us to succeed in London, but we wouldn't have a hope in Manchester.

Unlike those retailers, we sensed the signs of the times; we had insight into our market potential. There was the odd shop like us in Scandinavia, but nothing more. Seven years ago I discovered that there were 85 Habitats in America, all trying to copy us. They were ten years behind.

One important thing that we did was to fill our shop with stock. In other furniture stores 'we'll order it for you' was the approach. But we used the supermarket approach of making the goods available on the shelves. The stocky warehouse feel was very attractive to the customers. We provided an exciting environment for them.

After that early period of getting to know the ropes, and experiencing the frustrations of learning from our own mistakes, we began to realize we enjoyed retailing, and making ourselves visible on the high street. We believed it would work in Manchester. So the idea of a retail chain came to us. That meant we would really have to teach ourselves retailing, including distribution, stock control, and so forth. We also formed the very positive opinion that the future for retailing lay in creating something unique, something different from other people's shops. Habitat things were designed by us, not by manufacturer 'X'.

Conran proceeded to learn retailing by trial and error. That enabled him to discover his own path. Even if he strayed from his ultimate destiny, as in the abortive merger with Ryman, he learnt his lessons along the way. He also made a lot of money, through a subsequent sale of his Ryman shares to Burton, which enabled him

to expand into Europe. The lessons he had learnt from the Con-
ran-Ryman failure have also been applied since to the success of
Habitat/Mothercare. Conran had learnt the hard way how to seek
out the true complement of an amalgamation of interests:

> Selim Zilkha had built up a fine business which had many
> parallels with Habitat. Both companies were specialist retailers
> who did a high percentage of their business through mail order
> catalogues, and both addressed themselves to the same target
> customer. But Mothercare had slipped downmarket in recent
> years. Selim Zilkha, an extremely astute man, knew, when his
> profits began to fall, that it was because his merchandise had
> become lacklustre. He recognized the cure in the design-led
> Habitat concept. So I took over his business, and the alliance
> has proved a great success. Both companies have learnt a lot
> from one another. We now have the best retail systems in the
> world, along with our unique design philosophy.

GROWING LIKE WILDFIRE!

Mothercare is now responsible for something like two thirds of the
group's income. And opportunist that Conran is, and continues to
be, he has taken over Richard Shops, Heal's, and formed a joint
venture with Paul Hamlyn at Octopus Books. The Habitat design-
based approach to living has become aligned with Octopus's expertise in publishing and marketing. A new chain of clothing
stores, Now, aimed at teenagers past the Mothercare stage, has
been created. Conran is now operating in Europe, America and
Japan:

> We're on the edge of getting to my eventual ambition. The
> strength of the original Habitat design-based formula has been
> in selling furniture in a colourful ambience, partially created by
> the non-furniture merchandise. We have sold products which
> all measure up to a good standard of design, and appear to have
> been selected with 'one pair of eyes'. We have invested in a
> large design team, to ensure exclusivity, well-designed
> merchandise and strong graphic style. Moreover, we have never

been satisfied with existing standards. Now, we are really developing and diversifying our retail operations, well beyond furniture, and should soon be touching all socioeconomic groupings.

Two things are happening in the marketplace. Retailers are coming to understand that they can exercise their power to create products unique to them. Also, there is a new breed of buyer in the retail world who is a creative person rather than a number cruncher. So the buyers are able to work alongside designers and manufacturers to create innovative merchandise. Secondly, more and more people are realizing how bad so many shops are. At the same time a lot of electronic developments are giving the manufacturer the lead time they need. Shops have got to become less like a visit to the dentist, and more pleasant and exciting.

What I enjoy most now is the feeling that we can make any product we require, thanks to our designers' abilities. Richard Shops, for example, is a huge turnaround project, creating new products, new management, new systems. The same thing goes for Heal's. The great thing is to have things under your control, not to be the hostage of other people's fortunes. These are our products. This is our style. We will take responsibility for the manufacturing. Hence we have the courage of our convictions. We've created and stand by our own case in the high streets. Through Habitat, Mothercare, Richard Shops, Heal's and Conran Octopus, well-designed products are now accessible to people of modest means, whereas twenty years ago they were a prerequisite of the well-off. As Habitat's success has demonstrated, this availability has changed the way people furnish their homes. The Habitat look has gathered an increasing number of converts as their eye becomes educated to appreciate fresh, simple and imaginative furnishing. Now, not only in furnishing, but also in toys and clothing, we are making good design accessible to everyone. Perhaps I'm helping to create a self-sufficient British industry, with design at the centre of it all.

So the roots of Habitat/Mothercare lie in creative design (Conran) and in aggressively organized entrepreneurship (Zilkha). The respective branches, Habitat and Mothercare, have a common trunk of opportunism to draw on. Habitat endured, and was even able to overtake the larger and more aggressive Mothercare, because of its deep roots and profound stability. Both organizations, though, were merged at a stage of young adulthood in which product came before people. Product, interior, graphic and architectural designs have been integrated, but organization design remains separated. The two are likely to be woven together, with the onset of maturity.

DESIGN AND MARKETING

Again and again, during the course of my discussions with, particularly Habitat, management, I was struck by the emphasis on wholeness, an interrelationship, and upon integration – across functions, and between people. I was left in no doubt that at the centre of the whole business, if not Conran himself, were the products that his team created and sold. It was around the products that all else revolved.

The sense of coherence, of organic interrelationship, and of aesthetic harmony comes from a direct extrapolation of art and design into business and organization. The sensitivity to shape and form, to the rhythm of the seasons and the harmony of relationships, is shared by landscape gardener and Habitat board director alike. And the flow is not just one way, from product to person. It also flows in the other direction, from product to business. As John Stephenson told me:

> Designers often come out of the art schools with an arrogant sense of self-importance. Design has to be commercial. That is the essence. We're not, in absolute design terms, perfect. But the stuff must sell, must be marketable, must have a certain quality. It's a total interrelationship.

As Stephenson was talking to me I soaked up his own surroundings, his dress, his manner, the feeling of harmony that pervaded the whole atmosphere:

When you're involved in design you've got to deliver a whole package. That's the whole idea. You put it into one envelope. All you need for a home. All together. All sympathetic. An amalgam of style, that holds things together.

For many years, in teaching and reading about the principles and practices of marketing, I have been struck by the overall masculine approach to marketing. The emphasis is inevitably upon either market analysis or aggressive salesmanship. I have looked hard and long for what I have termed marketing's 'feminine' face. I found it at Habitat, and in John Stephenson's and Priscilla Carluccio's attitudes and words. Interestingly enough, Carluccio (Conran's sister), who is in charge of product development, associated marketing with facts rather than intuition. She sees them in a 'masculine' light:

I have an innate sense for what people want. Marketing, on the other hand, have the facts. That is what we look to them for. I have the intuition and they can analyse the market. But we all work together. Now the project is being taken over by the promotions people. But they will be working with the design people, in interiors, graphics and products. Then there's the fashion side. We sometimes get them to help with fabric and colour. We go and see what each other are doing. We all talk to one another all of the time. We talk to the promotions people about the style of packaging. The promotions people need us for the overall concept. It's an all-round conversation. Design is of prime importance, but we couldn't do anything without marketing and finance.

INDIVIDUAL AND TEAM

Even the hard edges of finance have been touched by the soft edges of design. Chris Turner, chief executive of Habitat, is an accountant by training who has since broadened out. While he was taken on 'to make things run more professionally', Habitat never lost its character:

There is a wholeness about it . . . I fell into accountancy by mistake. I love anything to do with buildings and furniture. I've been in property and investment banking, and I didn't enjoy either, particularly. I enjoy being a shopkeeper and selling furniture. I wouldn't like to be a grocer or a pharmacist. It's what I'm selling that counts, and, of course, being able to run the show. If you do a job you love, you must have found it by mistake. For you'd never know what you want at an early stage.

Most important of all, though, is that we work as a team, more than a team. There's an openness and self-criticism, and we hate anything less than perfection. That emanates from Terence. He's an amazingly detail-oriented person. That permeates down.

So the coherence extends, not only across functions, but also between vision and action – idea and implementation. I attended a marketing meeting, in the new Heal's building, and enjoyed a lunch that was laid out quite beautifully. The way the knives and forks, the crockery, the bowl of fruit, were set out was quite memorable. The sense of harmony, depicted in the organization and the product range, was reflected in this culinary detail. And the detail is the physical representation of the more abstract vision. Above all, it leaves a lasting impression.

FROM IDEA TO IMPLEMENTATION

The way that a vision, a sense and a feel get physically translated into action is very well illustrated through so-called 'orientation' meetings, which take place twice a year, for each company. The following is an extract from *Conran: the Habitat Story* by Bartie Phillips.

A buying brief is decided for a period. . . . They try and look at the merchandising with fresh eyes and discuss what it should consist of, which areas they should concentrate on, which styles they want to develop, what colour trends are to be. It is all considered in the broadest terms, yet these are not vague, policy decisions. They will try to reach a consensus of opinion and make positive decisions which can be followed by direct action. Orientation meetings are a forum for new projects, ideas and inspirations.

By the end of the meeting, when decisions have been summarized, the buyers have a clear brief and are ready to start searching for new products and, at the same time, looking at ways of updating existing ones. The orientation meetings . . . give buyers and designers an idea of the style of the new range and stimulate them into thinking in new ways and provide renewed motivation to them for finding more and varied products.

They may discover products at trade fairs, on a tour of factories in a certain country, or through businesses which approach the team with particular items. On some occasions they will find a manufacturer who has no products suitable for Habitat but who does have a particular manufacturing capability which Habitat could use. There may be a feeling that the factory is right to take the volume of work . . . but that it requires some design input. . . . The buyer will brief the Habitat/Mothercare Group Design . . . to come up with a product which will fill a gap in the market and can be produced at the factory. Occasionally, the design studio itself will come up with ideas for a product or a range. . . .

The design studio's brief originates from the orientation, working and merchandising meetings. . . .They are told in general terms what is required in the way of shape, colour and texture. A buyer may suggest that the range includes plenty of stainless steel cutlery but none with plastic handles – so why not design some. The studio will usually produce a proposal or a series of possible alternatives. The buyer may accept one of these or ask for some reworking of the idea. Then it goes to the stage of working drawings and is discussed again before the finished drawings or prototypes are handed over to the manufacturer selected by the buyer.

Merchandise meetings establish specifically which products will be included in the Habitat range over the next six-month period or even a year for each type of product, lighting, furniture, cabinet/upholstery, wall coverings, textiles, linens, floor coverings, kitchenware, tableware, toys and accessories. Conran always attends as does Priscilla Carluccio. Also there are the MDs of Habitat (UK) and France, Conran's USA, Seibu Japan, the sales directors, marketing directors, buying directors and the buyers for each area of merchandise. . . . Any products presented must already have been checked for suitability for mass production. . . . Conran has confidence in his team to make the right decisions but very occasionally he may refuse. . . . He is far more likely to suggest a final touch or change . . . a teacup may need to be a millimetre lower.

HARMONY OF INTEREST

Because the design function is at the heart of the company's business, Conran Associates, the design company that is part of the Habitat/Mothercare group, obviously has an important part to play in the group as a whole. On the other hand, it does run a separate design consultancy business. Stafford Cliff is the creative director of Conran Associates.

Design involves fitness for purpose. Some products can be helped enormously by redesign, recolouring, providing people with more of what they want out of them. We work within the limitations set by the client to create new market possibilities. The potential may be enhanced through presentation, pro- motion, product or price. Sometimes a client will come to us with a manufacturing facility and an overall strategy. We will look at their skills and facilities and design products accordingly. For Airfix Industries we went as far as to create a whole new company, for which we are designing new products to this day. An even further step would be for us to create a new product, find a manufacturer, and then market it. It's some- thing we've often talked about. We are one of the very few design groups that offer product, interior and graphic design, all under one roof.

Design, both within and without the business, is involved with the fulfilment of potential. Potential, in products or in people, is

171

normally unfulfilled to the extent that a harmony of interest lies unidentified. Such harmony is contained either in a merging of inside and outside – product and market, or of present and future – actual and potential. In both cases seeds of recognition are sown when patterns of evolution are identified. These material, commercial or social patterns are perceived by people with an intuitive sense for the spaces between words, for the common ground linking opposing forces, and for the natural flow of time across space. On the one hand, this involves visual sensibility. This is quite clearly in evidence within the group. On the other hand, it involves a sensitivity towards human potential. This remains, at best, implicit rather than explicit.

FROM HABITAT TO MOTHERCARE

The blend of design and marketing, one manager with another, an idea with its implementation, and a product with a customer, has been cultivated within Habitat over twenty years. This particular way of thinking and feeling is now being transferred to Mothercare, in particular, and to the other subsidiary or associated companies, in general. The way in which they now all come under one roof is best described by Ian Peacock, the group's director of finance and administration: 'We have had to ensure that creativity is allied to common sense and adequate discipline' (another example of loose-tight properties).

LOOSE/TIGHT ORGANIZATION

No one, least of all Conran himself, would claim that his primary interest is in organization and administration. Instead it is Ian Peacock, almost from Habitat's inception, who has taken up the reins in this respect. At the same time, Peacock has taken very much into account Conran's overall organizational philosophy, with its dual emphasis on smallness and togetherness.

One has to be sure one appreciates what the group now comprises. In essence, the main board is only six people of whom five – Terence, John Stephenson, Kevyn Jones, Terry Goddard and myself – are full time in a central, true, group management sense. Roger Seelig of Morgan Grenfell is purely non-executive. Underneath the board are our main operating companies, each with its own chief executive and board of directors. Both Habitat and Mothercare have separately constituted UK, European and American operations, and then there's Conran Associates, our design consultancy business, and now Richards.

One of the essences of the group concept is that we like to push authority down the line, and get the local boards to run themselves, provided it all remains consistent with overall group strategy and policy. Functional management is carried out at the local level. Decisions taken down the line are quicker and more effective. Among the five of us, at headquarters, Terence is the figurehead and continuing 'ideas man', whose primary interest is in design. John Stephenson is the marketing man. Between them they ensure that things look right – the merchandise, the stores, the catalogues, the advertising, basically anything visible to the customer. My job is to look after the backroom, the things that are not so immediately visible. And Kevyn Jones was more recently brought in to look after overall control of operations – in other words, making sure that the all-important stores work well, achieving the right balance between customer service and cost efficiency, besides looking good, the way that Terence and John have had them laid out. Terry Goddard looks after our properties.

On a day-to-day basis, John, Kevyn, Terry and I have regular contact with one another and with Terence. The same goes for ourselves and the chief executives and their local board colleagues. A lot of our influence is exercised informally, outside our regular business review meetings. Because we push out as much as we can, group operations, finance and administration is restricted to around twenty-five people. We only physically do, centrally, what we have to, like the published accounts, tax planning, financing arrangements, overall corporate planning and monitoring of performance against plans and budgets, City liaison, etc. John's side is a bit different. Because of the nature of design and the sort of environment designers like, we do a lot more centrally. Still, there are only one hundred or so people involved at headquarters.

Personnel management is very much delegated. We try to maintain centrally a consistent policy and implementation of terms and conditions applicable to the more senior managers throughout the group, but training and personnel development in general is undertaken locally. You have to take into account the local nuances, in different companies and countries. We have also always believed both in share incentives, for people running subsidiaries and above, and in more general share participation by all our longer serving staff worldwide. Philosophically, I always think small. The more independent the better. It makes for *esprit de corps*, and a sense of togetherness. It attracts better people, and helps maximize profits.

SHARING OWNERSHIP

We're an opportunistic as opposed to a straight line, narrow-minded business. And we are very, very flexible. I can adjust from 20 per cent over target to 20 per cent under targeted sales, and still make the same percentage profit. We react fast. I ring up all my shop managers and say 'For Christ's sake don't employ anybody.' They'll do it, but retailing is generally like that.

We don't make our decisions against an enormous bank of statistics, although we have reasonably good information systems. There are no statistics for new items. That's all very subjective. We have very close relations with our suppliers, which adds to our flexibility. We can ring them up and add to, or subtract from, our original order. Habitat has a reputation for being tight-fisted but friendly and fair. We'll always pay our bills on time. We know what's involved in running a business.

In fact, each operation is run as its own business. Habitat (UK) runs from here. There's little intervention from above. If I ask for something from the board it's generally accepted on faith. They trust my judgement. Anything under £100,000 I don't even have to get their permission. It's equally true here. I don't try and run people's departments for them. It's not for me to make their decisions.

As part and parcel of that philosophy, we were the first of a batch of companies, in 1976, to introduce a share ownership scheme, for our staff. In fact we believe we were instrumental in helping to shape the legislation on share ownership of the next Labour government. They adopted our approach almost entirely.

Our approach was to allocate a proportion of pretax profits to members of staff who had been with us a year and whose subsidiary was making profits. These shares were held in trust for three years, after which time, if the person was still in the group, the money became wholly theirs. Moreover, we got the Internal Revenue people to agree that the share allocations, as far as the group was concerned, would be tax deductible.

We have retained a similar arrangement for our staff ever since, and I know that it is something Terence is particularly proud of.

INFORMATION AND CONTROL

I leave it to you to imagine trying to control an exceedingly entrepreneurial business led by a designer. Having people listen to you, in my view, always depends simply upon first earning respect. But, in the early Habitat days, this was possibly a doubly difficult job, given the totally different backgrounds and training and perceived purposes in life of Terence and myself. (Designers by nature create, accountants conserve.)

The business, you might say, is design led, still carefully nurtured by its founder and present-day chairman, but suitably balanced by simple practical systems of controls. Throughout, my task has been basically to ensure that the company never overreached itself, always had the money to do what it wanted (within reason), and that the necessary accounting controls and administrative support kept pace with our expansion. In short, I have had to ensure that the 'backroom' was in good order, and that 'creativity' was allied with good 'common sense' and adequate 'discipline'.

In achieving this, there have been 'several bees in my bonnet'. Firstly, I regard cash control to be of paramount importance. As long as I remember, we've had a very keen and close control of cash. We prepare annually updated four-year corporate plans, with projected cash flows, so that I can get our financial structures and borrowing facilities right, well in advance. In support of that, for short- to medium-term control purposes, we have weekly cash projections. We always know, wherever in the world we are, what our cash position is. It's monitored weekly and regularly updated on a rolling twelve-month forecast basis.

Secondly, I regard financial management as very much a forward planning thing. Our whole approach starts with the four-year corporate plans, looking forward, so that we all get a clear idea, well in advance, of what our financial objectives are for the coming few years ahead. For operation control purposes, we then have a system of annual budgeting and monthly control of actual performance against budget. We specify generally what we want, and then our subsidiaries put it together in their own way. Each year, for each operating company, we draw up a balance sheet, a profit and loss account, and a cash flow. I use this accounting information together with the chief executive of a company, and his team, to look forward and to ensure, as far as possible, that the results we get are what we planned to achieve, not just simply what happens.

I believe, thirdly, in keeping things simple if I can. Often financial people create elaborations over and above what is basically needed. After all, most of the things that really matter are subject to judgement. 'What is our feeling about this market or that?' However clever you are with the numbers, in the end it's commercial judgement that counts. So our capital investment appraisal techniques, for instance, are relatively simple. We look for a three-year payback. So much, you see, depends on anticipated sales, and you can't quantify that precisely.

Fourthly, I believe in prompt monitoring of key information. Sales and cash figures from each subsidiary are telexed through weekly, compared with budget or forecast, and we look for significant trends which might require discussion or action to be taken. I also have my 'flash reports' in advance of the normal monthly management accounts. The key factors affecting the profit and loss account of retail businesses in the shortish term are gross margin rates and payroll costs. I also get a report on current merchandise purchase commitments. We have to make sure nobody is putting our cash position in jeopardy or storing up excessive mark-down problems. So I get these three flash reports just as soon as the figures are available after each month end, even before the management accounts are submitted.

Though I believe in close monitoring, forecasting and control, it's up to the operating company how they bring their figures together, and whether or not they use computers, but the general principles are set by me.

The important thing is that systems must be there to serve, and not to dictate. Selim Zilkha, of Mothercare, was very much systems minded. They had superb systems. But he seemed not to realize that they may have to change from time to time, as the nature of the business itself tends to change. Mothercare in the States is a different business from Mothercare in this country. Their business in the States is more fashion oriented. So you need a different system.

Now take Richards. We can't just take what we do in Habitat and transplant it. They are different sorts of businesses. That's not to say we shouldn't learn from each other. Habitat can learn from Mothercare and vice versa. We need to be flexible and pragmatic, and benefit from cross-fertilization. There's horses for courses.

Throughout we've developed close working with local management, making good use of informal contact. The philosophy is always to work closely with the guy who runs the show, to make sure he's putting together a plan which makes sense and we agree with and then to see, with him, that it is achieved.

BUSINESS OPPORTUNISM

With Heal's, as with Richards, we picked up a good property portfolio. The bricks and mortar are incredibly valuable. One thing we don't do is specifically to plan ahead as far as acquisitions are concerned. Our planning, long term, is never that precise. The best deals are the opportunistic ones. Mothercare, Richards, Heal's. What is important is that the opportunity fits in with the group strategy, what I see as the creation of a federation of speciality retailers. It's our sensitivity to the market, to people's changing needs, that gives us the edge, whatever the particular merchandise might be.

We now believe we can run many different sorts of business, as long as it's in retailing, and we're satisfying a particular niche in the market. Before Heal's, we'd been looking for ways of satisfying the older, more affluent furniture and home-furnishings customer. Heal's used to do extremely well and it suddenly came up as an admirable vehicle. As Habitat we have been considering Germany for years. But the exact timing of a final move will be in many respects opportunistic.

While Ian Peacock's viewpoint reflects a structured, organizational perspective, it nevertheless manages to accommodate the market sensitivity, and entrepreneurial thrust, that is so typical of Conran. Through a process of osmosis, Conran, Peacock and Stephenson have imbibed each other's perspectives, and evolved their own positions accordingly. More recently Kevyn Jones has added to the party his particular brand of forceful entrepreneurism. In addition Terry Goddard, who first joined Mothercare seventeen years ago, was appointed to the board to look after the property side. This means that the group is now in a better position to look after and direct the development of its property portfolio. The missing function in the group's structure is personnel. That could represent a problem or an opportunity. Problems could arise through dissatisfied people. Habitat/Mothercare has the opportunity to upgrade the design function to accommodate the fulfilment of human, as well as product and market, potential.

AUTONOMY AND ENTREPRENEURSHIP

Although Conran's mission is to remove ugliness from our world, and his joy lies in being a designer, he is probably best known in

Britain as an entrepreneur. His opportunistic deals, through which first Mothercare, then Richard Shops and now Heal's have come under the Conran umbrella, have consolidated his entrepreneurial reputation. In the last five years, his business empire has grown from less than one hundred to more than five hundred million pounds. This remarkable rate of growth and acquisition is indeed the mark of an entrepreneur.

And yet, because Terence Conran has so many sides to him, it is difficult to picture him in any single capacity. His entrepreneurial thrust is complemented by a missionary spirit, a strong aesthetic sensitivity, a boyish sense of humour, and a marked tolerance for diversity. In many ways, therefore, the Mothercare tradition is more a purely entrepreneurial one than Conran's.

Selim Zilkha had acquired a considerable amount of money before embarking on his new Mothercare venture. Together with Barney Goodman he ventured into maternity and babywear not because they were in love with the products but because – like good entrepreneurs – they spotted a market gap. Their approach to both merchandising and staffing was modelled on Marks and Spencer, so there was no fundamental innovation involved, either in a design or retailing sense. Once the company was formed, however, and the first few stores were successful, they grew at a phenomenal rate, particularly in Great Britain and America. Zilkha had installed sophisticated computerized systems, which made for supreme efficiency, so that it comes as no surprise that Kevyn Jones has recently been installed as the group's operations director.

Jones himself is very much an entrepreneurial manager, who therefore has carried forward a large part of the message that Zilkha and Goodman had conveyed.

I started out in the retail business. When I left school in 1960 I wanted to be an accountant, so I enrolled for a suitable course. But I got bored with the 'work after work', spending long hours at the desk. Although I found figures interesting I had too little contact with people.

So I joined a small printing company, on the selling side. After three months I became an assistant sales manager, selling office equipment and stationery. But the prospects seemed limited, and straight selling did not seem the route for me. Instead, I became interested in the more professional aspects of retailing. Although I thought Marks and Spencer would be interesting to work for, I felt it would take too long to gain real responsibility. So I joined British Home Stores as a trainee manager, and stayed for six years, becoming deputy manager in Swansea.

My career was then interrupted by a road accident. That put me back twelve months. I never felt quite the same when I came back. I'd been excited by quick promotions. I had become deputy store manager at twenty-four. I would then be competing with other deputy managers for promotion, and they had gained a year on me. Meanwhile I had got to know about Mothercare, who had been making inroads on our sales. Many of our staff had left to join them.

I was told about an ad in *The Times* that Mothercare had put in. So I rang Barney Goodman, Mothercare's cofounder, and he offered to come and see me. Mothercare was quite obviously going places, as the only specialist retailer of its kind in the world, and I wasn't ahead of the pack any more at BHS. So I joined as a trainee manager, in April 1969. That was in the Northwest. Two years later I took over the Midlands as well, and two years after that Wales and the West. I was made regional controller for the whole of the UK. Two years – again – later I was made director of store operations, and two years ago, after the merger, I was appointed managing director.

Interestingly enough, Zilkha is not the only Jew born outside of Great Britain to play a significant part in Conran's emerging business empire. Paul Hamlyn, a publishing refugee from Hitler's Germany, was also destined to play a major role. For, in creating a joint venture with Octopus Books, Terence has aligned his retailing and design skills with Hamlyn's amazing talent for publishing and marketing illustrated books.

In the cases of both Mothercare and Octopus, it was not Conran's entrepreneurial skills in particular which paved the way for a respective merger and joint venture. It was rather his market awareness, his company's design skills, and the ability to link product and market, that proved the telling force. In Mothercare's case, Kevyn Jones continues:

I had met Terence before the merger. Selim had begun to get bored with the business. I told him I wasn't satisfied with the way things were going. Market research confirmed my views. People wanted better merchandise, and were prepared to pay for it. They still respected us, though, as a specialist retailer. Before the merger Terence talked to all of us, the senior management that is, and we told him exactly what we thought. We were on a downward spiral.

Since I became managing director, after the merger, I've created a management committee. Each head of department comes along. They are accountable to one another at the meetings. I get people committed to various directions. It was different before. Selim and Barney operated on a one-to-one basis. The committee sounds formalized, but it's not. Everyone is represented – the directors of personnel, property, store operations, data processing and marketing. When the buying director left I took it on myself and have spent a happy year doing it.

After the merger, the personnel and systems policies did not change one iota. But the whole approach to marketing and design changed drastically. On the merchandise side we brought in our own designers for the first time. It was previously *ad hoc*. Now we have Jan Gale, from the design group. She's brilliant. She predicts the fashion for next year, on the textile side. The designers and buyers discuss a range before the season starts. At our orientation meetings, which are a new thing, the designers work up demonstration boards of fashion and style, for the whole of Mothercare. We agree a range for the following season, and then the buyers and designers work side by side.

We now lead our manufacturers, design wise, and we expect them to put the same investment as we do into design.

So much for merchandise. The second aspect that has changed dramatically since the merger is our catalogue. We started charging for the first time – 20p, now 25p – and last season sold a million. We went page by page, through the catalogue, to see how it should look. The design group produced a set of new graphics, for each page, the buyers put their input in, and Terence cast his eye over the whole thing, to see whether the mood was right, and so on. It made a dramatic difference. It became much more humorous and human.

The third aspect was store presentation. I had been dissatisfied for some eighteen months before the merger. I couldn't see anything, in this country, that I wanted to emulate, but I was influenced by the J.C. Penney revolution in America. They have been upgrading themselves drastically. After the merger, then, we opened a new shop. We then looked at the new, looked at the old, and worked out the best of both worlds.

We did a revamp on Kilburn. It was a remarkable success. Our customers responded. Last year we revamped 40 stores altogether. Over the next two years we aim to do them all. We shall also be extending and expanding in Germany, over the next five years, and we shall soon be creating the store of the future in America. We also want to move into 100 per cent own branding in the States, which has not been the case until now. Meanwhile I've set up franchise arrangements in the Middle East. There's not a chain like ourselves anywhere in the world.

In America, we presently have 200 stores, and I want to see us having 1000 in the next ten to fifteen years. We should be making a profit for the first time there, this year. We shall probably have 100 stores in Germany, in the same time period. There are presently three. I've taken on a German as our European chief executive. We're pulling out of Scandinavia but I want to develop the Far East. We already export to 118 countries round the world.

Mothercare now accounts for some two thirds of the group turnover. Yet it was Zilkha himself who first realized that his youthful business, successful as it had been, would never develop into a mature adult without the market sensitivity and design awareness that the much smaller Habitat could provide. Since the merger Mothercare has become transformed, but without losing the strong staff and systems base that it had acquired. Now that Kevyn Jones has become operations director, he will have the opportunity of lending some of Mothercare's operational expertise to the rest of the group. Conran, with his all-pervading sense of wholeness, of interdependence, has once more ensured that processes of osmosis and symbiosis will continue. His background in organic chemistry has not gone to waste. The entrepreneurial cells within Habitat/Mothercare, while semiautonomous, are at the same time held in balance by the design magic that is the company's hallmark. Problems may arise if the entrepreneurial thrust behind the Mothercare side of the operation overtakes the less commercially aggressive, and more design-sensitive, Habitat operation. There undoubtedly is a need for more interaction between the two largely autonomous entities.

FLEXIBLE SYSTEMS

It's still a very individual business and it breaks all the retailing rules. We try to create an atmosphere in which the products are seen as special.

Chris Turner, chief executive

OPPORTUNITY FOR SELF-EXPRESSION

Every time I walk into Habitat/Mothercare's headquarters, in the Heal's building, I am struck by the degree of individuality that is seemingly encouraged. Staff are dressed in jeans, in sportswear, in casual suits, and in formal dress. Men and women work together in an atmosphere of free expression that belies the normal, established corporate environment. The open-plan offices stimulate open communication and regular interaction.

The openness within is matched by an openness without. Conran is extremely accessible to the media, and to all walks of life. The important part that women play in the organization, as in the F International case, points to a flexible employment policy. Although women are not able to work from home, they have been able to progress through the organization in a very flexible manner. Alison Richards, buying director for Habitat (UK), is a good case in point:

> When I left school I was given the choice of nursing or secretarial work. I couldn't stand the sight of blood, so I was packed off to secretarial school. After two years as a secretary I saw an ad one day for a 'unique career opportunity'. Boots had about 36 new posts for people with my qualifications. They wanted buying assistants to take care of the merchandiser's administrative work. I should think 600 frustrated secretaries applied. I got one of the jobs, and worked as a buying assistant for two and a half years.
>
> In 1976 I was promoted to assistant buyer in the houseware department and I became involved with kitchenware and cookware. At the time we were developing plastic kitchenware, designed by Conran Associates. After a very short time my boss unfortunately became ill and was away for three months. To his dismay, I was either sitting at his bedside, in between the drips and tubes, or else operating on my own. It was sink or swim. When he came back I was promoted to being a buyer, during which time I continued to work with Conran Associates, meeting Terence from time to time.
>
> In 1979 I joined Habitat as buyer for toys and accessories. After a year I was given additional responsibility for kitchenware and tableware.
>
> Then along came the acquisition of Heal's. The former buying director, Geoff Davy, took over as managing director. I went through various phases of neurosis. Would I be seriously considered?
>
> I was finally appointed, in August 1983, probably because Terence and Habitat have an affinity for the devil they know. I must say I did find the prospect of not getting the job ghastly. I do have tremendous enthusiasm and commitment.

Rosemary Good, now marketing director at Mothercare, also rose to senior management via a diagonal route. Like many people at Mothercare, she started with a specific brief in the early days and then broadened out. Rosemary has been flexible in the past, and remains flexible in the present. Here she describes the nature of her work:

> We all need to be very flexible in the marketing department. Women tend to be more able than men to handle this kind of variety. I work very closely with the design group, on the one hand, and with our computer people, on the other. Take an hour of my life, in this department. We go through press cuttings . . . an idea for a press release comes up . . . I might come across something in a magazine . . . the phone rings . . . a piece of equipment hasn't arrived . . . I'm shown transparencies of Now merchandise . . . somebody changes a packaging meeting . . . I have to correct and proof some advertising copy . . . someone urgently needs some figures . . . one of the catalogue translators is off sick . . . there's a problem getting paper for one of our leaflets. . . .

Both Alison and Rosemary rose from administrative positions to posts of authority within organizations. Jan Gale, group fashion director of Habitat/Mothercare, also developed herself in a very flexible way, also spent time as freelancer before coming back into the organizational fold.

> Ever since I was a child I had enjoyed clothes. I loved designing and making my own clothes, and shopping in the stores, antique markets and new boutiques in London at that time for both fabrics and garments to satisfy my taste to dress in the latest fashion.
>
> My first job was as a secretary for the Commonwealth Development Corporation. I stayed there for four and a half years, initially as a junior secretary, working my way up to the senior secretary in the supply department . . . ordering spare parts for machinery in Third World countries worldwide. I learnt a lot about the exportation of goods and I really enjoyed the experience . . . geographically we were dealing with help for engineering and agricultural plants from Malaysia to Africa to the Caribbean.
>
> But time came for a change and looking through the *Evening*

Standard, I noted an ad for a secretary for a fashion consulting company. I applied and was accepted as secretary to Lee Rudd, partner to Nigel French in IM International Ltd. However, within nine months the company was liquidated and I stayed on with Nigel French, who formed his own reporting company, NF Enterprises Ltd, publishing fashion reports on European fashion trends and selling the information, particularly to America. He continued to sell the service and I took the initiative to produce and write the first report under this new company. It was printed and sent out and from then on I never looked back. That was in 1969.

For six and a half years thereafter I travelled the world to work with some of the biggest names in fashion retailing and manufacturing in America, Japan, Hong Kong, India, Australia and all over Europe. I covered the major fashion shows and fashion cities reporting on trends in colour, fabric and shape, and I worked ahead of the season too, predicting future trends. I learned so much from the Americans, especially on how to package and market a new range, merchandising concepts, display, price points, budgeting, etc. What I learnt in that six and a half years with Nigel is irreplaceable.

In 1974 Nigel's company was bought out and became a division of May Department Stores of America. At that time I met Geoffrey Wallis, who, with his brother, owned Wallis Shops. After nine months of talking with Geoffrey, I decided to leave Nigel French to go into retailing, as fashion coordinator with the only vertical fashion chainstore in this country at that time – a group with an image in the market I respected and with its own design team and manufacturing facilities. I managed a team of six designers and liaised with three buyers. Geoffrey taught me a lot about range planning . . . we engineered our ranges into an organized plan balancing price points, cloth types, garment fashion content and deliveries to stores. Every Monday morning the sales figures came off the computer . . . you knew instantly if you had a winner or not . . . that's the excitement of retailing. I also built up their import ranges while there, spending a lot of time in the Far East . . . it was hard work but very rewarding.

I left Wallis a year before they got into financial difficulties with an overoptimistic expansion programme. Late in 1979 I joined Jump Knitwear Ltd as fashion director having met Richard Caring, the owner of that company, during my trips to Hong Kong. But fate took a hand again in 1982 when, at a time when I had already decided that the work at Jump was not fulfilling enough, I received a telephone call from Jinty Stephenson, the wife of John Stephenson, who was design and marketing director of Habitat/Mothercare. She had been given my name by her sister in Montreal, Margaret Godfrey, whom I had worked with while at Nigel French . . . Habitat had merged with Mothercare and they were looking for the right person to provide fashion input into the new company.

I had lunch with John and Jinty that same week . . . we discussed a consultancy based on so many days a week. That same day, the telephone rang again . . . a voice from the past . . . Mr Segal of Chateau Stores in Montreal needed someone in Europe to report on fashion trends – two consultancies in one day! So I left Jump and started my own consultancy business. I helped set up the Fashion Design Studio for Mothercare immediately. Soon I was contacted by people from Hong Kong and New York. I had five accounts. That was enough.

Last year, Habitat/Mothercare bought Richard Shops. I was offered the position of group fashion director which I accepted and began to recruit more designers for a new Richards fashion studio.

What, then, do I do? It is my role in the Habitat/Mothercare group to research, analyse and evaluate fashion trends in colour, cloth, shape and detail . . . to extract the influences on tomorrow's fashion, and alert designers and buyers to those trends which will affect/relate to their market eleven to fourteen months ahead of the retail selling period.

Fashion is international . . . it is a reflection of today's lifestyles . . . it is more individual than ever before . . . to understand it means to feel, to look, to listen, to be aware of everything happening in today's world around us. On a continuing basis I am gathering information . . . watching what is currently selling at retail (or not selling) . . . what is being worn on the streets, not only here in London, but in Paris, New York, Tokyo, Italy, Germany too . . . what the established high-fashion designers around the world are showing for next season . . . what the fibre and textile mills are showing for the season following that . . . what is being projected by the various fashion services and magazines around the world . . . what art exhibition, pop group, world event, TV programme, new technological invention, ecological campaign, etc., may have an influence on design for tomorrow . . . and, of course, my own 'gut' feeling on the future direction of fashion based on a long experience in this industry.

We are always trying to improve our product . . . to maintain value for our money while improving quality and design . . . to help the customer coordinate her/his purchases easily, by planning their coordination right from the start, at the design stage.

I personally view fashion as a science . . . fashion merchandising certainly is a clever balance between good, creative design and sound, commercial realism.

A lot of planning goes into what we create . . . it's almost an engineering project. It can sometimes be a strain mentally. So much is going through my mind . . . I feel sometimes like a computer! You feed all this information in, add gut feeling and personal taste, and the shape comes out. I'm lucky I had the opportunity to learn early on, to meet key people in the trade. Everything I've learnt, I'm now able to channel productively, with the help of the strong team I've built around me.

Jan Gale, like Alison Richards and Rosemary Good, involved in processing information, combining personal feel with 'scientific' planning and control. Jan is the most entrepreneurial of the three and also the most explicitly scientific in her approach. In public relations, in merchandising and in monitoring fashion, each is functioning as some kind of gatekeeper between the organization and its environment. They need to be able to respond flexibly to the world outside, in the same way as they have responded flexibly to their own circumstances. Habitat/Mothercare has enabled them to do both. It is also a company that is noted for teamwork. Individual flexibility and collective activity are combined.

TEAMWORK

Habitat/Mothercare is strongly characterized by a family influence and by teamwork, which is both thrusting and supportive. Part of this 'spirit' is lodged in the merchandise, and part in the company's history. Because the history is being constantly relived, the spirit can be revitalized. The thirty young people working on the recent Heal's opening will never forget it. And, contained within that memory, will also be the opening of the first Habitat, as if contained within a time warp. Because the merchandise is on permanent display it cannot be forgotten.

Because display is visibly and repeatedly intermingled with graphics, interior design and product promotions, it cannot be isolated from the whole. So a team spirit not only infuses but is also infused by the merchandise, and its environment. Alan Hughes, the Habitat personnel director, made these comments:

> The management, here, are very aware that they are part of a team. We are part of a whole. Virtually every day we are approached by head hunters offering us up to double our current salaries. But there's a feeling of purpose to this business that we wouldn't find elsewhere. We each contribute to the whole. I'd find it very difficult to fit in with another culture. Here, I can contribute to the management committee in any way that I like, and also run the personnel and training function. We're encouraged by Chris, our MD, to develop as a team. None of us have left since he started. That's highly significant. We all believe that what we are doing is right. It's almost a crusade. We put out into the High Street something in which we all believe.

The family influence is not of a patriarchal kind. In fact there is a particular brand of outgoingness, an openness to change, and variety that complements the more inward-looking, family orientation. This particular cultural attribute has been represented very well by Habitat's marketing director, Tony Maynard:

When I went into a meeting at one of my previous employers, I would always feel nervous. If I opened my mouth in the wrong way I'd trip into a political minefield, and end up tongue-tied. One could never say what one felt. Here, I have a feeling of great relaxation and self-expression.

Terence himself has an amazing capacity to listen, and to observe. He has this wonderful power to hear what you're saying, and to see what you're trying to visualize. Creative involvement is high and combined with an urgent and exciting need to learn and develop new systems and methods. There's a refreshing reaction against the big company environment. And we feel that we're part of a major, influential change in the human environment.

Finally, all is not peace and love in the Habitat/Mothercare family. Business involves cut and thrust as well as sensitivity and collaboration. The strong entrepreneurial thrust has been provided by both Conran and Selim Zilkha, and has been internalized by not only processes of delegation but also by the inevitable stories. In the early days, Oliver Gregory tells us, Conran had an ambiguous reputation:

I was working for a bunch of architects. One day, one of the juniors came in late from lunch. I was bored. I'd just come back from Australia with a new wife. It was a stuffy office. I was used to the vibrant Australian scene. So I asked her where she'd been. She said she'd been out with this guy buying furniture. 'He's a bit of a shit,' she said, 'but the two of you should get on.' I rang him up and we made an arrangement to meet the same evening. That's how Terence and I met.

Conran's combination of assertiveness and humanity has been spelt out further by Alison Richards.

Terence sometimes can be difficult. But when he loses his rag, it's usually when I haven't been doing my best. There's always a good reason for it. He spots things before you do. He's very fair, and also I think interested in everybody who works for him as people. You know that if something goes wrong he'll be the first person to sort it out, as long as it's not your stupidity that has caused it. He's trying constantly to get the best out of everybody, and he's very approachable.

My favourite story, representing this blend of heat and warmth, is told by Alan Hughes:

I remember, when I'd just joined Habitat, Terence visited one of my stores. The lengths, incidentally, that they'd go to in my old place to prepare for a visit from someone important. . . . For example, all the toilet paper would have to be absolutely in the right place. Anyway, Terence found a grommet missing from one of our toilet seats. 'Young grommet' he used to call me, after that. So I sent him a packet of grommets. I said to him: 'I may not be so good at stock control, but I know a grommet when I see one.'

A couple of weeks later I was attending a summer school at Oxford. Terence was giving a talk. After the speech people trooped off. As he came down the aisle, with these dignitaries by his side, he spotted me. 'Hello, young grommet,' he said.

HANDS ON, VALUE DRIVEN

Immediacy, and action bias, are portrayed in Ann Sayer's description of the move into Heal's, and the final preparations for the Habitat/Mothercare/Now/Heal's complex.

It was planned to open all four stores in May 1984 to coincide with Habitat's twentieth birthday, and to invite press, suppliers and many VIPs to a great opening jamboree where they could inspect the new quads. To achieve this in ten months called for an all-out group effort.

Holidays cancelled, limitless supplies of black coffee consumed, midnight councils of war – everybody involved would remember May 1984 like old soldiers remember the D-Day landings.

Six weeks before 24 May (the proposed opening date), Oliver

191

'Winston' Gregory (head of Design Group Interiors) confirmed that he would be able to meet the deadline. Countdown began; Oliver Gregory's wife forgot what he looked like while he and his designers organized the shifts of builders who worked day and night.

Gill Lingwood (Habitat PR) and her team, in a great act of faith, sent out 1000 invitations to the grand opening, and got on with organizing the hundreds of other arrangements that would make the event go like clockwork.

Maurice Libby practically lived in the building, planning displays for the new Habitat and developing a totally new, and very elegant, display style for the rejuvenated Heal's.

On 23 May the Habitat store still had a long way to go, but help was on its way . . . TOC was doing his bit. At 2.00 a.m. on the 24th he was still there with anyone else who could be pressganged – polishing glasses, painting, sweeping and mounting displays.

Design for Business Evolution

At this particular stage of Britain's economic and social development, design awareness is spreading considerably. We now refer to the design not only of products and buildings, but also of software and hardware, and of organizations and whole environments. Interestingly enough, 'design groups' do not incorporate 'organization design' within their repertoire, although corporate image and identity certainly overlaps with it.

Design for business and organization evolution, as a conscious and strategic activity, must lie at the roots, if not in the branches, of excellence. Organization is to my mind what product design is to Walter Teague, the American car designer:

The function of a thing [organization] is its reason for existence, its justification and its end, by which all its possible variations may be tested and accepted and rejected. It is a sort of life urge thrusting through a thing [organization] and determining its developments. It is only by revealing its [the organization's] destiny with candour and exactness, that a thing [organization] acquires significance and validity of form. This means much more than utility, or even efficiency [in organizational structure and function]. It means the kind of perfected order we find in natural organisms [natural organizations], bound together in such precise rhythms [formalities and informalities] that no part [subculture] can be changed without wounding the whole [corporate culture].

Just like a product, a business, and its organization, is forever evolving – its destiny is continuing to unfold. Habitat/Mothercare is currently poised to evolve, from a managed organization to a developing corporation, as it faces up to the implications of its proliferating joint ventures.

Three Stages of Development

The tale told so far bears witness to two significant stages of development in the group. There was a time to be pioneering, and there is a time to manage. The successful, adolescent organization transcends both as it evolves, rather than omitting or obliterating either. Habitat ran the danger of being too much the gifted amateur, and Mothercare of being too much the sophisticated professional. Now they are united in the best form of marriage, whereby each draws from the other so that, both separately and together, they become more whole.

Yet time and evolution never stop. There is, in fact, a third stage of development, as has been revealed in the case of the giant ICI. People, civilizations and organizations evolve from childhood to adulthood, and then to maturity, and each stage contains its own separate phases. Habitat/Mothercare, although only twenty-five years old, has begun to enter the phase of integration, of interdependence, of wisdom.

The company is better prepared than most for this stage of evolution. The preoccupation with wholeness that Conran has had from the start, carries distinct evolutionary advantages with it. For it is the accommodation and development of both individuality and wholeness that become essential, at this third stage.

Habitat started out as a single entity, albeit with the coexistence of Conran Associates. It grew out of a furniture manufacturing enterprise into a retailing one. To that extent, Conran was familiar with interdependence as well as evolution. However, the first major attempt to create separate but linked identities, between Habitat and Ryman, failed. Habitat was not yet ready for interdependence on a large scale. It still had not progressed sufficiently, through its second – managerial – stage of development, to assimilate the third. We need to become fully assertive and established young adults, before we proceed towards maturity.

By now, of course, the situation is quite different. Not only has Habitat become Habitat/Mothercare, but, through a series of joint ventures, the company has changed its fundamental shape and form. Not only has it acquired Heal's and spawned Now as a natural extension of its vigorous adolescence, but it has also formed two joint ventures, with Richard Shops and with Octopus Books. These joint ventures, whereby association rather than acquisition is the form of development, are very characteristic of the third evolutionary phase. In this respect the merger with Mothercare was poised neatly in between young adulthood and oncoming maturity. For in one sense it was an acquisition, and, in another, a genuine association.

DESIGN FOR EVOLUTION

For some time now, perhaps ever since the demerger with Ryman, Conran and his management team have been feeling their way towards a new stage of organizational development. Though this has not been made a conscious part of its design awareness, the issue is bound to be raised. In fact, I was first made conscious of the feeling for such an evolutionary organization design by Priscilla Carluccio, who heads Habitat's product development team:

> We're now becoming large, professional and well founded. There's a need for logic and organization. But, for me, the titles are irrelevant. It's a fantastic team effort. We have hierarchies but we don't acknowledge them. I don't believe that those of us who have the titles have a feeling of importance because of them. We all work alongside one another. I don't like

hierarchies. I don't understand them. It's a way of protecting yourself from the outside world.

The human being, like a child, needs structure. But it mustn't be rigid. What it's all about, at the end of the day, is enthusiasm. Lots and lots of it.

Carluccio started off by presenting a picture of the open, interdependent, wholesome world that characterizes the truly integrated organization. However, understandably, she concludes that 'enthusiasm' – very much a characteristic of the pioneering enterprise – lies at the roots of excellence. To that extent she is looking backward rather than forward. For the core attribute of the maturing organization is an enabling one, rather than enthusiasm *per se*. Together with enabling goes the recognition and enhancement of potential in people, and in products and markets, particularly by virtue of association. The enabling company, in essence, is one that fosters both individuality and interdependence in both its products and its people – as both staff and customers.

This combination of individual identity and collective association is something that Tony Maynard was striving towards:

. . . we can't rest on our laurels. What we must ensure is that, as the business grows and Terence's role changes (as it must), Habitat retains its identity. We have a terrific ability to be self-critical, and then to resolve the issue at hand, and do something exciting. We've got to go on developing, and retain that sense of never having done enough. We have always had to fight for what we believe in. If at any stage the feeling arises that a big group is developing, and people begin to say 'enough is enough', that small company will be gone, and it will be very difficult to get it back.

Again Maynard was struggling, like Priscilla Carluccio, to marry up the past and the future. The yearning for smallness is a call from the past. The call for identity, that reaches into the future, has to transcend smallness. For Habitat, whose turnover is now less than Mothercare's, needs to develop a new identity. As the creative force in the combined group, I suspect that Habitat needs to develop more of an originating identity. Such an originating impulse would need to spread beyond Habitat's traditional product lines, if it is to become a transcendent force and gain a composite identity, across the whole of the group. In fact it is rather intriguing, if not curious, that there is not a more extensively established research and development function within Conran's innovative business.

Such a research and development function need not be confined to products. That would go against the grain of the integrated organization. The integration of product and organization design, under the aegis of a transcendent corporate identity, would be a way forward. After all, if the company has developed such a unique culture and identity for itself, should this not be part of the product line it offers others? In fact, Tony Maynard, in casual conversation at least, seems to be paving the way:

> We need to develop sensitive and creative structures, retaining that ability to react responsively, as the need arises. In fact, the structure is evolving now. Inevitable change will result. I can see it coming. We are beginning to develop venture or project groups. I hope we won't fall into the textbook management tree. A paralytic management structure would lead us away from our product identity. Our organizational fabric is worth fighting for. The key lies, as always, in personalities, and in not hiding in preset stylized notions of what, for example, a director should be or have.

He is quite consciously feeling his way towards an integrated organization. In order to take that further step, towards an integrated company, it is important to magnify the significance of the joint ventures, in contrast to the independent units or acquired interests. For joint ventures require synergy. Synergy requires the recognition and enhancement of potential, in the individual and in the association. Synergetic structures require organizational designs quite unlike those with which most of us have been familiar in the past.

The key lies, in the first instance, in Terence Conran's personality. The fact that we can identify several distinct subcultures within the organization – entrepreneurial, harmonious, familiar, flexible, active, creative, and open – is no accident. For Conran himself operates on all these levels, personally, and these qualities have been infused, and personified, within the organization. In addition a 'managerial' subculture has been implanted through Conran's recognition of his own weakness, and search for a compensatory balance. Ian Peacock, the financial director, and Kevyn Jones, now the operations controller, personify this complementary, managed operation.

What has not yet emerged is an organization design that enables these diverse attributes to take deep organizational root. Hence there is some anxiety in anticipation of the day when Conran is no longer at the helm. ICI bears witness to the trials and tribulations that can result from the absence of a founder's imprint, particularly insofar as innovation, entrepreneurism and culture are concerned. The particular challenge and opportunity that Habitat/Mothercare faces is to nip things in the bud, to design in advance for evolution.

8. ICI

Innovating Pioneers

1862   Ludwig Mond emigrated from Germany and arrived in England.

1864   Ivan Levinstein, also from Germany, established the forerunner of British Dyestuffs.

1870   Nobel launched his detonator, and dynamite, on to the market.

1871   The British Dynamite Company was established by Nobel in Scotland.

1873   John Brunner set up in business.

1874   Brunner and Mond went into ammonia production.

Expansive Diplomacy

1880s   A period of worldwide industrial diplomacy began.

1926   Imperial Chemical Industries was formed by Alfred Mond and Harry McGowan, incorporating Nobel Explosives, Brunner-Mond, British Dyestuffs and United Alkali.

1929   Mond introduced, as chairman, early principles of industrial organization, on a 'scientific' basis.

1931   McGowan took over as chairman.

1930s   Inauguration of the great chemical cartels.

1938   McGowan's dictatorship was overthrown.

Emergence of a New Chemical Industry

1938   ICI went into nylon.

1940s   The seeds for pharmaceuticals were being sown.

1943   The rise of terylene.

Structuring a Modern Industry

1940s	Formalized structures were extensively established.
1947	Wilton was established as a large, fully integrated plant.
1951	McGowan fully retired.
1952	The new chairman, Alexander Fleck, introduced thorough principles of management.
1957	Pharmaceuticals Division was born.
1960s	A major period of imperial expansion.
1970s	Activity redirected into Europe.
late 1970s	ICI goes into oil production.
early 1980s	ICI incurs its first losses for forty years.

Corporate Renewal

1982	John Harvey-Jones takes over as chairman.
1984	Profits of over £1000 million for the first time.
1984	ICI launched on the US stock market.
1985	Toshiba's chairman is appointed as an ICI non-executive director.
1985	A major acquisition is undertaken in the US.

ICI: The Developing Corporation

ICI's ROOTS

I left in early youth
A home for distant lands beyond the sea.
But strange to say, even when the ocean spread
Its grandeur round it struck me not as new.
My mind has pictured oceans far more wide.

Alfred Nobel, cofounder

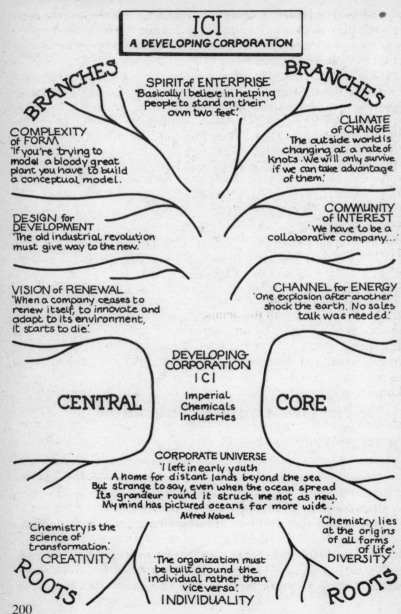

ICI
A DEVELOPING CORPORATION

BRANCHES

BRANCHES

SPIRIT of ENTERPRISE
'Basically I believe in helping
people to stand on their
own two feet.'

COMPLEXITY
of FORM
'If you're trying to
model a bloody great
plant you have to build
a conceptual model.'

CLIMATE
of CHANGE
'The outside world is
changing at a rate of
knots. We will only survive
if we can take advantage
of them.'

DESIGN for
DEVELOPMENT
'The old industrial revolution
must give way to the new.'

COMMUNITY
of INTEREST
'We have to be a
collaborative company...'

VISION of RENEWAL
'When a company ceases to
renew itself, to innovate and
adapt to its environment,
it starts to die.'

CHANNEL for ENERGY
'One explosion after another
shock the earth. No sales
talk was needed.'

CENTRAL

DEVELOPING
CORPORATION
ICI

Imperial
Chemicals
Industries

CORE

CORPORATE UNIVERSE
'I left in early youth
A home for distant lands beyond the sea
But strange to say, even when the ocean spread
Its grandeur round it struck me not as new.
My mind has pictured oceans far more wide.'
Alfred Nobel

'Chemistry is the
science of
transformation.'
CREATIVITY

'The organization must
be built around the
individual rather than
vice versa.'
INDIVIDUALITY

'Chemistry lies
at the origins
of all forms
of life.'
DIVERSITY

ROOTS

ROOTS

The organization must be built around the individual rather than vice versa.

Sir John Harvey-Jones, chairman

CHARISMA

Sinclair Research behaves like a small pioneering enterprise, though Sinclair's roots lie much deeper within European soil than those of an average entrepreneur. F International and Habitat/Mothercare have both become managed organizations, but without losing either their individual flair or their wider social purpose. ICI, however, is the one company cited in this book which has reached maturity. It has a long-standing tradition which is imperial, chemical and industrial. Its geographical, scientific and commercial roots reach deep down and stretch out wide. And John Harvey-Jones, its current and charismatic chairman, is trying, and probably succeeding, to draw upon these roots of excellence in order to create a company that is in tune with its environment.

ICI is rooted in imperial, chemical and industrial diversity. Imperial diversity, with the demise of the old British colonies, has in fact been replaced by an international orientation that spans Europe, America and the Far East. There has always been industrial diversity and there increasingly will be. ICI spans mining and agriculture, manufacturing and services, as well as the new knowledge-based industries. At the root of it all lies chemistry.

What John Harvey-Jones has been trying to do, since he became chairman, is to bring back a personal and charismatic presence into an organization that had become depersonalized and rule bound.

DIVERSITY

Chemistry lies at the origins of all forms of life.

Francis Crick, discoverer of DNA

ICI has a very mixed heritage. Interwoven with its uniformity and conformity is variety, diversity, and a tolerance for eccentricity which I shall be highlighting in this case study. ICI is full of paradoxes. After all, what business do a Swede (Nobel) and a German Jew (Mond) have in creating Imperial Chemical Industries, aided and abetted by a fiery Scotsman (McGowan)?

ICI's roots are all too visible for anyone who sets out to find them. Unfortunately, all too few people have set out! At the present time in particular, we are so busy condemning tradition that we run the risk of bypassing history. We do so at our peril. For therein lie the roots of excellence. If ICI fails to draw from them, its family tree will eventually wither away and die.

TRANSFORMATION

Chemistry is the science of transformation.
Encyclopaedia Britannica

Chemistry is the science of transformation. The mechanisms of chemical reactions are the detailed processes by which chemical substances are transformed into other substances. Chemical reactions involve changes in the bonding patterns of molecules. What, then, lies at the roots of chemistry? How might we transform 'organization molecules' as well as physical ones?

The roots of chemistry lie in the ancient practice of alchemy. The root word, 'chem', is found in many languages and generally denotes change or transmutation. The language of chemistry employed by the alchemists was in fact a metaphor for personal transformation. In other words, the transmutation of base metals into 'gold' is an analogy for the transformation of human energies from an impure, obstructed state to a high-frequency state of responsiveness. The precious metals were regarded as the most evolved members of the animal kingdom; so, by analogy, to 'make gold' was to become more highly evolved.

During the setting up of their laboratory experiments, many of the original alchemists became more concerned with the nature and composition of external substances than with man's inner nature. Hence modern chemistry was born, which, in time, proliferated into a wide range of specialized subdisciplines. While science and industry developed in leaps and bounds as a result, the original human connection was lost. In a mature corporation this connection needs to be reestablished. If this is to happen, physical chemistry, organizational psychology, business enterprise and corporate culture have to develop hand in hand.

THE DEVELOPMENT CYCLE

An evolutionary approach recognizes the interdependence between people, technology and the marketplace over space and time. The seed of inspiration is planted by a creative scientist in a research department. At the root of development, therefore, is an underlying science, or even art form, promoted by an individual and supported by the surrounding culture. The individual is thus intimately connected with evolving science and society, as well as with the 'corporate universe'. The creative outcome, or invention, is then nurtured and developed by a cultivator, an enabler, a 'gardener', who establishes the environment in which people and things can grow. In being converted into a prototype, designed for fitness of purpose, adapted to need, a product or service needs a complex organizational structure. This conventionally project-based structure is rendered dynamic by the spirit of enterprise. Business is secured when product, market skills and resources are profitably combined. Yet business is only maintained if the enterprise and its environment are closely monitored, and adaptive responses are made as and when required. At the same time, unless there is a community of interest, in that all departments within and customers and suppliers without, are involved, continuous momentum will not be maintained. Such a lack of momentum will affect morale, reduce learning, stifle enterprise, corrode the structure, and dampen the climate for innovation, so that the development cycle will go into reverse.

If the development cycle is continually energized and revitalized, then the progression from birth and infancy, to adulthood, and then to maturity, will renew itself. In postmaturity, fundamentally new materials are discovered by a group of people who form a growth culture. The biotechnology-based new venture groups in ICI's Agriculture are a good case in point. These groups form an experimental venture which, if their plans come to fruition, become new enterprises. As such enterprises become

more robust, they build up management structures (see pages
259–60). This can promote further expansion. Subsequently, growing
interdependence with the environment calls for a new style of developmental management. Then, in maturity, a fundamental transformation takes place. A new division is created, as was the case when
Organics spun off Pharmaceuticals. The company image is transformed, revitalized, renewed. The corporate universe is nourished
and enriched. Agriculture returns to its roots, both literally and
figuratively, and discovers a new reason for being. It grows even
further down into the soil. No wonder ICI has recently acquired a seed
company! A business based on fertilizers, spread over the surface of
the ground, turns to seeds, which are potentially alive. The underlying
chemistry of life is further probed. A new role for the division, and for
the company, is consciously evolved.

THE CORPORATE UNIVERSE

The image of development is not one of separately isolated
functions, but of richly interconnected forms. The appropriate
physical structure is hexagonal and interactive, rather than rec-
tangular, with separate boxes. At the core lies chemistry, with its
increasingly interconnected base. On the periphery lie the business
or industries, the managed relationships, the core activities,
together with the geographical bases on which ICI rests.

THE ICI CORE

THE DEVELOPING CORPORATION

Unlike the managed organization, a developing corporation like
ICI has consciously to develop not only its products and markets
but also its people and organization. That is why John Harvey-
Jones has deliberately focused on corporate renewal. In addition,
and unlike Habitat/Mothercare, the design and development of
learning environments has become as important as the design and
development of new products.

The structure of an evolving and mature corporation is a very
complex one. All three phases, pioneering, managerial and de-

International Focus

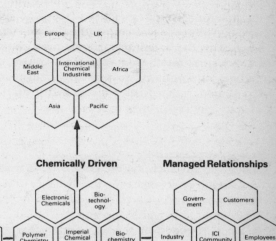

Development Functions

Chemically Driven

Managed Relationships

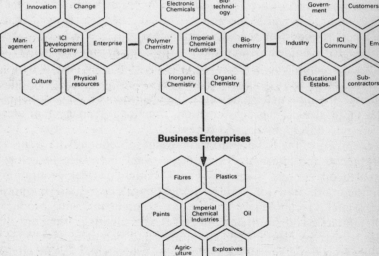

Business Enterprises

velopmental, need to be accommodated. That is the rule. But the developmental phase should dominate. At a presentation to the ICI project group concerned with the move to new headquarters, I put forward the idea of a 'development centre' which arose from the mature corporate functions (see page 208). The reaction was mixed. The group was both enthralled and daunted. How does this fit in with our intention of creating a slimmed-down, lean and hungry corporate headquarters? Of course, as you might expect, mature corporations are presently caught up with the image of 'adulthood' rather than evolving maturity. ICI is still in the midst of transcending its managed organization.

THE ENABLING BOARD

If ICI, or any such mature company, is to accommodate·the full 'tree of life', encompassing the diversity of its origins, its 'universe corporate', its powerful visions and its branch activities, the function of both leadership and the 'board' needs to change. That is what Harvey-Jones is currently attempting to achieve, and although I cannot envisage the board disappearing altogether, I can see it being reconstituted. In fact, the existing board might be divided three ways to reflect pioneering, managerial and developmental orientations respectively. The chairman would coordinate the three groups: business creation, functional management and corporate development, and renewal.

Members of the ICI organization would subsequently have three distinctive and alternative lines of personal and career development. Conventional managers would continue to seek promotion to the more traditional side of the board's activities: finance, personnel, technology. The sales, commercial and product champions could set their sights on the 'pioneering' functions of the board: acquisitions, new ventures and patent exploitations. The innovators, enablers and managers of change could angle their efforts and ambitions towards 'development': of products, of people, and of systems. . . .

The board would thus evolve from standardized parts towards an integrated whole. The synergy between the pioneering, managerial and developmental sectors could be achieved, through the

Threefold board

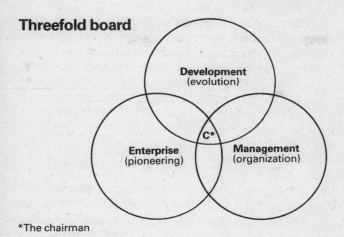

*The chairman

chairman. The board's overall responsibility would be to inter-relate, and to integrate, the economic, technical and social activities of the company as well as the increasing amount of interdivisional activity. It would now symbolize both the diversified and the coherent nature of ICI, its evolving maturity. It would be international, interdependent, interfunctional, interdisciplinary.

This new structure would be replicated lower down the organizations in two ways. Divisional boards would also assume each of the three primary functions – enterprise, management, development – but the respective weight and influence of each would vary. In fact there could be three kinds of 'division'. In a youthful division, like Electronic and Speciality Chemicals, pioneering is primary, and the managerial and developmental functions secondary. In a mature division, like Organics or Mond, it is the developmental arm which should hold pride of place. A 'middle-aged' division like Pharmaceuticals lies in between. This variation

The Development Centre

Core	Function Subsidiary	Core 'Director'	Proposed Facility	Activities Existing (E) plus Prospective (P)
DEVELOPMENT ↑ ↓	Vision and innovation	Innovator	**Innovation Centre**	(E) Technological/social Forecasting
				(P) Science forecasting Living chemistry – audiovisual, interactive display service
	Evolution and development	Enabler	**Training/ Development Centre**	(E) Environmental analysis
				(P) Organization development 'Living archives' update service
				(P) Research and development
	Learning and communications	Change-agent	**Communications Centre**	(E) Management services Contingency planning
				(P) Audio visual information, technology education service
MANAGEMENT ↑ ↓	Leadership and organization	Director	**Board Room**	(E) General administration (secretarial, registry, contracts) Personnel management (negotiations, pensions, appeals) Financial management (purchasing, financial control)
				(P) Technology management Marketing management
	Community and culture	Animateur	**Cultural Centre**	(E) Catering, travel, editorial services, public relations
				(P) Cultural information, services and entertainment activities
ENTERPRISE ↑ ↓	Enterprise	Entre-preneurial manager	**Trade Centre**	(E) Managers/acquisitions Investments
				(P) International business ventures New ventures and patent Exploitation Permanent exhibition and Business club Business services (subcontracted)
	Energy	Adventurer	**Health and Adventure 'Playground'**	(E) Security, building maintenance
				(P) Health shop, sports and fitness activities

on a 'three-note theme' would build both logic and flexibility into divisional operations. It would also alter the function of both divisional and overall chairman.

THE ENABLING CHAIRMAN

In the central board, over time, as the image of development becomes dominant, the role of the chairman would change. In fact, the changes are consistent with the way Harvey-Jones is now operating, in that:

- instead of seeing himself at the top of a pyramid, in splendid isolation, he has shifted to the *centre of the organism*, at a point where all channels of communication meet
- instead of making heavy-handed decisions and exercising ultimate authority, he selectively *guides, encourages, stimulates*, asks questions, gives support, recognizes potential and inspires confidence
- instead of focusing momentarily on the management of change, he regards the present as a snapshot on the *path of development*, towards which an objective is still to be discovered
- instead of merely competing with companies outside, and resolving conflicts inside, he *strives for association* with enterprises and institutions, and reaches decisions through *mutual agreement*
- instead of pursuing business, technical and organizational change as separate goals, he strives to *integrate business, technological and personal development* within a transformed business and social framework

In order for this developmental perspective to take genuine root, all of the attributes of excellence need to be transformed. Transformation takes place from the roots upwards, so we need to go back to ICI's origins.

BRANCH ACTIVITIES

VISION OF RENEWAL

> When a company ceases to renew itself, to innovate and adapt to
> its environment, it starts to die.
>
> Dick Hudig, marketing manager, ICI Americas

Alfred Nobel was born in Sweden in the early nineteenth century. He
came from a family of inventors and studied languages and natural
sciences at school. Throughout his life he was apt to express his
feelings in imaginative English prose, but, after his education, he
entered the family business. His mind wandered along many bypaths
of chemistry, but his curiosity was never purely theoretical. His
deepest reverence was for pure science, but he was no ordinary
scientist. He spent most of his time acting as a man of business, while
cherishing a deep yearning to live for science alone. The laboratory
was his sanctuary and the field of business his testing ground.

Experiments in his father's factory had convinced the young Nobel
that explosives offered a source of progress. There had been re-
markably few developments in road and canal building methods since
the days of the Romans, and he saw tremendous potential. Nobel had
heard of nitroglycerine, invented by an Italian chemistry professor,
who had used it for purely medical purposes. Nobel foresaw its
potential as an explosive, but he needed to invent a detonator. This he
duly did, but not without many trials and tribulations. Nitroglycerine
eventually proved too dangerous and, by 1886 – twenty years after he
had invented a detonator – Nobel created dynamite.

In between his inventions he travelled incessantly, seeking or
making opportunities in Europe and America, and creating new
businesses in both. His ultimate ambition was to move to Britain,
which he saw as the workshop of the world. He eventually set up his
first factory there, but not without experiencing enormous difficulty
in finding backers. The great lengths he had to go to in order to
attract interest, is described by one of his biographers:[1]

---

[1] N. Halasz, *Nobel* (Robert Hale, 1960)

Back in England he invited mine owners, railway builders and
engineers to a demonstration. He ignited charges of
nitroglycerine and powder mixture. A case with these contents
was dropped from sixty feet high. The onlookers were stunned
as they followed the frail, small body of the scientist moving
fearlessly. One explosion after another shook the earth. No
sales talk was needed.

Ludwig Mond, like Nobel, was an extraordinary man.

In the mind and in the action of Ludwig Mond the dream of
Francis Bacon came true. As in the case of Benjamin Disraeli,
it required a great Jew, with the divine fire burning brightly in
his spirit, to express and to embody in action the somewhat
vague hopes and aspirations of the British race.

Professor F.G. Donneson

While Nobel's dynamite business was enjoying its earliest suc-
cesses in Scotland during the mid-1870s, two young men in
Cheshire were struggling to establish the alkali business of
Brunner-Mond. Ludwig Mond emigrated to Britain from
Germany in 1862, because he realized that – as a Jew – his
prospects in his home country were limited.

Mond had studied under Professor Bunsen at Heidelberg and
gained a love for chemical science, as well as a disciplined mind.
But, by his second year, he had had enough of university. He
already had intentions of setting up in business, and was drawn to
Great Britain's tolerant environment. His ambitions were also
fixed on the soda industry, where England had taken a lead.

Soon after his arrival Mond took up a post at Hutchinsons, of
Widnes, where he met another young man on the make. John
Brunner, whose father was Swiss, left school at fifteen to set up on
his own. Mond's strength was on the technical side while
Brunner's was on the commercial. So they teamed up. In 1871
Mond heard about the Belgian Solvay process. He secured
agreement to set up a plant in Britain, and, in the early years, the
pressure of work was so great that he would sleep in the factory.
Through his bedroom wall he could clearly hear the throbbing of

the engines – sweet music to his ears! He would also spend many hours talking to the factory workers, who gradually came to trust this strange character with a foreign accent.

Many people have commented on the uniqueness of Ludwig Mond's character and abilities. Albert Cerasoli, an artist at the time, described him in these terms:

> A noble and commanding figure, his eyes remarkably keen and scrutinizing, his figure ever moving and revealing an excellent and exuberant vigour . . . I had never seen such a man before, and I must say that I haven't seen his equal since. He looked at my eyes for a few seconds, then asked me a few questions about my studios – I could see that he was a man for whom every side of human activity was intensely interesting, that he would see and scrutinize for himself.

Mond never tired of studying art, and some of his happiest evenings were spent with friends – lawyers, teachers, chemists, writers, artists – at the 'Qu'est-ce que c'est' club. His biographer, Jean Goodman,[2] described Mond's innovative mind thus:

> His unique sense of predestination enabled him to visualize the result of an experiment long before it could be established – as one sees the light at the end of the tunnel, although the tunnel itself is dark. With a wonderfully rapid and nearly always unerring intuition, he decided whether a scientific discovery could be used in practice. If it could, he proceeded immediately to overcome all kinds of material difficulties which for him didn't exist.

A pattern of innovation, then, both in character and in new product development, had been laid by Nobel, by Mond and – to a lesser extent – by Brunner. Ludwig's son, Alfred, was able to build upon the innovative foundations that they laid, and proceeded to champion the role of science and technology in the development of Great Britain as a nation. He ensured, at least within Brunner-

[2] Jean Goodman, *The Mond Legacy* (Weidenfeld and Nicolson, 1982)

Mond, that the tradition of scientific research should continue, and ICI's subsequent record in innovation is due, to a considerable extent, to these solidly laid foundations.

However, the dazzle, the sparkle, the imagination and the flair that Nobel and Mond brought with them has been substantially eclipsed by the organizational trajectory of subsequent years. Those who recently called for a new spirit of innovation would do well to rememeber the founding fathers, the creative spirit, of Nobel and Mond. It is time that modern technology, like interactive video, was used to resurrect the image of these men and their science – the living chemistry – with which they grew up. I see a great danger in allowing the spirit of independent enterprise to eclipse the interdependent roots of excellence that Nobel and Mond, and the chemical sciences, have brought with them. And we need to ask the question, at the same time, what is the new chemistry of our day?

DESIGN FOR DEVELOPMENT

The old industrial revolution must give way to the new.

Alfred Mond

From Innovation to Entrepreneurism: 1900–50

The accidental preservation of a gentleman's house, right inside the Brunner-Mond factory, had a profound and lasting effect on the tone of the business. Unlike Nobel, who died, a lonely foreigner, in France, Mond and Brunner were keen to become part of the British establishment. According to the official history of ICI, they were 'anxious to become squires if they could'. A management club was founded at Winnington Hall – the former gentleman's house – which, over the years, 'proved an efficient magnet for the sort of young men, technically and socially well qualified, whom Brunner and Mond wanted to bring into their service'. So a dynamic or tension was created, which could be productive or destructive for ICI's future. Mond's eccentricity was juxtaposed with his conformity. The question was, would the standardization build on the innovation, or quash it?

In fact, by the year 1900, both the Nobel dynamite company and the Brunner-Mond Solvay Group had become rather set in their ways. It was almost as if history had come to a stop, especially for the comfortable classes to which most of the managers belonged. Ludwig's son, Alfred, vacillated between politics and business, though he was a man of considerable business talent when he did apply it to his company. He personally carried with him both his father's vision and his own developed sense of organization. The creative pioneer and the organized manager coexisted in Alfred Mond, as the following reveals:

> The chemist today is the great adventurer, the true world pioneer. To him must fall the task of feeding, clothing and providing for the teeming generations of the future.

> The old industrial revolution must give way to the new. The old one was the age of steam and the application of power to production. The new one will be the age of the machinery of organization. The economic entity of the British Empire awaits it.[3]

The Advent of Industrial Diplomacy

But the immediate future, at least until the Second World War, rested more with industrial diplomacy than technology. The diplomacy was directed towards regulation of competition and expansion of markets, particularly within the Empire. The architect of expansion was Harry McGowan. It was McGowan, an industrialist and organization builder, and definitely not a scientist, who, in 1926, created the new company. ICI (Imperial Chemical Industries) combined Nobel Industries and Brunner-Mond with British Dyestuffs and United Alkali. The motive was to protect British interests against hefty German competition, by taking full advantage of imperial markets:

> The company has, of deliberate purpose, been given the title of Imperial Chemical Industries. The British Empire is the

[3] A. Mond, *Industry and Politics* (Macmillan, 1928)

greatest single economic unit in the world, and it will be the avowed intention of the new company to extend the development and the importance of the chemical industry, throughout the Empire.

Sir Harry McGowan.

McGowan had assumed, since the earliest days of the merger, that ICI's main profit centre would be in the fertilizer plant at Billingham. The investment in that plant had been based on the faith ICI had had in the heavy chemical industry. Yet the real development lay somewhere else, in the organics side of the industry.

During the 1930s, the heavy chemicals industry was suffering from intensive competition. Yet, to someone brought up with bulk chemicals, the 'pot and kettle' batch processes of the dyestuffs industry were unremarkable. So, at first, ICI's founders took very little notice of them. The technical revolution which would in time completely transform the industry went unnoticed. Plastics, man-made fibres, antibiotic drugs and agricultural chemicals lay beyond the horizons of ICI's decision-makers.

When Alfred Mond, the first chairman of ICI, died in 1930, Harry McGowan assumed full command. McGowan, unlike Mond, dealt in power. He enjoyed international wheeling and dealing, and building up a wide range of power-sharing agreements. It was the era of international cartels. McGowan's favourite instruments were commercial and financial, not technical or scientific.

The Development of New Technologies

Fortunately, though, because McGowan had no real understanding of technology, control in that area was delegated. As a result, ideas bubbled up to the surface from scientists working down below.

From 1933 to 1935, 87 new products had been added to Dyestuffs' manufacturing range. While ICI found themselves having to buy into plastics, and teaming up with Courtaulds in fibres, both Pharmaceuticals and Agrochemicals were spawned from their own Dyestuffs Division.

In fact, the birth and growth of Pharmaceuticals is a fascinating

The Roots of Excellence

case study, illustrating only too well the pioneering, expansive, and potentially integrative phases of business development.

Innovation

We started in 1938 as a small group of chemists. There were originally no biologists. Then the war intervened. From then on we never looked back. Our early research was directly related to the problems associated with modern warfare — trying to control infection and particular diseases originating in the Middle and Far East. The antimalarial agents were prompted by the disappearance of quinine as a source, what with the Japanese occupation of Malaysia.

So we expanded rapidly. It has been said that more people have been lost in wars through disease than through battle. We also got involved, at the time, with penicillin. The British government had been doing research into penicillin and we were asked to take the research effort over. We were successful on all these fronts. Out of the work on malaria 'paludrin' was created; out of the work on sulphonomides 'dulphodimidine' was born; and we also produced a penicillin drug for the armed forces. So the original investment of £15,000 proved extremely important for Britain.

The fact that we were so successful is due to several things. Firstly, the discovery of one drug led fairly directly on to another. Secondly, we were chemically driven totally. Thirdly, we were doing interesting chemistry in those early days. Fourthly, the targets were nice and clean. They stuck out like a sore thumb. There were just a small number of clearly identifiable infectious diseases. You only had to go back to the 1914–18 war to realize how many people died from infectious diseases. And the great hazard of disease was immediately apparent from the start of the Second World War.

Entrepreneurship

The personalities in those days were also clear for all to see. There was F.L. Rose, a really imaginative chemist, and Garner

Davis, an extremely creative biologist, who later got his OBE. One major difference between then and now was that, if you identified interesting biological properties, the route forward was relatively simple. The environment encouraged the entrepreneur. One man could have a major impact, right through from discovery to the marketplace. In 1962, with thalidomide, that all changed.

Come the middle forties we were quite small in the world scene, but we had shown that there was an ability, within ICI, to turn up compounds with biologically interesting properties. Gradually, the financial commitment increased. The decisions made in the early fifties brought us into the game seriously. It led to the opening of this separate, purpose-built site in 1957. Up until then we had been together with Dyestuffs Division, at Blakeley.

Expansion

In the mid-fifties Dyestuffs saw our separate development as a natural progression. They were proud of their offspring. We were very fortunate to have been working in those times. Expansion, in the fifties and sixties, was the order of the day. Nothing was deemed impossible. Something had to be created. We also look back with pride at our commercial predecessors, who had the guts to sustain their investment. Pharmaceuticals didn't make a profit until 1958–60. That was the first time, in twenty years, that there was a positive cash flow. The flavour we recollect, from our early days, was one of considerable excitement. The individual could make an impact across the board. Jimmy Black, the inventor of our heart drugs – beta blockers – almost single-handedly transformed our industry. Without him, we would not be here today. In the fifties there was still a tremendous suck from the outside world.

Scientific Management

Today, if we discover a product, it will take ten to twelve years to bring it to market. Such have been the changes wrought since 1962. Now, for the individual working as a scientist, the most that he can achieve is to produce one drug in a lifetime. It means that the individual can no longer have the same sense of product ownership. The experts now make all the decisions. The number of people involved in a product's development has increased inordinately. Take the three stages of development. Stage 1: We take it into man for the first time. £1 million. Stage 2: We do a clinical evaluation involving many patients. £10m. Stage 3: We get into the market. £100m. It's big business. Big money. This year we spent £93m on R and D. In the thirties we spent £15,000. The end result is that management is caught on the horns of a dilemma. We want people to be imaginative entrepreneurs. But it's big money we're talking about now, and we're cautious guys. So we have this conflict, trying to motivate people within severe constraints.

Interdependence

We live in an industry which is not only highly regulated, but also in the public eye. This is a big problem. In the industry, during the late sixties and seventies, we began to feel that the day of the big winner was over. The targets now are less visible. We are now dealing with the quality of people's lives rather than the quantity of births or deaths.

Bill Duncan, deputy chairman
Brian Newbold, research director,
Pharmaceuticals Division

The inventive pioneers did their formative work while still part of the Dyestuffs Division, in Blakeley. Pharmaceuticals' subsequent expansion and structured development took place on its own new site, in Alderley Park. It took a full twenty years before it became wholly profitable, but in 1983 Pharmaceuticals worldwide contributed about one third of ICI profits. In its third stage of development, the division is having to learn to live a truly interdependent existence with society as a whole. At the same time, the structured organization, which its very success has generated, is now being seen, by some, as a bit of an encumbrance. Early seeds have been sown for the essential organization 'crisis' that can open the way for development into a truly integrative phase.

The Twist in the Entrepreneurial Tail

The foundations for structured organization, in ICI as a whole, were laid many years before 1957, when the new Pharmaceuticals Division was created. The seeds were sown by the gentlemen of Wilmington Hall, and carefully planted by Alfred Mond when chairman of Brunner-Mond. His twin philosophy, of 'big is beautiful' and 'organization is efficient', was in part espoused by McGowan, when he created the mighty ICI. However, by temperament, Harry McGowan was more of an entrepreneur than a manager. He led from the front, manipulating the levers of power, rather than operating the machinery of formal organization. The world around him, in the period from 1926 to 1951 when he was all-powerful, suited his style. In 1939 ICI's business was regulated by 800 agreements with major competitors, many of which McGowan had negotiated himself. These international agreements, supporting major cartels, were the stuff of power politics within the chemical industry.

When McGowan finally retired in 1951 the chemical world had changed. The plentiful scope for wheeler-dealing, for carving up territory between the chemical giants, had been shattered both by the war and by American antitrust legislation.

From the time McGowan departed, the ICI board agreed that never again would such a dictatorial, if also entrepreneurial, individual, be allowed to lead their way. A succession of much lower profile professional managers, rather than dynamic leaders, took over ICI's reins.

Yet McGowan had served his purpose, at the expansive phase of the company's development. After all, the primary purpose of setting up ICI was to concentrate power. The Empire needed defending in 1926 from the industrial and trading force of Germany and the United States. From that point of view McGowan was successful. ICI had become an imperial force in the chemical industry and, in the fifties, looked well set for consolidation. But there was a twist in the tail. In quashing the image of the entrepreneur, as personified by the swashbuckling and manipulative McGowan, ICI was to pay a price in the longer term future.

FROM ENTREPRENEURISM TO SCIENTIFIC MANAGEMENT: 1951–82

THE EMERGENCE OF MODERN MANAGEMENT

Once McGowan retired from the scene, Alfred Mond's original philosophy, of integrating scientific research and development with the machinery of organization, was more fully implemented. As a result, perhaps unfortunately, the image of the gentlemen of Wilmington Hall eclipsed that of the original innovators Nobel and Mond. We therefore entered into an era of scientific management, which substantially supplanted the phases of innovation and entrepreneurship.

In many ways the construction of the Wilton Works in 1947 was symptomatic of this change. The world of the cartel makers was seen to pass away. In the new site, the plant for dyestuffs and intermediates would stand alongside the manufacturing plant, for primary inorganic chemicals. This was a large-scale integrated complex which had to be scientifically planned, and subsequently organized and controlled. As Reader, author of ICI's official history, said:

> It was a site of a kind quite new to ICI, needing a new kind of organization. The necessary independence of divisions to run their own factories would have to be reconciled with the degree of central control required to provide the cheap common services which were essential to the whole conception.

After the war, the British nation, and ICI with it, was dedicated to the pursuit of a well-coordinated programme of research and development. As the sums of money increased, together with the scale of organization, it was proving less and less possible, and desirable, to rely on individual inventors and entrepreneurs. So research, development and subsequent commercialization had to be carefully managed.

This is how Alexander Fleck, ICI's chairman from 1952 until 1956, put it:

The Managerial Revolution

In the last fifty years there have been great changes in industry – far greater than any which took place in the previous hundred years and comparable only to those of the early Industrial Revolution, say from 1780 to 1820. From the point of view of management, the most important of these changes has been the increasing divorce of ownership from management. In 1900 the vast majority of industrial enterprises were directed and managed by those who substantially owned them. Today the contrary is the case. In practically all large concerns the directors have reached their position by promotion from the ranks of executive management and not by virtue of being substantial shareholders. Thus most of modern industry is directed, controlled and managed by a new class of man – the career executive, the professional manager.

Parallel with the decline in owner-managers has been a rapid increase in the scale and complexity of industry. Production used to be a craft and is now a science. The scale of operations is larger; the processes are more complicated; far greater technical knowledge is required; staffs are larger, better educated and less amenable to demands for unquestioning obedience; planning and control have to be more accurate; the division of labour is more sensitive; the technical and economic consequences of error can be more far-reaching; the burden of taxation is heavy; public opinion is vigilant and politicians are critical. All these make greater demands upon management – and top management in particular.

These two trends – the divorce of management from ownership and the increasing complexity of the management function – taken together have led to what James Burnham has called the managerial revolution. Whether in the long run this evolution – I think evolution is a more accurate description than revolution – will prove to have been a development for the better or for the worse it is too early to say. We ourselves are too much part of that process to be able to judge it objectively. But looking at it subjectively we can already identify some of the strengths and some of the weaknesses.

Managerial Strengths

What are the more obvious strengths? In the first place, the modern managerial system is more democratic – promotion shall be by merit and not by birth. The highest posts shall be open to all. The only test shall be that of ability. Every apprentice shall have a chairman's gavel in his tool kit. This means that, in theory at least, the ablest men should always get to the top, and consequently British industry should have the best leadership possible. It should also mean that managers should be more acceptable to those whom they manage. All shall know that the opportunity is the same for all and that merit, not nepotism, is the path to promotion. But I wonder whether in practice the system works as well as this.

The weak link in promotion by merit is how to establish objective standards by which merit can be measured. This is a problem which has not been solved, for it is a very difficult one. In want of a solution it is easy for promotion by merit to relapse into promotion by seniority – the dismal ascent of dead men's shoes; or promotion by luck – 'the right face at the right moment'.

The second advantage which modern management should possess is a far greater technical knowledge than their predecessors. The technical nature of modern industry is obvious to everybody, but what appears to be less obvious to some people is that to manage and to direct a modern manufacturing concern it is necessary to have acquired a working understanding of the technology concerned. The question of what subjects a man took at school or university is far less important than what he has learned in later life. You can come to terms with the technology of your own industry without having a doctorate. Nor, incidentally, is the possession of a degree in the humanities any proof that the holder knows anything about human beings. Although we have the problem of technological education and training still very much on our hands, I am satisfied that modern managers are technically abler and better qualified than they were fifty years ago.

The third advantage of modern management is that it has a greater sense of public responsibility and public accountability. This springs from two causes. The first is that by divorcing management from ownership the test of profitability becomes less keen. The continuity and the stability of the company becomes more important than the immediate maximization of its profits. The modern manager is less interested in actual money-making than the old entrepreneur and more willing to take a longer and wider view of his company's interest.

The second cause of this greater sense of public accountability lies in the social and political ideas of our times, which differ greatly from those of the Victorians. The managerial director of today sees himself not only as a servant of his company, but also as a trustee for three interested parties – the shareholders, the customers and the employees. He has a duty to all three, as well as a wider obligation to the community. I would suggest that his sense of triple trusteeship is a new and, I believe, desirable feature of modern management.

Managerial Weaknesses

On the other side of the coin there are weaknesses latent in professional management against which we should guard. The first is a tendency towards conformity and an excessive adherence to precedent, for promotion in some organizations depends more on making neither mistakes nor enemies than on any positive accomplishment.

The second is that not being their own masters, managers may develop a fear of risk-taking, whether it is in trying out a new method or launching a new product or simply expressing an opinion which is unpopular with their superiors. I wonder how far young William Morris would have got with his hare-brained schemes for making motor cars if he had been the dutiful servant of a modern corporation. Here the manager is at a disadvantage over the independent master. A manager is a

223

member of a team with a hierarchy and therefore by nature of his position must subordinate his ideas to what is considered best for the organization as a whole. This is obviously right, for unless it were done a state of internal anarchy would arise.

But, if we are to encourage initiative and risk-taking on the scale necessary for Britain to retain her position as a leading industrial nation, we must try to devise some systems of promotion and reward for the manager which combine a reasonable degree of security with a real incentive to develop his more venturesome instincts. In the last analysis the habit of initiative in a firm is developed or retarded by the example which the directors and the senior managers set. So if we as directors or general managers complain of lack of initiative on the part of our subordinates, we may find like Cassius that the fault is not in our stars, but in ourselves. Earnings, hours of work, conditions, amenities – all play their part; but in the last analysis it gets down to the character, the personality and the example of the people who lead the enterprise. This means good leadership, and the heart of good leadership lies in the two simple words: 'Follow me'.

Alexander Fleck heralded the new era of professional management, with the maverick McGowan now retired to the sidelines. Interestingly enough, Fleck was also a Scotsman, but with a very different background from his illustrious, if not notorious, predecessor. He was a chemist and university lecturer before joining the managerial ranks of ICI. He rose to the top from an original position as research chemist and then works manager.

PURSUING EFFICIENCY AND EFFECTIVENESS

The basic form and style of management of ICI between 1951 and 1981 has remained fundamentally the same. The essential pattern of a central board overseeing the semiautonomous, but centrally coordinated activities of several major divisions – each with its own board and managerial hierarchy – did not change for thirty years. When Sir Maurice Hodgson retired as chairman at the end of 1981, his apparent leadership style was not at all unlike that of his predecessor, Alexander Fleck. When asked what he set out to do, during his term of office, he responded:

> . . . reducing our cost base, improving our manpower productivity, improving our energy efficiency. . . . We have been increasing the proportion of our business in higher value added products. . . . But these are differences of speed rather than real changes in objectives.
>
> *ICI Magazine* (January/February 1982)

His emphasis was very much upon efficiency and effectiveness, the conventional preserves of the traditional manager. Of course, Hodgson did have the misfortune to preside as chairman when ICI's results for a quarter showed a loss for the first time in over forty years. Yet Hodgson's reaction was sensible and moderate, rather than imaginative and radical. He left any fundamental organizational change to his successor, and current chairman, Harvey-Jones.

1982 – FROM STRUCTURED ORGANIZATION TO MANAGEMENT OF CHANGE

FROM IMPERIAL TO INTERNATIONAL

Although Sir Maurice Hodgson was somewhat conservative in his approach to the chairmanship, he did emphasize that the company needed a new approach. It now needed to have plans which were robust enough to withstand changes in external circumstances, and to have an organization which was able to respond quickly and flexibly to them.

Of course, ICI had by no means stood still in the period 1950 to 1980. While the overall structure and style of management was conservative, there were pockets of innovative and entrepreneurial activity, as exemplified by the Pharmaceuticals Division. The board maintained and developed a style of management that was sufficiently open-minded to accommodate evolutionary change. Perhaps the greatest change had been the shift in emphasis from the old Empire to Europe and America as key export markets. The comparative value and distribution of ICI's overseas business, between 1963, 1973 and 1983, is given below.

Overseas Sales Distribution 1963–83				%
	1953	1963	1973	1983
UK		52	43	29
Western Europe		11	17	21
North America		11	13	22
Pacific (inc. Australia)		9	11	18
Others (Africa, India, Eastern Europe)		17	16	10
Total Sales	£282m	£624m	£2166m	£7448m

Besides the very rapid increase in overall turnover, almost a thirty fold increase, the distribution of sales has changed significantly. Over the last ten years in particular, there has been a dramatic increase in the proportion of revenue generated from overseas. ICI has become a truly international company, with Western Europe and North America now easily surpassing the old imperial countries as markets for the company's products.

The change in product line, over a similar period, has been equally dramatic. If we look at the changes in relative profitability over just the past few years, these are interesting enough. Oil and Pharmaceuticals between them accounted for almost 50 per cent of ICI profits in 1983, compared with less than 10 per cent in 1975.

METAMORPHOSIS

So, both market forces and technological breakthroughs have changed the shape of ICI's business over the last twenty years. There has also been a deliberate strategy to expand in Europe and America, and to develop high value-added products. But these factors alone have not been sufficient to change the basic style of leadership, and shape of organization. The combination of three factors have caused that to happen.

Distribution of Profits amongst Product Lines   1975–83

	£m	
	1975	1983
Agriculture	111	170
Fibres	(33)	(5)
General chemicals	68	115
Industrial explosives	22	26
Metals/engineering	18	–
Oil	–	95
Organic/speciality chemicals	15	(10)
Paints	6	28
Petrochemicals	47	–
Plastics	–	
Pharmaceuticals	25	200
Miscellaneous	9	–

First, ICI has had to cope with an ever-increasing rate and variety of change. In fact, during the seventies, not only was the world economy in a state of turmoil, but society's rapidly growing awareness of environmental and social issues, including the impact of automation, was also having an effect. Then, secondly, and spurred on by the economic recession, came the first loss ICI had incurred in a quarter for over forty years. That created massive shockwaves through the ICI system. Third, and by no means accidentally, a chairman with a very different style and background to his predecessors was appointed. For John Harvey-Jones is neither the scientist nor the 'company man' that most former chairmen had been. He sees his role as very much one of 'managing of change', as an article in *ICI Magazine* (spring 1983) revealed.

Would you like to say something about regeneration of ICI business?

I think really there are two different types of regeneration. First of all . . . the industrial problem is that a company has to continuously renew itself. The world is littered with the remains of once private and powerful companies that are now just names, and that is because they were outstanding in their time but they failed to make sure they were continuously renewing their company to meet the market demands of the future.

There are umpteen ways you can do this, but there is only one normal way in which it has happened in ICI. By and large, the operating units have sought to renew themselves, and they have done that mostly by looking at their own portfolio of activities and then seeing whether there are bits on the edges that they can develop, or where they have some relevant technology.

Now some of those attempts have been outstandingly successful. The Dyestuffs Division gave birth to the Pharmaceuticals Division and the Plant Protection Division. The Fibres Division was again a spin-off from other activities.

To some extent we have been lucky because in the past that has enabled us, by and large, to move across into most of the new developments. That will still continue and that is still the responsibility of the individual operating unit.

But increasingly we now look at the world markets and the future world growth. We see areas where, to exploit that market, the drive will not necessarily come from one operating unit. I suppose the current example of this is probably electronic chemicals, where ICI has got quite a clutch of chemicals which apply to the high-growth electronics industry. There is nobody in the world who has a very large electronic chemicals business and, when we first started looking at this business, we realized that we had a lot of penny packets which had not been pulled together to constitute a whole. Moreover, we have a number of new technological thrusts inside the group which we believe are very relevant to this, and we have some fundamental scientific skills which we believe are very relevant and necessary. Therefore this is one of the regeneration areas that we have selected, where we have asked Charles Reece, the technology director, to make a particular effort to push, and we have allocated money for research. He has set things in motion in various ways which will become clear as time goes on, and he is pulling together the activities that we already have, and making sure that we have got a developing business there, which may involve the acquisition, some time, of other companies, or acquisition of products or of tehnology or the development of new technology, so that in ten years' time, or thereabouts, we have a significant electronic chemicals business.

Does not all this involve altering attitudes and getting people to approach their tasks in a different way?

That is what the end result has to be. You see, the whole basis of my belief is that no individual, or group of individuals here, can manage the company. The management of the company has to be done at much closer range to the real problems. I don't believe that ICI has performed up to the capability of its people. This is only part of the truth because I start off with the view that we have very, very good people — not just managers, but first-class people in the weekly staff area as well.

Are you confident that the calibre of people already in ICI can make this change or shift in attitude?

I am confident that they will, but I think *they* are much less confident. There is always an ICI hope that somewhere there is a Big Daddy who will make the decision for you. Indeed, what we have had in ICI is a series of brakes so that if anybody at the bottom had any ideas of wild excess, there were so many cautionary things that stopped the wild excess, that by the time they got through them all it was presumably fairly safe or fairly sound. The problem with that is first of all it is extremely slow, and secondly it does mean that you rely very much on the chaps at the bottom having the incentive to push their way up through these layers.

Actually, there has always been a lot of headroom for people inside ICI to do things, but not many have believed that. Many struggle hard to achieve things. However, you are far better off in ICI if you don't realize how restrictive the basic system can be; you can do almost anything the moment you realize that truth! Most people tend not to start or even try.

Are you looking for more entrepreneurial, more risk-taking management?

We have to, because this isn't just a question of a personal piece of action, it's a question of the reality of the outside world, which is very unstable and changing at a rate of knots. We will only survive if we are able to take advantage of those changes. And the reality of the changes can best be read close to the scene of action.

ENABLING DEVELOPMENT

Interestingly enough Harvey-Jones has grasped the new banner, with a dual emphasis on 'the management of change' and 'business entrepreneurship'. The notion of 'change management' dates back at least to the sixties, as far as management academics are concerned. Of particular evolutionary significance for ICI is the juxtaposition of change, entrepreneurship and development in the context of being an enabling company.

There is a world of difference between an organization that enables development – in people, products and technologies – and one that creates change (innovation), exploits it (entrepreneurship) or channels it (management). To what extent ICI has become such an enabling company is still very much open to question, but it certainly is evolving in that direction. I want to close this section by introducing one of ICI's research directors who comes close, in my mind, to performing the role of a genuine enabler.

Rob Margetts read chemical engineering at Cambridge and, at the age of thirty-six, was the youngest man ever to be appointed to the board of ICI (Agriculture). In his early years at ICI he worked on the first three prototypes of ammonia plant in the world.

We developed our skills together

. . . they put me in as technical manager of the fertilizer and acids factory. That was like being sent to Siberia. People sent there never seemed to come back! It was regarded as low technology. Ammonia and mined potash plus phosphates from North Africa were converted into fertilizer for farmers. It was a big works. The industrial relations were complicated. It was desperately in need of technical innovation. I was five years there, out in the cold!

I had a whale of a time, in fact. My team was absolutely first class. What talented people. I was thirty. 1976. It was a key time in my life. The person who was my deputy is now works manager. Another colleague is now personnel manager at Plant Protection. One more now heads up the building of a methanol plant. And so on. Marvellous. We developed our skills together. There was tremendous interaction. We added to each other.

Building conceptual models

1979. Biotechnology. I was brought in out of the cold to head up this biotechnology thing. It had already been going for ten years and we had this Prutein plant. I couldn't see any logic in the choice. Why me? I had no background in biology. But I guess they were looking for something else.

Chemical engineering is really good for management you know. It teaches you to build models. If you're trying to model a bloody great plant, you have to build a model, a concept, something that describes it, and helps you play about with variables, thereby enabling you to modify the plant. Then you get the plant to work better. You know, you can model almost anything in life. You can use the model too, as an analogy. The more analogies you can build on, the better. Without a model, the manager is lost. You can act all the bloody time, but what if you get it wrong?

We helped each other climb a mountain

Two things about my position with the Prutein plant. It was a battle situation, and a number of people weren't up to it. We worked for two years, seven days a week. My role wasn't just management. The technology was very difficult. There was a high level of uncertainty as to how to approach the design and operation of the plant. Testing and learning. Bloody great monster. The seven days a week stuff sorted out the men from the boys. It left me with a dozen top-quality managers. Now they're spreading their wings to have a go at new ventures. All have gained confidence. We climbed a mountain together. There were marketing problems, technical problems, political problems. That was the most formative period of my life.

I put my whole soul into it

Then out of the blue, fifteen months ago, I was put on the board. The youngest ever, at thirty-six. Why? I had been out of circulation. I hardly ever saw any other part of the company. Yet I wasn't distressed. I put my whole soul into making the business go. I was given the portfolio of research director. I was also made director of a couple of fertilizer companies. We set up this new venturing activity, of which I'm now chairman. You see, I don't design my personal future. That's not right and proper in a large company. But I do look ahead. I work like hell at what I think needs to be done. I am totally committed at any point in time, totally oriented to the success of the activity.

I get my satisfaction out of harnessing potential

I'm paid well enough. I can get access to the resources I need for my new ventures. I'm not interested in empire building, in any shape or form. I get my personal satisfaction out of building, constructing. I try and tackle one significant problem every few months. I don't aim for anything grand, actually. What it's basically about, for me, is enhancing the scientific capability of my bit of ICI, exploiting it firmly and positively, across a broad front.

So my role now is to connect it all, technology, customers, organization. I still get a lot of fun out of the technical side, but it's getting the whole act together which now particularly appeals. The whole thing is better than any of its separate parts, and to harness its full potential you need a combination of people and skills.

Margetts is not simply a manager, not quite an entrepreneur, and probably not a conventional leader. He loves to construct, to develop, to model, to build, to combine, to enhance, to harness potential and to make whole. These are the skills of the enabler, developing people, products and technology. ICI (Agriculture) have in fact created a New Ventures Division which is inviting collaboration with anyone, anywhere, who has an idea worth developing. Thus the division is reaching down to its underlying roots, into seeds, and into cultivation. In acquiring a large seed company in America, the division, and hence ICI as a whole, is further deepening and widening its roots. In evolving towards an enabling company, however, it would need to erode much of its conventional structure much further.

THE BUSINESS MISSION/PRODUCT LINE

ICI's basic mission has remained largely unchanged since its for- mation, as a combined entity, in 1926. All that has changed is the scale of the operation, and the distribution of products and markets. In particular, the emergence of pharmaceuticals and oil, as products, and of continental Europe and the United States as markets, has led to a distinct shift of emphasis. But none of this has altered the underlying mission – to exploit science and technology within the chemical industry so as to serve, profitably, ICI's international customers, employees and shareholders. In fact, it is remarkable how seldom the internal organization has changed, over the space of almost sixty years. Perhaps in the last three years, we have begun to see significant changes for the first time.

Nobel and Mond sowed the scientific seeds for ICI, and grew them into fledgling plants. If they were the fathers of invention, the mothers were Great Britain, Europe and America, who received the products of Nobel and Mond – in the first case more reluctantly than in the second. While Nobel conducted his own technical and commercial business, Mond brought in Brunner to handle much of the latter. Moreover, Mond's son Alfred was very adept, when the time came, at turning a pioneering entity into a well-structured organization.

The 'children' that 'grandparents' Nobel and Mond bore, together with the construction, munitions and heavy industries, were bulk chemicals. When ICI was created by the 'foster parent', McGowan, United Alkali and British Dyestuffs were adopted as additions to the original family. All four 'children' retained strong elements of individual autonomy, while forging a new identity with their parent company. The extent of this autonomy has increased and decreased over the years, but its basic nature has remained unchanged.

Today, ICI has nine major divisions of activity and an equal number of territories in which it operates. The divisions range from Agriculture, Explosives, Fibres and General Chemicals, to Oil, Paints, Plastics and Petrochemicals, to Pharmaceuticals, Speciality and Electronic Chemicals. The territories span the entire world, but most particularly Europe, America and the old Empire.

THE STYLE OF MANAGEMENT

The company as a whole has always had to manage product lines, business functions and geographic territories at one and the same time. In recent years, board directors at the centre have had responsibility for one or more of all three. So, inevitably, some degree of matrix management has been involved. The frequent reorganizations over the years have involved reshaping the product lines, the territorial allocations, and the extent of divisional and functional autonomy. They have led to variations on a basic, and not unconventional, organizational theme. The feature that has been relatively unique to ICI is not its basic structure, but its approach to management development. Staff have tended to remain within ICI for a lifetime, and the company, through selective and challenging new placements at regular intervals, has kept their high-flying managers on their toes. There has been substantial fluidity between divisions, but strong rigidity in terms of job grades and descriptions.

When John Harvey-Jones assumed the chairmanship he was dedicated to two major organizational changes. The first was to delegate power further downwards. So each divisional chairman became chief executive of his division with considerable powers of authority. Harvey-Jones's own background and style of leadership help to explain this first change.

Harvey-Jones's father was a 'professional prime minister' in India, and John was brought up with a Maharaja almost as his elder brother. That provided a colourful early setting. He survived schooling, in England, with some difficulty, before going on to naval college. John was 'attracted by the life of adventure'.

When I finished at college, I went to sea. It was during the war, and I was under seventeen. We were sunk a couple of times before I was eighteen. I became a sublieutenant specializing in the submarine service. After the war was over, the submarine I joined was in a mess, in fact so much so that the first eight months of peace were more dangerous than ever.

At the time they were looking for volunteers to learn

Russian. The bait was Cambridge. I had always wanted to go to university. I wanted to go to Cambridge and have a good time. But it wasn't to be.

My submarine experience did a lot of things for me. There was rigorous discipline, but it wasn't hierarchical. We all worked in close proximity. There was a high degree of mutual respect. After all, we were all capable of sinking the sub. So it was friendly and uninstitutionalized. The discipline was real, but we mucked in together, officers and men. It was a team thing. This had a profound effect. It taught me that the difference between individuals is marginal. It's basically the luck of the draw. Everyone has the same difficulties.

That's where my left-wing predilections emerged from. The background and conditions of the sailors touched me deeply. The unequal society raised its ugly head. I'm still in touch with some of the sailors to this day.

In between submarine service and joining ICI, Harvey-Jones did a mixture of command and intelligence work, working at close quarters with both the Russians and the Germans after the war. When his daughter contracted polio, he decided to stop globetrotting and to get a job that would keep him at home more. At this point he also needed a vocation to follow, rather than a career.

I stopped wanting to have a career. I had had a very good one, and that was it. I felt the need to get into something basic. I had a need to perform a service, something socially responsible. Money doesn't do a thing for me.

What makes me run is achievement. I need to live up to my own standards. My cardinal sin is pride. Self-pride. I don't care what other people say about me, but I care what I think about myself. I know what I think a 'man' ought to do. I have this inner compulsion. I have to perform, and to ensure that I can make things happen. I must feel that something has my name tag, for me to see and nobody else.

I'll give an example. There's a refinery in Teesside. I know

ICI

that it only exists because it was a concept I created, a deal I put together. It's still there. Every time I go near it, and take a look, I feel great. It's still running, still employing people. To see it gives me an inner satisfaction worth a guinea a box. It hasn't changed the face of the world, but it has given me the satisfaction of a creation that's working.

I'm not interested in calling it the Harvey-Jones Works. I know what I did. I know the struggle. I know the deals.

He ultimately became division chairman, at Wilton, and doubled the profits there for every one of his three years in charge. He was then ordered to amalgamate Wilton and Fibres.

I created a new outfit, with a new identity. That's the art of amalgamation, to create a third, and completely new entity, rather than have one company take over another. If you go to Petrochemicals now, people wouldn't remember whether they were originally this division or that. Then I was put on the main board. I'm a strong believer in group leadership, but not in consensus. My job is to manage the board, and to make sure it makes decisions. I have to polarize things. Good boards don't operate on a basis of no conflict. But, no way do I want people to row, and to hate each other. Argument there must be, but good-humoured stuff. I'll listen and change if I can't carry people. If anyone is bypassed, then they still must be heard. They must have a kick at the ball. And if things turn out wrong for me, I shall always say, 'Well they did say this might happen.'

What I want to create is an adaptive company that has got some of the values you need to survive in tomorrow's world. I believe passionately that you should not have any organization layers, unless they visibly add to the party. The board's job, meanwhile, should be unique. It is concerned more with the what than the how. When you mix the two you get into trouble. The art of jacking any business up is to continuously set people targets a bit beyond their perceived capability, and then ensure they achieve them.

We need to become the chemical problem-solvers of the

237

world, by the year 2000. Whenever you have a chemistry problem, you ring up ICI, and, of course, we get paid for it. We're not doing good for love. But our customers must profit from working with us.

I envisage that when I've done this job, I'll retire and do something with my family. By the time I'm done, I'll be knackered. I give this job everything I've got. I'll be ashamed if I'm bounding with vigour at the end of it. I think I'm leading the best large company in the country, but neither my wife nor I get our pleasures from driving a Rolls.

The extent to which the chairman's leadership style rubs off on the divisions is illustrated through David Barnes, chairman of ICI (Paints); one of the younger and more recently appointed divisional executives:

I spent ten years as part of a team building up operations in Europe. In nearly every case we were founding a business from scratch, sometimes as a joint venture with an existing distributor, and other times on our own. I was part of a small team that set up a dozen operations in eleven years, involving, in most cases, manufacturing facilities. Finally, I became manager of the European department. This was all in Pharmaceuticals.

The average age of our European department was twenty-seven years old, and the average length of service three and a half years. It was fabulous. There was a tremendous element of good fortune in it all. We had extremely good business leaders. There was enormous delegation. We had to sink or swim. It was a marvellous way of learning.

If you've got to set up your whole new operation you learn about things you would never otherwise do. Even as division chairman I don't have to worry about my overall bank account. It's all pooled with ICI's. But in those small ventures I had to be concerned with finance, pensions, industrial relations, the lot. I had a total overview. What a fantastic learning experience.

As commercial manager for Europe, I was the spider in the

middle of the web. We were territorial managers, business promoters. Also, I could call in the expert bits and pieces – lawyers, financial experts, and so on – as needed. I was also put on the local boards of our overseas operations. That helped me enormously, at the tender age of twenty-eight. They were tiny companies, but it was a whole experience in miniature. Much more broadening than being the product manager of this or that. I opened plants, established bank accounts and pension schemes, was exposed to European forms of joint consultation, and got that all-round experience. I admired ICI's courage, in putting me on the local boards at such a tender age.

In other parts of ICI, these sort of decisions were taken most commonly by the divisional board directors, who were wise men, but probably too remote. In the case of Pharmaceuticals at that time it was the operators down the line who decided. It's much better to be there, on the spot. We were blessed with the opportunity, and our superiors trusted us. Had we been in a bigger division it probably would never have happened. It was circumstances.

I was then appointed overseas director with a view to utilizing that European experience in a much wider inter-national context. Once again I was fortunate enough to have the opportunity to form new pharmaceutical operations in a very wide range of territories such as Japan, Argentina, Mexico, Iran, Indonesia, etc.

Then, a year ago, I was tapped on the shoulder and asked to become chairman of Paints. I had mixed feelings, I have never had ambitions for myself. I really don't care about status or title as long as I can bring something to the job, and be kept occupied 110 per cent. I've always been fortunate in having a range of tasks that have kept me fully engaged. It was with great sadness, though, that I left a business which had come from nothing to something very big and important. I came from a place where I knew lots of people to one where I knew just four; from a business where I knew the competitors and customers to one where I knew none. I didn't understand the technology, and as a family we were uprooting from a house we loved dearly and from friends and relations.

But a division chairman's job is the best one going. I believe everyone cherishes it, and would always accept it if offered. So I asked myself, and those who tapped me on the shoulder, could I bring anything relevant to it? Could I honestly do the job to the benefit of Paints? I line up, personally, with a Japanese philosophy. I don't believe you have 3500 people (as in Paints) working for you. You are working for them. So I said to myself what can I bring to this group?

My impression of Paints was that it's geographical axis was still in the 'Imperial' image. Back to Pharmaceuticals in 1960. Paints had only one operation in continental Europe, in Germany. So my learning curve may be of assistance in rebalancing the geographical portfolio. We see the growth of international branding everywhere. Macdonald's is simply lifted from America to this country. So why shouldn't our decorative products have a market in Europe and America? As for motors, that's quite obviously an international business.

What every division chairman also brings to a division is a personal style. I hope that it is seen as aiding the division. I believe in involvement, delegation and communication. I also wish to give sharp, clear-cut decisions. I want to give people clearly defined tasks and challenges. They should then be allowed the discretionary room to get on with those tasks.

Again, I am very lucky. I have arrived at a time when there are some very promising new technologies. Solid emulsion paints have just been launched. In all sectors waterborne technology is going to be of enormous importance, as a response to environmental and health pressures. Bits and pieces of technology are coming through which will provide us with 'breakthrough' products.

One of the tasks I have is to switch from an almost exclusive cost reduction mode, which has characterized the last few years, and get into controlled expansion as the external economy begins to grow again. We've got to develop and enlarge particularly our development departments and overseas.

Where I came from in Pharmaceuticals, the stuffy institutional image just did not exist. I find this division extremely friendly, but more hierarchical and less irreligious than the one I left. Individuals here have not had the opportunity to experience growth of the same magnitude as Pharmaceuticals. Paints is a more mature business sector. They need to get fresh air at the moment. So it is important to enable change, by making some new and significant appointments, by being more open with everyone, by encouraging new product and market developments.

I'd also like to work towards a less safe remuneration system. Salary should be no more than, say, 85 per cent of total reward. I believe 15 per cent should be available according to results. This discretionary portion should be distributed only if division profits improve by a certain targeted amount. It would bring greater realism to the business. People would participate more directly in business improvement. I also like the idea of 'box maxima', whereby people can improve their grade within an existing job. You then encourage each individual to develop, within his existing position. You do need orderly systems, but they must never stifle anyone. We need both technical and commercial innovation, financial strength, but above all energetic and well-motivated staff.

Each division, in turn, was broken down into business areas, each of which were assigned managers with delegated authority. There was nothing revolutionary in all this, but rather a change in flavour and emphasis. It offered new chairmen, like David Barnes, the opportunity to apply their spirit of enterprise – as well as their scientific background and managerial experience – to ICI's development.

THE FUNCTIONING OF THE NEW BOARD

The other major change was in the functioning of the central board itself. Firstly, it was drastically cut down in size; when the deputy chairmen left they were not replaced, and staff support people were dramatically reduced in number. Charles Reece, ICI director:

> When I joined the board, in 1979, I had 69 staff support people serving me alone. Now I have two. Staff are great at generating questions that others have to answer. There used to be a whole staff department looking after India, for which I have been responsible. Now there are none. My secretary acts as gatekeeper. I don't have lots of guys dreaming up problems to solve.

So, in the past five years not only has the entire workforce in the UK virtually been halved – as part of ICI's rationalization policy – but the central staff have been considerably slimmed down.

Secondly, there has been a major structural change, not only quantitatively, but also qualitatively. Reece explains what has happened:

> We got rid of policy groups and the deputy chairmen roles. Board members also lost their responsibility for a particular part of the company – as advocate for particular divisions. As individuals, we directors now have very little responsibility. Our power resides in our small group, in our team. The team has all the power, the individual has virtually none. Whereas the head of an operating unit can spend £5 million, without referral, directors have no powers of discretionary spending. Well actually, the finance director and myself can each spend £2 million for specific purposes, but that's all.
>
> The rationale is, firstly, if we are going to concern ourselves with the strategic direction of the company, without the bias of advocacy, we need to work with a spectrum of skills. Between the eight of us, because of our knowledge and experience, we have these. Denys is trained as a lawyer, and has been a businessman. He's now a friend and a help to five business divisions. Robin trained as a physicist, became a barrister, and then a planner. He has a good political understanding of the outside world. I'm the scientist and technpeople both as individuals and as groups. Phil was a physical chemist who got

involved with the production of heavy chemicals and latterly has taken a considerable interest in organization development. He's knowledgeable about energy and general chemicals. Bryan is a fibre technologist who has been exposed to the cut-throat commercial world of textiles. Clement read economics at Oxford. He's a tax man who runs our finances. And John has to be a jack of all trades.

Our function, then, is to think through, devise, and manage the portfolio of the company, to make ICI highly profitable, more international, and less capital intensive. The key words are *portfolio management*. Our job is to define what strategies one can afford in relation to what is desirable. We have to bring together a whole spectrum of goals and ambitions, to eventually win. We have to reconcile the short and long term, and define the pushes and pressures that we face. We need to decide what must grow and what must shrink, all in the interests of driving up the profitability of the organization.

In many ways the board's functioning is in a state of flux. While it has shifted away from individualized responsibilities, its new role as a coherent force, and one that accommodates variety, is still unfolding. It takes time to adjust from one position to another. The new organizational blueprint has not yet been fully absorbed within ICI's managerial psyche.

THE AMOEBA FORM

The new form is in fact more complex than the conventional organizational chart. It accommodates much more fluidity, interdependence and evolutionary development than a static chart allows.

I liken it to an amoeba form rather than the conventional family tree. The amoeba can change its shape as it takes in nourishment from the environment.

It can also form anew, as its nucleus splits in two. The boundary between itself and the world outside is easily crossed and transgressed. So the old Dyestuffs Division which begat

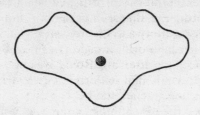

Pharmaceuticals and Agrochemicals may have been seen to change its form rather than detract from its own existence. People leaving ICI to set up their own business serve to extend its organizational form rather than remove themselves from it. Links across divisions, between manufacturing units and marketing facilities, can be easily demonstrated within the amoeba-like structure, which cuts across divisional lines of authority. New ventures become elongated arms of the original amoeba, until such time as the divisional nucleus splits in two or three, and new amoebae are formed. Finally, and in similar terms, a board is able to change its shape and form, as individuals discover their intrinsic value, so that its overall dimensions change, unpredictably, but synergetically.

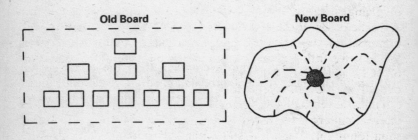

This organic development brings us to the new forms of entrepreneurship emerging within and alongside ICI.

The picture of the new board is indicative of its potential, rather than of its actual structure. It will take a long time still for

ICI to shed its traditional form of organization and take on a more complex form; one that is capable of genuinely accommodating the immense variety and diversity that it has generated for itself. Relics of the old world of rigid stratification are still very much in evidence. But, after all, Rome was not built in a day. What is exciting today is that under Harvey-Jones's leadership a creative tension is being generated between not only the old form of bureaucracy and the new spirit of enterprise, but also between the old controlling and the new enabling structures. A worry does remain that once the influence of Harvey-Jones's charismatic character is removed, there might be a slide back to old forms. This puts a high priority on developing the richer, complex form as indicated earlier before his chairmanship comes to an end.

THE NEW ENTREPRENEURS

Basically I believe in helping people to stand on their own two feet, and facing up to the consequences.
Brian Codling, business manager, ICI (Paints)

After the McGowan era, scientific management took over from entrepreneurship, as the ICI approach to business. Entrepreneurism was restricted to isolated pockets within the company, involving, notably, Pharmaceuticals in the fifties and sixties and Agrochemicals in the seventies. The forces of structure and organization, of planning and management, had taken over. When new venture activity was undertaken, within the heartlands of ICI's managed organization, it often failed. There was no overall spirit of enterprise to infuse it with life.

Times have changed. Changes in the environment and in the internal culture have led to a new spirit of enterprise. In fact, I soon found (although it is still a minority pursuit) that this spirit is blossoming in various shapes and forms. It is extremely important to appreciate the varied forms that the enterprising spirit is taking. We cannot rely on the old entrepreneurial stereotype. Life is never as simple as that. We cannot merely go back to an age of merchant adventurers.

The Roots of Excellence

Within ICI, therefore, I shall be identifying six essentially different variations on the entrepreneurial theme. I call these individual varieties:

- the high-flier
- the entrepreneurial manager
- the product champion
- the enabling entrepreneur
- the 'gamesman'
- the 'marketeer'

High-Flier

'High-fliers' are well known in management circles, in name if not in essence. To put it simply, they make it to the top, or thereabouts, and they fly there quickly. Denys Henderson, ICI's youngest member of the central board, is a typical case in point:

> People say that to reach a senior position in ICI you need judgement, intellect and experience. That is absolutely true but, for me, there are three things which are of paramount importance – luck, stamina and determination.

In his early days, luck played a particularly important part:

> I have been incredibly lucky, in more ways than one. I had very good parents, for a start. They gave me an extremely happy home life, as a good Presbyterian in Aberdeen, Scotland. I grew up in an atmosphere of some financial insecurity, but underlying stability in the background.
>
> My second bit of luck was being extremely happily married. My domestic life has always been terribly important to me. As they say, when you're put out to grass, you need something else in your life. My wife and I are very complementary. I'm mercurial and impulsive. She's calm and relaxed – a marvellous support to me.
>
> Thirdly, I have two supportive daughters. Fourth, I have very good health – touch wood. Fifth, I enjoy working in the UK.

246

And sixth, I've worked for ICI for twenty-seven years. If I had my time all over again, I'd have done exactly the same. I've had a very secure and exciting time.

Before joining ICI, Henderson, who had a legal training, was called up into the army:

In the army I was lucky to be given a post as a staff captain, doing prosecution work. I was allowed to handle a very wide variety of cases. You were entirely on your own and, for a lad of twenty-three, to be thrown in at the deep end was really exciting. It began to convince me that I was an achiever.

Henderson took up his first position at ICI in the secretary's department.

We were living at the time, my wife and I, in a very small flat in Harrow. 'How much will you be paid?' my wife asked when I came home. The fact is, I didn't know. When I asked I was told, 'My dear boy, in ICI we breed a certain type of individual. We don't ask such questions as how much will I be paid?' Times have since changed!

I spent three months in the secretary's department, before I was sent on to Paints for two years. I nearly left. I was bored to death. After being a staff captain in the army, here I was drafting three-line letters to complaining customers. I tried to leave, but fate saw to it that I didn't. Instead I was moved to Billingham, and from then on I never looked back. I got involved in an exciting lot of negotiations, many to do with the licensing of technology.

Towards the end of 1963, I was asked to join Nobel Division in Scotland as their division secretary. All good Scots are supposed to want to return to their native heath. Yet I knew after a week that I'd made a mistake! The division had been shrinking for some time and there was a total lack of excitement or forward vision. For one thing, the National Coal Board was declining. For another, every emerging nation wants to manufacture its own explosives. Though the division had been ICI's largest, prewar, this was certainly no longer the case. My God, I thought. I can't stand this. Then, incredibly, luck entered into my life once again. ICI decided to locate a nylon salt plant in the vicinity, partly to offset the run down of Nobel's traditional explosives business. The very large plant was to be built on what had been our golf course. I had the happy job of negotiating the change of use! I got considerable visibility as a result, and was consequently noticed by the division chairman. At the time, they thought at Nobel that it was necessary to start looking out for new ventures. I was asked whether I'd head the team.

I was somewhat taken aback. But I said I'd give it a whirl. Despite my lack of technical background, I went into the job with a fresh mind. Perhaps I was the sacrificial lamb. . . . We looked everywhere for possible new ventures. The world is your oyster, they said to me – which was palpably rubbish! Where shall I look? I thought to myself. What if I want to promote Caithness as a tourist centre for Americans? Of course they wouldn't buy anything like that. What they cared about was explosives. They were half-hearted about all the alternatives. This all went on till 1968, with only modest success, till I was rung up from Billingham by Phil Harvey, currently on the ICI board with me. He was technical director at Agricultural Division at the time. The ammonia and fertilizer business was going through tough times. But they had been very successful in licensing their naphtha steam reforming technology all over the world. Now they were intending to set this up as a separate business area by adding in the many catalysts used in their traditional processes. Phil asked me to come and take over the job as general manager, and again I didn't hesitate. Even though Nobel's chairman made me a promise of a seat on their board fairly quickly, I wasn't interested.

Excitement, pain and suffering

When I joined Billingham again, I found that about 90 per cent of our catalyst sales had been made to British Gas to make something like 70 per cent of all the UK's towns' gas from oil. Then North Sea gas appeared on the scene. I could see our market drying up. So I spent four exciting years securing export markets, eventually to the tune of 90 per cent of our business. From this I derived my philosophy that all young men should have such prolonged periods of excitement, mixed with pain and suffering, getting new businesses off the ground, designing new plants, tackling costs, or other such solid achievements over a period long enough to prove their mettle, other than on a 'passing through' basis.

The breakthrough

That takes me to 1972, when I was thirty-nine. I was beginning to get itchy feet. I was summoned by the division chairman. The big career breakthrough comes in this company when you join a division board. Nowadays men are asked if they want to join. I was told. I can remember to this day. It was a Monday and when I came home to let my wife know, she said, 'Very nice, but our elder girl has a Latin exam tomorrow, and she needs help with her homework!' That put things in perspective. Then, by Christmas, I was made director in charge of fertilizers. In my previous appointment, in charge of catalysts and licensing, I had been left entirely on my own because it was very profitable and relatively small. Now I had to pick up a really big business in which everyone was interested. It was a marvellous period. The business wasn't in the highest morale at the time. The overall motivation of the sales force had slipped. So I did a lot of customer liaison work to improve that situation. Then I was summoned by the division chairman who said to me that I'd done well, 'but you've ignored production and distribution'. I was livid. I'd killed myself with customers and all he could say to me was that, seeing I was naturally good at that, it deserved no Brownie points. Ever since that time I've put a disproportionate amount of effort into doing things that don't come easily. Another useful bit of management philosophy.

After two years at Billingham, on the board, I was appointed to a staff job as commercial general manager at ICI headquarters in London. Being essentially an operator, I wasn't too keen on that prospect. On the other hand, it did represent a considerable promotion. It was quite close to being a division chairman. And ICI was a very hierarchical company where movement up the ladder was a challenge.

In that job I acted as a senior adviser to the board on purchasing, public relations, government relations, and the whole commercial interface right across the group. That's when I began to learn about ICI as a whole. I commuted for a year, from Teesside, so as not to interrupt one of my daughters' 'O' level preparations.

I did that job between October 1974 and May 1977 when I was appointed Paints Division chairman. That job gives you tremendous power and authority. Paints was already a fairly big business in 1977. £200m turnover. But it hadn't been doing particularly well for a year or two although in the sixties it had been one of the jewels in ICI's crown. They'd tried to diversify, unsuccessfully. I cut out the extraneous activities by divesting a number of activities and also reduced 25 per cent of the cost base.

We'd inherited the German company Weiderholdt. It had to be tidied up. Acquisitions always are difficult to absorb. Things crawl out from under the woodwork that you don't discover until you've bought the company. I don't believe there are undiscovered nuggets around today. Either you pay a high price for a good business, or you pick up a jaded business for a modest sum and have to put a lot of resources into putting it right.

I stayed at Paints from 1977 to March 1980 through a period of considerable improvement and then I was appointed to ICI's main board. I would happily have stayed longer at Paints, but it wasn't to be. It's turned out, in fact, that I'm still the junior director, but during these last turbulent but exciting years I've broadened my experience still further by looking after Planning, Commercial, Europe and Explosives initially, and then lately dropping the first three and picking up Pharmaceutical, Aero-Chemicals, Colours and, my old love, Paints. Plus two outside directorships with Dalgety and Barclays Bank – so it certainly hasn't been dull!

Henderson's rise to the main board, while still in his forties, is rare, but not unprecedented in ICI. There is a path that high-fliers can follow, one which passes through different divisions and functions. The developing manager is deliberately provided with a series of testing challenges, and stretching experiences, along the way. If he is successful, and luck is on his side, he can rise to the top. But not everyone can fly so high. So what other entrepreneurial routes, or cells, are there in the company?

Entrepreneurial Manager

The entrepreneurial manager may not have the same aspirations, or even capabilities, as the high-flier. He may become, and remain, an able middle or senior manager, and fit comfortably therein. But he will be the sort of manager who adopts an entrepreneurial style. He will have no particular product to champion, no special new ventures to develop, but in his overall style he is entrepreneurial. Brian Codling, business area manager for 'Autocolour' in ICI Paints Division, is a very good example. He lies somewhere in between a manager, an entrepreneur, and an agent of change.

Codling, in typical ICI style, moved through a rapid succession of posts, locations and functions, before he ended up, in his mid-thirties, as a business area manager in Paints. Over the years he has formed distinctive views of management. These are views which are accommodated within ICI, but no clear path has yet been formed for their ongoing development. The entrepreneurial manager has no automatic succession route laid out before him.

Basically I believe in helping the individual to stand on his own two feet, and face up to the consequences. If you can do that, within the framework of where the business is going, you're on the right track. To use a seafaring analogy, you need people who know how to set the sails, to scrub the decks and to do the cooking, and who get on with these tasks. The yachtmaster sails his ship in a particular direction, and doesn't call all hands to the deck unless there's an emergency.

I've found that approach works very well. Unless you're

251

achieving some social and economic purpose, though, the typhoons come pretty regularly. In other words, in business if you keep making profits in a manner acceptable to those people around you then the typhoons won't often come, and you can sail in the direction you want. If you don't have the retained earnings to be able to replenish and to renovate, the water will start seeping through the bilges. You also need to take the occasional risk.

I suppose you'd say I have a higher risk-taking profile than most. I do trust people. That's taking a risk. Ninety-nine per cent of people, I find, don't let you down. The other one per cent you hang, draw and quarter!

In meetings, for example, I give people full scope. Recently a guy told me in no uncertain terms not to interfere with his part of the business. If I'd have said, 'You will do it or else', I'd have lost all credibility for my open and participative style. I found it exhausting to get him off his 'petard', and to get him to go through a different door. But I succeeded in the end without him losing face and to the benefit of all of our management team.

Economically, I also take risks. For example, I am ploughing a lot of money into research, to yield long-term gains. And yet, it's not really a risk, in the gambling sense of the word. I am a bridge player and I love poker. They are games in which you carefully work out the odds. You balance the real odds against the personalities of the people around the table, and the professional usually comes out ahead. The people who lose at poker just sit down at the table, and casually play a few hands. They haven't taken a professional approach or studied the people involved, and are often surprised when they lose. I almost don't accept that I'm taking risks. The payback is always greater than fifty-fifty. I actually hope it's eighty-twenty.

Systems: a means to an end

You see, I was always interested in maths and logic, in probability and philosophy. What is truth and so on. Of course, business isn't all about philosophy. You need to have your methods and procedures, your systems and strong controls. But they must remain a means to an end, or else you have no freedom. The systems have to be there. Without them the business would fall apart. We don't want 15 sails, 5 masts, and 25 different ropes to pull on. Then the crew wouldn't know where to go, which rope to climb. You need concise, simple controls, and a proper feedback loop, so that you can change your course when appropriate. The trouble is, all too often people confuse means and ends, and they get things out of perspective. What we're trying to do, ultimately, is to run a successful business.

People are of paramount importance

In running a business, people are of paramount importance. I have to make my business as participative and friendly as possible. We have lots of social activities, taking people to the pub on their birthdays, playing rounders and skittles in the evening. These are small things, but it includes people as part of the family. I've also introduced this teleprompt device, up in the entrance hall. Like a small version of the flashing screen in the shopping arcades, it's a means whereby anyone can say their piece.

There is no doubt that the kind of organization I am creating is looser, more free-wheeling and individually oriented than the norm. For a start, I always build up my organization, and the jobs within it, round the people, rather than vice versa. I try and get individual responsibility down to the lowest possible level. Get the guys to feel they're running their own businesses. For example, we've formed a team of demonstrators who are being employed, within a separate company, by one of our people. He has formed a £100 company, with its own share capital, articles of association, operating systems and so forth. Normally, he wouldn't have had this kind of responsibility in ICI. Although he's still on a salary, he has to run the business as an independent entity. If his 'baby' does well he will see the rewards directly. He's now contemplating adding an additional service to his business, with my blessing, and his satisfaction. People can get more experience of running their own businesses under the safety net of ICI or other reputable large companies.

Exploding a dilemma

Where then, does that leave me? When I left university I had a clear vision. I was going to acquire knowledge and experience by working in a large company. In my twenties and thirties my vision remained clear. I was working my way up the promotional ladder. Now that I'm approaching forty, I'm not so sure. I already have the authority, the power, the freedom. I have been stretched aplenty. I have developed and, God, have I been lucky! Now I'm like Janus. One side of me wants to continue along the well-worn promotional track, and the other feels that this won't be enough. Sometimes I think of taking a three-year sabbatical, as Visiting Professor at Otago University Business School, or something like that. It's the frustrated intellectual in me coming through and requiring stimulation – the philosopher of science. I also like the idea of turning companies round – a kind of company doctor. Perhaps I can do both! It's a dilemma that will have to be exploded. Whatever I do, I can't see myself remaining in the background for long!

Product Champion

The third, and perhaps best-known entrepreneurial post, is that of the 'product champion'. A company that is strong in science and technology has a great need for the sort of person who can drive a project through, from a point just after conception to one just before full commercialization. Someone like Vaclas, or 'Vaci', as he is popularly known within ICI Paints, is an example of such a champion. He takes up a position in between the innovator and the salesman. Vaci's background is an interesting one, and serves to illustrate not only his own entrepreneurial heritage, but also the company's international base.

Vaci started as an ICI research chemist in Australia. He was promoted to technical manager, for ICI Paints' (Australia) automotive division, before being brought over to the UK, as a project manager-cum-product champion:

Developing an instinct for survival

I was born in Greece, and lived there during the war years. When you're young, in those circumstances, you develop an instinct for survival. You try to exploit situations to your advantage. For example, when the bombs are dropping, you think pretty quickly about where you can hide. When you're not faced with such decisions you are inclined to procrastinate. But I learnt to think and act quickly. At a young age, it's not a question of logic, but of attitude. There were food shortages at the time. I learnt to bargain, and to get the best out of the little that was available. It led me to assess carefully every situation, with a view to getting the best out of it. And it's different, say, from bargaining over the price of a car, when it is a matter of survival.

Relying on your own resources

After the war I left Greece for Australia. It was one of the few countries that seemed safe at the time. Again, going away to live in a foreign country is an education. I had to rely on my own resources. There was nobody else I could depend on, I just had to become self-reliant.

I decided to go to university, and needed a part-time job to support myself. I was always without enough money to enjoy things. I measured everything carefully, because nothing was plentiful. I became resourceful.

Learning to understand people

I also had to learn about people and their motives, if I wanted to get anywhere in my life. I had nobody else to make introductions. That gave me a certain acumen, an ability to analyse people that I have relied on ever since. It also gave me a certain compassion for others. A man with a full stomach can't understand a hungry man. It helps when you've been through it yourself. You stop being arrogant and become sympathetic. You learn to understand people from all sorts of backgrounds.

A lot of people can go through the same sort of experiences I did, of course, and not pay attention to what's going on around them. They fail to use their experience. Because I have used mine, I have become more demanding of others.

Developing commercial acumen

My university years were hard ones. I couldn't enjoy myself the way fellow students did, but the struggle did mould my character. I studied chemistry. Although I didn't particularly like it, I wanted to do well. I have always wanted to do whatever I tackled to the best of my ability. After university I started work with ICI. Not being an Anglo-Saxon, I had to do better than others. You only have yourself. It makes you think twice about everything you do. You never take anything for granted. Gradually you develop an acumen, whereby you think about a problem from many angles. When I see a cup, I wonder what's behind it. To try to get the most out of a situation you have to look around it. To exploit a situation you have to act as an explorer.

The role of project manager

Once you've identified a good idea, you must find someone who really cares about it. Then you must develop a project and a project team. You need people in their twenties and thirties with a good technical understanding and a flexible nature. The project manager, then, needs to carry the technical activity as a whole, as well as the promotional and customer contacts. I can discuss future trends with customers, for example. And, if I identify trends early on, I have the best chance.

What it is all about, actually, is channelling the output of research towards fruition. Ideas need to be protected at an early stage. In projects I have which are still at the stage of technical development, I have to protect them from the critics, while judiciously creating some customer interest. Many ideas have never seen the light of day because nobody is strong enough to stick their neck out.

The project manager needs to be flexible, when you stay within the lab, you deal with people like yourself. There are some very different and sharp people in the industry, and you have to recognize and act accordingly. I speak very differently to a research scientist as compared with the customer outside. I have to use the right approach with the right person.

People in research labs are paid to develop ideas. But often they are not familiar with the industry. You need a project manager who knows the industry and can perceive the importance of one or other idea to it. He has to listen and to participate.

It is best if he is outside the normal line management structure and responds to a very senior and appropriate manager(s) for the fulfilment of his remit and hence success of his venture. This gives him the necessary freedom to act.

The project manager must be in a position, and possess the personality, to push the project forward in spite of 'problems' and be unencumbered by most day-to-day matters.

How to get the best out of people is such an important question. How to see that ideas generated are not lost. How do you distinguish seed that produces an oak tree? So often we throw away the acorns and keep the weeds! How do we create these people in the middle, who have both the technical knowledge and the market awareness and the right personality? How far do you expose a person to his benefit and not to his detriment, to a new discipline? How can you get creative scientists to look after their babies, rather than putting them out on the street, for some other person, like a social welfare agent, to take care of?

A business of my own

As you might have gathered, my mission is to look after what the company has entrusted to me: that is, the products of the automotive market. I always was a company man, which may have been a mistake. But I do also have an independent concern. I have no hobbies outside of work, as such. I cannot see the wisdom, for example, in hitting a ball from one point to another. But I can drill a hole, put up a fence, keep some sheep, and make a return on it. I have an interest in a farm in Australia, you see. To be successful in the technical area, it helps to have a business of your own. It enables you to calculate finances and to measure effort. You learn from bitter experience that if you delay something you lose.

Enabling Entrepreneur

The high-flier and the product champion are relatively well-known 'entrepreneurial types' within a company like ICI. However, the first is more visible than the second, and has a clearer career path. We now come on to a newer and rarer breed that I have termed the enabling entrepreneur (a mixture between an entrepreneur and an enabler).

Although large companies have been engaging in 'new venturing' for years, particularly in America, only 3M, has been overwhelmingly successful. In virtually all other cases, the companies have found it difficult to combine new venturing with existing lines of business. The cross-cultural forces tend to get in the way of successful development, and ICI, in the seventies, was no exception to the rule. However, in the eighties, and drawing on the lessons of hindsight, some new ventures are beginning to come good.

A few years ago, the Agriculture Division board decided to make a strong and concerted effort to develop new ventures, particularly in fields related to biotechnology. This formed part of an overall strategic development that extended beyond the development of individual products. The board drew on both American experience and their own lessons, from the past, in taking a concerted and fresh approach. Today there are ten new ventures in the process of development.

We can see from Rob Margetts's new venturing example that it is a complex process. It calls on a good mix of old-fashioned entrepreneurship and newly fashioned enabling skills. The board at Agriculture has come up with a rich mixture of organizational forms to accommodate the different ventures. It has collaborated with outsiders, on the one hand, and formed a stand alone unit within, on the other. Rob Margetts is neither high-flier nor product champion in their simplest terms. He is some kind of amalgam of the two, with enabling skills as well:

New business ventures

New business is significantly different from the mainstream. We've got two new ventures in agriculture, where our mainstream business has a strong presence. Each of the two teams has a combination of technical and commercial people. The team leaders report to the head of the fertilizer business. When they need help, they'll need the undivided support of the sales force. You need that synergy between separation and togetherness.

Biopolymers is a new concept. Biodegradability. We've discussed the new concept with a couple of local entrepreneurs, and formed a joint company. One of the entrepreneurs is chairman, and I'm director. We needed their flair in knowing how to assess a market we don't know, and nobody else does! They've entered in development contracts with 25 companies, internationally. We own the polymer and the 25 companies will own the downstream uses. They're teaching us, those two entrepreneurs. One of them, incidentally, is an ex-ICI man. Basically, they're venture capitalists. One of them has started up a lot of new companies, and sold them off. They have a unique selection of skills between them. They are able to focus single-mindedly on one product, at any point of time. They can organize finance with dexterity. They know how to coach others, and they're good at picking people. Their thinking is sharp and clear.

For all our new ventures, we're trying to go on to a bank account principle. There's a lot of clarity got out of pursuing value for money. Most of us are working twelve hours a day.

In one particular case, we've formed a stand alone business, within ICI, to market a particular device we've developed. It's a mixture of software and hardware that, when plugged into a significant-sized plant, can provide terrific feedback on the efficiency of materials used. The cost of each device is £50,000. We've used them ourselves, so we know the benefits. So we've formed this separate business to take it to the outside world.

We looked at a whole lot of potential linkages, within our organization, and found no good fit. None of the existing sales forces was ideal. The market could be anyone who uses energy and materials in bulk. So we've formed a separate unit which will buy in technical support. We've also appointed sales agents. We then had the problem, who would own it?

Oddballs and misfits

People say there are not many entrepreneurs in ICI. You tend to find them amongst the oddballs and misfits. We found one. He hadn't quite fitted in at Billingham, so they sent him off to help start up firms in Teesside, as part of our social and economic contribution to the area. He did very well. He happened also to be ideally suited, technically, for our new venture, as an electrical instrument engineer. So we got him in to do the tail end of the feasibility study, and now he's running the new venture, and is busy assembling his team.

As a stand-alone, he reports to a 'godfather', that is, a senior manager who was involved with the very same technology ten years ago.

Guardians of the faith

If any concept is to have a chance, it needs the people in support, in high positions. If organizations will behave like elephants, you need guardians of the faith. Each godfather has a growing interest and faith in venturing. We also have a New Venturing Executive. Three out of the seven on the division board, and four business managers, act together as a ginger group to stimulate and initiate new business concepts or acquisitions. They examine the robustness of each proposition, looking at staff, finance, recruitment, training and development. We distribute involvement as best we can through the whole organization. If you don't involve people you can't expect support. You need to sustain an umbrella of such support for at least a decade, to succeed overall with new venturing. One or two of the ventures are bound to be disastrous.

A point of focus

All of our new ventures have had their focus in or near our technological skills or market base. Our technical skill is in chemical catalysis, agriculture, biotechnology and process engineering. Give us a bug on a plate and we'll turn it into a process!

We'd like to see a high proportion of our new ventures having an agricultural or bio base. We have a big organization here, with sales of three quarters of a billion pounds. It's quite profitable too. The organization will reject anything that doesn't have significant potential.

Learning from success or failure

Three quarters of the ventures are going to fail, but they must fail cheaply. We must learn our lessons quickly. It's playing the numbers game. We're playing with a dozen concepts. Could do with a dozen more. Also, you can never be sure where the businesses that are created will eventually land. We have two daughter companies that were sired at Billingham, Petrochemicals and Plant Protection. Dyestuffs was the mother of Pharmaceuticals. Ten years out we may have another major division. You can't control that sort of thing.

It's like the analogy with a baby. When it's in the cot, it needs the strength and robustness. Skills, people, money and experience. We approach our financing in a similar way. A baby in a cot doesn't pay taxes!

But you can't do without risk. Perhaps the greatest risk is to do nothing at all. I'd regard myself as a high-profile risk-taker, on some occasions. But I don't enter into it lightly. I would never want to see anything I believe in deeply go down. I take significant but judged risks. I always back my judgement. I believed for two and a half years that we could turn our prutein experience into a major business opportunity. We have learnt technically and managerially. It's now coming to fruition. We've built up the new businesses, to demonstrate it's true. We've got an asset base like nobody's business.

'Gamesman'

The product champion has a discrete responsibility for championing one, or even two or three, new products. The enabling entrepreneur develops the organizational forms and linkages, to enable new ventures to succeed while retaining his connections with the relevant techologies. The 'gamesman' is a mixture of change agent and entrepreneur. He plays a symbolic as well as an entrepreneurial role in getting a new venture off the ground. He represents a new wave, a new technology, a new style within the company. John Mellersh, in Electronic Chemicals, is just such a person. He combines technical knowledge and a background in marketing, with a sense of theatre and a capacity for 'brotherly love'. He is aware of his symbolic role in the company, as his story reveals.

Being involved in expanding situations

I've spent twenty-one years in marketing, at ICI. Since 1968, the whole of my career has been involved with the commercialization of new products. I've been very much involved in expanding situations. Three years is the longest I can take in one job. When a stable pattern emerges it's time for someone else to take over, someone who can pay attention to detail, police things, fine tune.

We enjoyed a bit of theatre

Not many people have had a string of experiences like mine. At one stage there was a group of us, a gang of four who had come together in Organics. We were all very inventive. We enjoyed a bit of theatre. The other person's success wasn't my failure. There was a fair bit of brotherly love involved. Now they're calling for people like us in ICI all of a sudden.

In 1981, Organics began to realize that it needed to create some new businesses. The division that had spawned Pharmaceuticals had contracted. So I was called in, a marketing man, to work with the researchers. I hadn't been through those research portals for years. The scientists had been insulated from the marketplace. It became obvious to me that something would have to be done about this.

Letting people know you care

I came in and let people know that I was interested in them. I cared. I was also looking for commercial opportunities for their ideas. Some of the research going on was in the area of 'electronic chemicals'.

Seizing opportunities

Then in 1981 I got a letter from Harvey-Jones. He'd been up here in February, just six weeks before he was appointed chairman. He had visited the Corporate Laboratory and listened to the research managers. They got talking about electronic chemicals and referred to the relevant work I was doing in Organics Division. He asked me to come and tell him about it, and then invited me to come up with a proposal. So we put our thoughts down and Charles Reece, the ICI director responsible for research and new business development, put up a paper on my behalf. We had said that the electronics industry was growing, diversifying, diverging. There were opportunities there for molecular science. We wanted a small business team with a small budget, to get things rolling, and to find out how to make money out of electronics. Because we didn't know the market we needed partners, and we needed access to other technologies. We got board approval, and away we went.

Experimental organizations

To try and fit our kind of organization into the ICI matrix is difficult. We're a bit like Sinclair, developing innovations, or securing them from the divisions, and subcontracting out their subsequent manufacture, having found a market. We have contractual arrangements, joint ventures, autonomous divisions. Here are three examples.

Take what has now become ICI Masks. We produce masks for circuit boards. The original company was in a bad way, and the Californian equipment manufacturer was about to reclaim the leased equipment. Then we were approached by an associate to save the company. We thought it could be a good window on to the electronics market. We liked the American manufacturer and they liked us. The idea of bringing the equipment and chemicals together appealed. So we got together.

Fibre optics fits our business of twisting molecules. There's a government-funded consortium, of which we are a part, researching organic, non-linear, optical materials. The electronics companies are looking for something to replace silicon. So a research consortium, including Plessey, GEC and ourselves, have come together to research the new possibilities.

Then there is optical and magnetic storage. That prospect came out of our roadshow when Organics went over to Japan. Initially the Japanese got interested. Now the whole world is looking for a disk that can be written on with a laser, and then erased, like a magnetic tape. By now, nine months into our programme, people are beginning to come to us.

Our organization involves myself, the ideas man and the driving force, and John Reynolds and Bill Barlow – on the commercial and research sides – who can organize things and attend to the detail. Bill Barlow has project leaders under him, to develop the science. John Reynolds, in time, will have a similar number of commercial managers to keep tabs on the marketplace. The two together, research and commerce, make a successful combination. And they've got to work together. I want no *prima donnas*!

We're not a research group. We're a business. We have to find what's partly below the surface, that causes change and discontinuity, and which we can cash in on. In five years' time I want a billion-dollar turnover. That's the dream I presented to the board last week. In a way I'm a model for Harvey-Jones – a pawn some people say. But I'm willing to be one. I had an idea, and I was given the opportunity. If we fail, it will be a public failure.

'Marketeer'

Last, but by no means least, we have the case of the 'marketeer'. More than a salesman, and not quite an entrepreneur, he represents the many people in marketing who have commercial acumen and flair, like to try things out, and will occasionally champion a new product from the market end. Because of the greater emphasis that ICI is now placing on the market end of things, this sort of person will be increasingly in demand.

David Macleod, sales manager for ICI Decorative Paints, is a good case in point. He is in his early thirties, full of bounce and energy, and not someone who fits into the more traditional and conventional ICI mould. Macleod has been responsible for introducing 'Natural Whites', one of ICI's most successful, recent, market-led innovations:

Our crisis

In 1980/1981 our market share fell from 28 per cent to 23 per cent, almost overnight. The competition grabbed 5 per cent of our market share. That was the end of our complacency. Philip Handscombe took over Decorative Paints. He sensed the need for innovation. His philosophy is that if you have a bright bunch of people, set them loose to identify opportunities, encourage them to do more, and allow them to fail, you can get results.

My opportunity

We had this sales conference coming up and I was asked to produce something new to help build confidence amongst the sales force. I believe that in the creative area you have got to cast your net incredibly wide. The odds against innovation are very high. So I went to four design houses. I was given a big budget. I went to PR and advertising people. I asked one of our people to present to us on what was happening in the paint business worldwide. He gave us a presentation of his findings. One of the colour cards he showed us seemed to have something in it. I gave it to one of our colour consultants who took three shades and arranged our whole colour range around them. He came up with a whole set of names. I chose three – Rose White, Apple White, and Fleece White. Then we gave the concept to the advertising agency. It was all zap, zap. Rolling fast. Two particularly creative guys there, together with my boss, helped create the magic. The advertising agency produced the commercial and helped produce the artwork for the can. Both had style. It was very new and different. It felt right. All of it flowed terribly well.

A personal crusade

At that stage nobody thought we had anything very big. It was only after we started selling to customers that we realized how enormous the thing was. Natural Whites now amounts to 25 per cent of our turnover. It was the biggest single impact we have had for twenty years. It worked because it was a personal crusade. I kep a pad on me wherever I went noting down anything and everything. I had the strong overwhelming belief that we could do something, and I worked pretty hard and there was time to be creative and to develop lots of ideas.

Our supportive climate

The atmosphere here is now good and positive. We are incredibly free of politics. My immediate boss, who is a woman, gets to the point rather than beating around the bush, as men sometimes do. Women tend to be more intuitive. They have a feel for things.

My vision for the future combines aesthetics and function. Our consumers are becoming more and more interested in creating an atmosphere rather than buying just paint. So we have to offer people the colours to create the rooms they are looking for. Our new colour cards include pictures of colour combinations to fit different styles, different tastes and different

ICI

rooms in the home. We now work with our retailers to develop
impactful and relevant point-of-sale displays.

We have to enthuse each other

People are becoming more individual in their tastes so we have to
create more variety. Research is therefore becoming more important, because we need textures, new finishes, new applications.
So the interchange between R and D and ourselves is crucial. We
have to enthuse each other. Each new product needs an individual
to champion it, and an environment that supports it. Successful
individuals need to be reinforced by the culture. Relationships with
people outside the company are crucial.

VARIATIONS ON AN ENTREPRENEURIAL THEME

There are, therefore, six variations on the entrepreneurial theme.
Three are well known – the high-flier, the product champion and the
'marketeer'; three are less familiar. They are the entrepreneurial
manager, the enabling entrepreneur and the 'gamesman'. Each is a
hybrid of entrepreneur and, in the first case, a manager; in the second,
an enabler; and the third, what is often called a change-agent. As ICI
evolves towards a state of true integration, more and more of these
hybrid forms will develop. Management, in the pure sense, will
become very much a minority pursuit.

In fact, if these hybrid forms are not developed, the remaining
forms of pure entrepreneurship will gradually be rejected or eroded.
The development of a spirit of enterprise within a mature company is a
more all-pervading thing than the encouragement of individual entrepreneurs. It calls for a transformation of all roles and activities so that
each combines existing elements with entrepreneurial ones. Cross-
breeding rather than exclusivity becomes the order of the day.

INFORMATION AND CHANGE

The outside world is changing at a rate of knots. We will only
survive if we can take advantage of them.

Dr Rodney Armitage, management services manager

If money is the blood of ICI's organization, then communications constitute its nerve centre. Communications include both personal face-to-face interactions, and also the ever-changing information technology that is revolutionizing our lives. In the sixties and seventies in particular, ICI played a prominent part in the OD (organization development) movement, that was involved with the improvement of personal communications and organizational change. Programmes ranging from sensitivity training to Coverdale approaches to improving group dynamics were instituted. Two of the current board members, Phil Harvey and John Harvey-Jones himself, were heavily involved with one or other of these.

In the eighties, the emphasis has shifted from personal communications to communications technology. Although OD work continues, it has slipped out of the limelight; sadly, some feel. In ICI, as well as nationwide, computers and telecommunications have captured everyone's imagination. As the chairman said in an interview for *Chips*, ICI's newspaper on the subject:

> I believe that the opportunities for using computers are limited only by the creative imagination of the people in our business.

Information technology, as we now know it, has arrived in two great waves. The first wave began around 1950 and was driven by mainframe and, in due course, minicomputers. 'First wave' computer applications are now mature, and no one questions their ability to improve the productivity of the business. The major applications have been on the administrative and engineering sides, to cut costs and to optimize plant performance, respectively. But the whole situation has changed in the last ten years.

The second wave came two decades later, driven by the microprocessor. Microprocessor-based devices such as word processors and personal computers are relatively small and cheap. Managers at the sharp end are now beoming involved with them. They are demanding not only numeric but also text-based systems. They are saying, 'I refuse to schedule envelopes on Concorde. We need a system of electronic transfer.'

Most of the developments in the communications technology, to date, have been applied to internal communications and control.

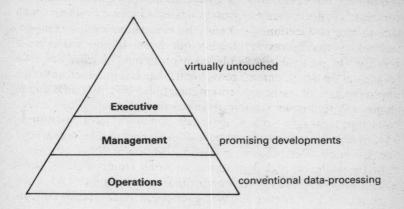

The diagram above illustrates the state of communications in the past. The diagram below points to the future. The left-hand triangle refers to internal communication, and the right-hand triangle to external:

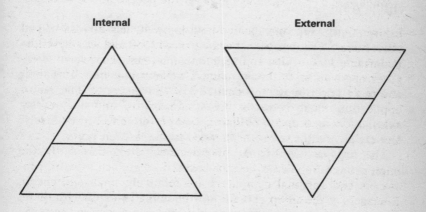

The development to come is on the external side. A whole raft of new technologies – text-based systems, personal computing, international networks and office automation – is helping to bring this about.

269

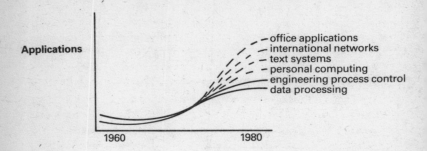

THE ROLE OF CHANGE-AGENT

The theme that unites those concerned with the design and implementation of new communication systems is the 'management of change'. They are all, in their different ways, change-agents.

Office Automation

Rodney Armitage, management services manager for ICI head office, is managing the prospective change in headquarters location, as far as office automation is concerned. ICI's head office may be moving from the imposing Thames-side edifice to smaller and more contemporary premises. The decision creates a golden opportunity for the company's first full-scale investment in office automation. In a portion of the existing building, Dr Armitage is already paving the way for the new development.

The sorts of facilities Armitage foresees, once the project is implemented, include:

- the preparation and editing of documents, using word-processing facilities
- the sending of documents, electronically, from one office to the other
- the filing, indexing and retrieval of information, electronically

- the sending of messages, electronically, to any desk, room or site in ICI worldwide
- the planning of appointments and maintenance of 'action lists', using an electronic diary, thereby enabling boss and secretary to work together more efficiently
- the use of Viewdata Services, or Prestel, for easy access to commonly required external information
- consultation with external data bases, the world's electronic knowledge banks, on anything from trade figures to toxicology
- the use of personal computer-style software for 'what if?' projections, spotting business trends

As a result of all these facilities, management should be in a position to learn faster, react more quickly, make better informed decisions and communicate more effectively round the world.

Viewdata Systems

ICI was the first pharmaceutical company to become a Prestel information provider to doctors. High on the head of Pharmaceutical Marketing Alan Barnes's list of priorities is the need to improve his service by adopting the latest in communications technology, and his reps had Viewdata since October 1984. Pharmaceuticals Division has launched a magazine called *Practice Computing*, which tells doctors what they want to know about computers. Meanwhile, Agricultural Division has been using Viewdata for order processing since 1982.

Personal Computers

A computer system has been developed which managers at the Stowmarket paint factory now use to plan production four weeks ahead. Marketing and production managers can get together in front of a computer screen and play a 'TV game' in which both sides stand to win. Productivity at Stowmarket has risen 30 per cent since the system was installed. It is believed that production scheduling systems of this kind will be very valuable to ICI, since it is from batch products such as paints and organic chemicals that the company now makes a high proportion of its profits.

These are just three areas, among a myriad of examples, in which change-agents are altering the shape of ICI's communication systems. They are not creating new business, nor even new products, but they are designing and implementing systems that improve efficiency and effectiveness. They are building more flexibility into the business functions, enabling ICI to accommodate greater diversity of product and market. By enriching and refining the organism's nervous system, the change-agents have enhanced its ability to adapt to change. At the same time, there is a sense in which technological change has raced ahead of people's ability to both cope with, and also to magnify, its effects. As I have already indicated, organization development has been overtaken by business enterprise on the one hand and by the new communications technology on the other. When the company's learning and information systems truly come of age, a closer relationship will be established between organization development and management services. In fact, I believe the time has come when both should be disbanded in their current form and recombined together in a new form. Both have had their separate day.

COMMUNITY OF INTEREST

This whole period of being chairman, for me, has involved creating the social framework, for ICI, befitting the opportunities of the twentieth century. All I have been doing is directed towards that goal.

Sir John Harvey-Jones

Peters and Waterman's *In Search of Excellence* has placed great store on 'corporate culture'. Such cultures are, I believe, suitable for the managed organization. Once we approach the degree of diversity that an evolving and mature company needs to accommodate, then we need a different, a more wide-ranging approach – one that is capable of accommodating great variety.

The following is taken from an interview with Sir John Harvey-Jones (October 1984).

When I think of culture, various adjectives come to mind. Being *open* is the most important one. We've got to be more so than most companies. I want to develop a culture where differences of opinion are expressed clearly and openly. People must try to solve their problems rather than hide them.

Second. We have to be a *collaborative* company, working together as a team. Friendly. We need to respect one another. There isn't another way. We have to tolerate individual differences.

Third. High tech. We must seek technical excellence. *Technical preeminence*. And the technology has to be *linked* to the marketplace. It's no use being the world's best polymer chemists. We must be more responsive, more sensitive, more linked up with, more switched into, the marketplace.

To a large extent I'm reacting to, rather than reshaping, the ICI culture. I'm letting the lion out of the cage, rather than being the sea lion, myself, bouncing the ball in the air. I'm doing a number of things to let the culture out. We run our board meetings in a very open way. We have arguments. I expose the politics. We debate them. The other day a personal issue came up at a board meeting. So we dealt with it, rather than hiding away from it. I welcome criticism.

Symbolism helps. I attend all the management courses at Warren House. I speak bluntly. I go out of my way to heighten our awareness of the way we make mistakes. It's a sort of public striptease. After all, the company isn't run by a bunch of supermen. We have the same limitations as anyone else.

The model I've spoken about, for ICI as a whole, is a sort of federation of free men, with maximum freedom and information. Part of our job, as a board, is to hold a mirror out to the company, and to give people the opportunity to see where they fit within it. Given the totality of the picture, what part do they play? It's almost like a patchwork quilt.

Look at the painting over there. If somebody in the company saw it, he might feel he's the boat in the left-hand corner. But how does he relate to the man in brown, and the hat in red? You have to blend in, in harmony with the totality. There needs to be a process of self-aligning.

273

The problem is that you need the large company to deploy the resource, but the big corporations don't switch people on. People want to belong to a regiment, but don't want to turn out for the parade. We have to be able to align the advantages of the large with the motivation generated by the small. The company can only operate near to its potential if individuals operate near to theirs. They have to be switched on by the opportunity, and not just by the task.

At the present time there's tremendous goodwill and excitement in ICI. Some people's expectations are unlikely to be met to the full. We could slip back to the old and comfortable existence. Become nice chaps. Don't grow. At the other extreme, of course, people could seize their freedom, if encouraged to do their own thing. The key problem that arises is one of collaboration. All depends, once again, on mutuality of respect. That needs to be reinforced, and not too early.

One of the keys to it, is the executive directors acting as a band of brothers. We've got to subordinate our individual enthusiasm for the whole. That depends on me, managing the situation. I've got to convince my fellow directors that the whole is greater than the sum of the parts. I have to punish advocacy. That is under my specific influence. The big change I have wanted to introduce is to give the executive directors the feeling that they, collectively, own the company. Each one of us then feels for the health of the organization as for his own. Genuinely, in large corporations, things do start at the top. People are quick to discern if the metal is flawed. That coherent bell has to keep sounding.

We are a team of co-equals. They can outvote me. I will hear them. They are the corporation. Before it was always someone else's responsibility. 'Poor old Joe,' I'd say. Now we all wear a worried look when something goes wrong. In the olden days one guy would have been left to carry the can. 'Oh, John's got it round his neck again.' No more!

What you're seeing, and hearing, is a response to the company's own history, and values. It has always had outstandingly able people. It has always worshipped excellence. It has always been caring. Only the openness is a new dimension, and the emphasis on the marketplace. The rest is a heightening and a revision.

Anyone, now, can have a meeting, you know, on the sixth floor. I often have a pie and a pint in the staff cafeteria. I can't remember the last time I passed someone, who didn't speak to me.

I don't want to foster a personality cult. This is no ego trip. But I do a lot with the press. That is because the public must understand the role that industry plays in society. Industrialists are not squeezers of sales for personal gain. People need to know what I value, and what I don't. You've got to be approachable. I like being called by my first name. I loathe being called 'Chairman'. I'm no better or worse than the next man.

I make these gestures, quite sincerely, because I believe you must create the conditions in which people can learn. You can't teach people to respect each other. But every act betrays your values. I'm not an 'unguided missile', as some people think. But I must be prepared to be as open outside as I am inside the company. If I feel our performance is lousy, I'll say so. I don't intend to appear publicly, waffling on about this and that.

In year one I had to grab the board, and change its style. In years two and three, we had to work out the strategies for the individual businesses. In years four and five . . .

Nobody would dispute that Harvey-Jones has had a dramatic impact on the culture of ICI. The question is, exactly what impact? People call him charismatic, charming, colourful, extrovert, outspoken, and even eccentric. I see his fundamental role in ICI, in this period of its history, as one of enabling its culture to evolve to a point of what Stafford Beer, in his book *Design for Freedom* (Wiley, 1974), calls 'requisite variety'.

Stafford Beer is a management scientist, and former president of the Society for Operations Research, who is probably best known for his attempt to create a computerized democracy in Allende's Chile. The basic idea behind 'requisite variety' is that we have to design organizations that can accommodate as much variety as is contained within the hearts and minds of the people with whom they are connected. If they fail to match such variety, through their overall structure and culture, they will inevitably limit their business and human potential. That may sound obvious, but it is all too true.

Organizations, both large and small, characteristically limit variety. The pioneering business, in focusing on the economic task in hand, inevitably ignores some of the personal and social consequences. The large organization, in focusing on its institutional requirements – including those of stability and survival – ignores some of the economic and human consequences. Entrepreneurs are often creative and aggressive, but disorganized; managers are often organized and logical, but unimaginative. As a business genuinely matures, it needs to develop what I call a 'metaculture' that can accommodate several subcultures. My metaculture, in a sense, matches Beer's 'requisite variety'.

COLOURFUL CHARACTER

A colourful character has a better chance of creating a community of interests than his conventional counterpart, because he sports 'a coat of many colours'. That chance will become a reality if such a colourful character is able to spread his many colours around. So let us take a deeper look at ICI's current chairman.

When we refer to 'colourful' personalities, we imply that they possess a wide variety of traits. Earlier (page 15), I referred to the whole person in terms of creativity, awareness, organization, initiative, perception, enthusiasm and physical prowess. Each of these elements, when magnified, constitutes a business subculture: innovative, enabling, bureaucratic, enterprising, informal and energetic in turn. To the extent that these elements are both transmitted and received within the organization, they will form part of the culture.

Colours originate, physically, from the light spectrum. We refer, as a result, to the 'social spectrum'. ICI truly embraces people from all walks of life – from all classes, all nationalities, all branches of science, and all the disciplines of business. Its fundamental task, as a metaculture, is to assimilate such diversity. As the company matures, internationalizes and becomes more interactive with its environment, so it needs both to accommodate and bring together variety. The key to development lies in communication between different sections, different social groupings, different business disciplines, and different branches of science. Divisions no longer stand on their own, but, like Organics, become increasingly interwoven with the rest of the company. Organics has not only spawned two major divisions; it has also become a manufacturing centre for the rest of the company. In so doing it has consciously to transform itself. In losing its old identity it still needs to find its new one.

ICI's culture, its binding force, is scientifically and chemically based. Yet there again, as it evolves, it needs to assimilate and integrate diversity.

CHEMICAL DIVERSITY

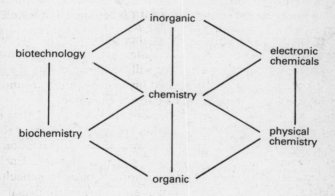

Most of the new developments, both technologically and commercially, lie at the crossover points between chemistry and other scientific disciplines. So communication between these disciplines, as well as between the technical and commercial people, becomes all the more important. Also, as we have seen with the new ventures in Agriculture and Electronic Chemicals, there is a need for different kinds and sizes of businesses to combine forces. It is almost as if a new paradigm of communication across cultures, rather than conflict between them, is taking over.

ICI'S EMERGING CULTURE

In their pioneering days, Nobel and Mond compressed and radiated several 'cultures' within their own being. Nobel was scientist, travelling salesman, accountant, financier and philanthropist, all wrapped up into one. Ludwig Mond and John Brunner shared out the roles between them. When ICI was created in 1926, two subcultures gained particular prominence: those of the organization man – personified by Alfred Mond – and of the high-powered entrepreneur – personified by Harry McGowan. After the Second World War, the scientific culture reemerged to join the bureaucratic one, at the forefront of things. An entrepreneurial subculture survived and prospered only in fast-growing divisions, particularly in Pharmaceuticals and Agrochemicals, and, to some extent, at the marketing end of Decorative Paints.

As we have seen, in 1982 ICI entered a new phase, in which the so-called bureaucratic subculture lost its traditional and stabilizing appeal. What has emerged in its place is a new entrepreneurism. Brian Codling of ICI Paints summarized the situation:

> You used to get on if you were scientific and conservative. Everyone strove for approval on capital expenditure. Things have changed phenomenally. You now get Brownie points for profits and change.
>
> Our image is changing rapidly. We used to be thought of as highly respectable, traditional, paternalistic, fatherly, a good employer. But we've become more aggressive in the last three years. We're expecting people to stand on their own two feet. Instead of 'pat, pat' it's 'get out and about'.

Charles Reece, the main board director who overviews research and development, elaborates on this theme in the context of the new and high-powered international managers that ICI have established. These newly created posts are a spur and a response to the company's increasingly international orientation. The new entrepreneurism that Reece extols is a mixture of aggression, flexibility, authority and tolerance. It brings together the roles of manager, entrepreneur, and change-agent. These are all roles with which John Harvey-Jones is very comfortable. Phil Harvey, who had taken a particular interest in organization development, put it this way:

> What we're trying to bring about, I don't know altogether consciously, is a very strong federal feeling, so that we can hope to get the economy and other benefits of size and yet retain the culture and values of a small organization.

The fact that I have identified such hybrid roles as entrepreneurial manager, enabling entrepreneur and gamesman, is further evidence of cross-fertilization between management, entrepreneurship and change. The following are Charles Reece's comments on this new entrepreneurism:

> There's a tremendous cultural change. We've given our new international managers clear responsibility and authority, as individuals. That's not an easy thing, culturally, to do. We have to set the right tone, from the top, and heavily encourage people in the divisions to be helpful to these appointees. They each represent a single power source, and will have to pull themselves up by their own bootstraps.
>
> There's another leg to the story. We've had enough matrix management in ICI to realize it results in decisions of the lowest common denominator. You have to have clear responsibility and authority. The man in charge is responsible for the overall thrust, and those in the locality for specific implementation. He is a powerful business manager. Both he and the person responsible for developing new business opportunities need flair and imagination, without necessarily having a detailed understanding of the technology.
>
> So the bureaucratic approach is on its way out, but slowly. Often, it's still used by the old guard to defend themselves from the new path set by the board. There's a tension. John Mellersh, for example, has access to me in forty-eight hours. In the old bureaucractic system it would take a month. The divisions are cohesive cells with their own ambitions for their

longer-term future. However, it is difficult to cut costs and gamble in the same structure, hence the need for some organizational experiments in managing new business opportunities.

The key message, then, that we're projecting is 'watch this space'. There a number of experiments going on. We want a rapid and consistent response to changing circumstances. We need to be tolerant of differences.

MULTIPLE ROLES AND CULTURES

There is still work to be done, however, if ICI's culture is to evolve so as to fully assimilate its internal and external variety. As a community of interests, in the best sense, it needs to grow to accommodate a diverse base of customers, suppliers, employees and freelancers as part of its extended and interdependent organization.

A metaculture that serves such a purpose will both absorb and combine multinational/multifunctional/'multiscientific' activity, and also accommodate the multiple roles described below:

Role	Manifestations	Subculture
Innovator	Inventor, social transformer	Creative
Enabler	Gatekeeper, enabler, developer	Developmental
Manager	Leader, director, manager	Formal
Entrepreneur	Enventurer, entrepreneurial manager, high-flier, product champion, gamesman, marketeer	Dynamic
Change-agent	Manager of change, project controller	Flexible
Animateur	Social catalyst	Enthusiastic

For the first time perhaps in its history, ICI – in the person of its chairman – is accommodating and strongly projecting the role of 'animateur' throughout the organization. The question is, how can it best be received and magnified? The role of enabler still remains hidden within the corporate psyche. The gatekeeper in research and development, and the OD man in personnel or training, keeps a low profile. At the same time I have heard rumbles that the function of the board has changed from one of authorizing change to enabling change. The notion of enabling 'development' remains one step removed. ICI is hovering at the edges of becoming an 'enabling company', but still has some way to go.

Finally, ICI has always recognized and rewarded innovation. Yet, ever since the days of Nobel and Ludwig Mond, innovators have been relegated to the sidelines rather than occupying centre stage. Centre stage has been occupied by the chief executives and the high-fliers. The uniform board structure reinforces this central tendency. If a metaculture of diversity is to be created, the concept of the board would have to be reformulated even more fundamentally than it has been. As it now stands, however, it neither represents a 'community of interests', geographically, stakeholder wise (suppliers, customers, employees, shareholders) nor culturally (managers, entrepreneurs, innovators, etc.). Yet the most fundamental interest that the company serves, physically speaking, is that of chemistry.

THE C-CHEMISTRY BETWEEN THE I'S

What counts in ICI, concretely speaking, is neither culture nor change, neither enterprise nor organization, neither development nor innovation, but tangible, chemically based products. The huge plants dotted around the country, the pipelines and pylons connecting energy source and destination, the distribution networks carrying people and products, materials and equipment, are all physical manifestations of ICI's continued existence. Unless people physically come to work and make their presence felt, in the same way as machines are made to work, and provide the necessary power and energy, there would be no ICI. In the final analysis it is the C-Chemistry between the I's that provides the company, and its personnel and customers, with its substance.

Increasingly, the physical processes in ICI are being undertaken by machines rather than people, so that heart and mind rather than muscle power become the forces behind human endeavour. As physical work enters increasingly into recreation, mental and emotional energies, and intelligent machines replace human labour on the factory floor. The ages of work, development and recreation are crowding in on each other. Can it be that ICI is being called on to manage another boundary crossing, between work and leisure, household and factory, as well as between business and community? Therein lie some further clues in the puzzle of whether ICI is moving towards the roots of excellence.

9. The Tree of Business Life

We have now reached the stage when all the threads – the social and historical foundations, the individual and collective roots, the stages of business development and the phased criteria for excellence – need to be woven together. It still remains for me to work through the unifying theme or metaphor. That is to say, I have not yet developed a holding concept, or image, for the component parts mentioned above.

When I invited a group of MBA students to put up on the board whatever business ideas they had, a mature student, with extensive managerial experience behind him, drew this simple sketch:

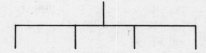

He called it a 'family tree'. We all use the term 'family tree' to describe something that is an organization chart, which is inherently lifeless. In fact, my student seemed to be saying to me, indirectly, that as an 'organization man' he had lost the liveliness to create a business. Yet a tree is very much a living form. What had the organization chart done to it? It was at this point that I decided on the 'tree of life' for my holding image. After all, I have entitled the book *The* Roots *of Excellence*.

THE SEEDS OF BUSINESS LIFE

The tree of life is an ancient symbol of the Judaeo-Christian tradition. It is a picture of Creation. It portrays universal principles. Cast in the form of an analogic tree, it demonstrates the flow of forces in man and the world around him, from the most intangible to the most tangible.

The point of origin is the seed. The seed is formed through cross-pollination between the person and the environment. Sinclair Research has emerged from cross-pollination between Clive Sinclair, electronics and personal recreation. F International has emerged from a combination of Steve Shirley, computer services and personal freedom. Habitat was created when Terence Conran linked his own imagination with creative design and individual lifestyle. ICI was initially formed when Alfred Nobel, and then Ludwig Mond, linked themselves with the chemistry of life.

THE DOMINANT STRAINS OF BUSINESS LIFE

ENTREPRENEUR

The entrepreneur, by virtue of his personality, is hero of the pioneering stage. He carries the physical, social, perceptual and emotional strength that brings the business into being. But as the enterprise develops into a managed organization, the entrepreneur moves from centre stage to the wings. What he loses in power, he gains in autonomy and in security. He is given scope to expand his division of the business, but in the context of a strategy laid down by the centre. Personal heroism is turned into managed achievement. Hard work, spontaneous enthusiasm and mental agility turns into hands-on activity, productivity achieved through people and the establishment of flexible systems. Structure takes over from personality.

As the business matures, the main focus turns from the pioneering entrepreneur and from autonomous profit centres, to the cultivation of a spirit of enterprise. Managed activities, people and systems, become released energy, nourished communities and enabled change.

MANAGER

The manager, by virtue of his knowledge and ability, occupies the central position in the *expansive* stage. He carries the business product, its market, its organization and its systems, in his mind's eye. He is reasonable and practical, just and impersonal. He may have emerged from the sidelines in an improvised structure with a lean and simple form, and grown into his new position. As the entrepreneur loses ground, so the manager gains it. In the managed organization, he has responsibility for balancing centralized and decentralized, loose and tight structures and systems. As the business matures, so he is required to assume leadership of a more complex structure.

INTRAPRENEUR

A 'leader' conventionally assumes responsibility for a large and mature corporation. If he is to be more than a trumped-up manager, he needs to understand social and industrial evolution. He should also be able to tap the 'corporate universe', reveal its vision, and transform its physical, economic and cultural fabric accordingly.

At the same time, a leader can only succeed if he is supported by not only capable managers, but a whole band of *intrapreneurs*. Such innovators, enablers, entrepreneurs, change-agents, animateurs and adventurers, as well as managers, represent the totality of the mature corporation.

Thus the innovator transforms, the enabler develops, the manager structures, the entrepreneur energizes, the change-agent adapts, the animateur animates, and the adventurer moves things, people, places.

THE STAGES OF BUSINESS LIFE

Finally, we come to the stages of business life which have been this book's main concern. The roots, the trunk, the branches grow in phases – *pioneering* enterprise, *managing* organization and *de-*

veloping 'intraprise'. Each phase carries with it characteristics which are cumulatively transcended. The entrepreneur, for example, as we have already seen, becomes depersonalized (entrepreneurship) and then 'spiritualized' (spirit of enterprise). In ICI's case, Ludwig Mond, the innovator, had a son, Alfred, who became a leader. Subsequently, the spirit of Mond lived on in the form of Mond Division. To what extent that spirit has been continually revitalized is open to question.

THE ROOTS OF BUSINESS LIFE

The root grows, like the business organism as a whole, in cumulative stages. When it is young it consists of *personal identity*, like Sinclair's. As far as the general public is concerned, Sir Clive and his products are like one.

As the root expands into middle age, it remains connected to, but gains a separate identity from, its youthful origins. So F, for flexibility, International gains a *cultural identity* apart from its founder's. Habitat merchandise and shop fronts gain an identity apart from Terence Conran's. While excellent middle-aged companies retain a link with their originators, they also form a unique identity which sets them apart.

Finally, as the root matures it becomes deeply embedded in the underlying physical and social environment. It has now grown beyond both the personal inspiration of its founders, and the product identity of its unique company. It now has to consciously rediscover itself, through the evolving technical and social environment which it both follows and shapes. The mature root turns into a *universal identity*, the all-inclusive, multicultural reason for the business's being. For ICI, this lies within a new chemistry of life, which links science and man, technological and social foundations.

THE CORE OF BUSINESS LIFE

With roots but not centre, the business lacks substance. The central core, the main stem, the 'trunk' of excellence, makes concrete the invisible and the abstract. For the young and pioneering company the core consists of an individual's *enterprise* – the tangible outcome of human individuality. So Sinclair, as an innovator, has produced his personal computers, his flat-screened television, and his electric car, as extensions of his personal enterprise.

For the middle-aged company, a depersonalized *managed organization* takes over from the personalized enterprise. F International and Habitat/Mothercare stand for more than distinctive products or services. They each have a unique company ethos that is reflected in their personnel, their facilities, their organization, and their way of doing business. While F prides itself on its flexible and efficient project management, Habitat/Mothercare oozes good taste and value for money.

As the business matures, so its visible centre develops from the personal and the impersonal towards the universal. It acquires for itself, if successfully mature, a powerful vision that radiates across time and space. Such radiation extends beyond a single company's image to represent the shared vision of a whole community of interested parties, including customers and suppliers, associated businesses and institutions. It is the kind of vision that Olivetti and Acorn computers may share together, now that they have developed an interdependent relationship. It is the vision of an international group of chemically rooted industries, rather than of a monolithic ICI. It is the visible manifestation of the corporation's invisible 'roots'. It is a multifunctional, multicultural *developing corporation*.

THE BRANCHES OF BUSINESS LIFE

Out of the central trunk, and supported by the underlying roots, grow seven branches, or excellent attributes. Each branch grows and develops these attributes, through the pioneering, managed and developmental phases.

Entrepreneurial flair

We start with pioneering, and with the entrepreneurial flair that is central to it. Conran, describing his early days, remarked, 'We made every mistake under the sun, but we had enough energy and life to ride over the problems.' Iona Eichner, who established Interlingua's Far Eastern operation, is another person with such flair. 'Being short of money isn't a problem,' she says. 'I can make money if I need it. I will always fall on my feet.' Clive Sinclair, together with his inventive mind, has a capacity to take huge, if calculated, risks. David Potter, the founder of Psion, who knows him well, told me, 'Clive is prepared to risk his all on a favourite project. He seems able to sniff out a market and then go for it, hell for leather.'

Entrepreneurial flair is instinctive, largely subconscious and composed of 'gut feel'. It is something people either have in their blood or they don't. It is very different from the more cultivated 'autonomy and entrepreneurship' that can emerge during a company's middle age.

Personal contact

In the pioneering phase, a family feeling and closeness to the customer, to employees, even to the bank manager, come naturally. Interlingua exemplifies this. Sinclair only deal with people that they personally like. Spontaneous enthusiasm and gregarious behaviour are part and parcel of the pioneering spirit. Salesmanship is an extension of personal enthusiasm rather than any cultivated 'interpersonal processes'. Personnel, management, and the development of social skills, only come into play once the pioneering days have gone.

Mental agility

The third feature of pioneering days is mental agility, including the ability to learn fast from experience. Jack Dangoor, who created a business worth tens of millions in two years, told me, 'We are fleet

288

of foot. While others bury their profits in overheads, we develop new products.' He kept his staff down to seven people while creating and distributing his Advance small-business computer, via Ferranti and W.H. Smith. Sinclair is noted for trying things out, rather than formulating long-term plans. Anita Roddick, creator of Body Shop, loves the buzz of the high street, the quick turnaround of products and people, and the opportunity to switch from one line or store to another, at the drop of a hat. Such mental agility is innate. It is only once a fully fledged organization and training function is developed that we begin to think in terms of 'learning to learn'.

Simple form, lean staff

Within even the largest corporations, this harks back to early pioneering days. Certainly the Eichners, as well as Sinclair, Jack Dangoor and Anita Roddick, love simple structures. The entrepreneur likes to keep his organization simple, basic, unencumbered by undue overheads or complicated systems. Yet there are occasions when a PhD physicist starts a new business, alias David Potter of Psion, and does see things in a more complex light. 'The structure that is right for us', he says, 'is like a string of pearls. It's beautiful, it works well, and people work well inside it. Psion is the string, the whole work of art.'

Hunch and intuition

Hunch and intuition are an intrinsic part of the entrepreneur's world. For him, they are instinctive qualities. But, if we choose to analyse them, they have some connection with an aesthetic sense. Richard Cutting, director of Sinclair's Metalab, remarked about Sinclair: 'Clive has a rare ability to combine his unique grasp of electronics technology with skill in spotting consumer applications. He is also able to come up with the most economical and elegant solutions to technical problems.' There is a link, somewhere, between intuition and a feeling for the harmony, or natural links, between things. As a result, once we lift intuition out of the instinctive, entrepreneurial realm, it begins to rub shoulders with design. Design, in its broadest sense, has a significant, cohering part to play as a company develops. It is a powerful integrating force in product, if not also organization development. The role of design in business becomes, in fact, most strongly identified as companies mature.

Personal creativity

Sinclair has been characterized as a creative originator. What does this have to do with his entrepreneurial flair? The short answer is: not much. Few entrepreneurs are very imaginative. There are not many Mary Quants or Clive Sinclairs who have the kind of creative imagination that can transform products or people.

Because of Sinclair's wide-ranging alliances with not only the British public, but also with Timex, Thorn EMI, Hoover and so on, he is able to leap across from his entrepreneurial branch to his transforming one, without the mediating structure of a strongly managed organization. In fact, other organizations, like Timex, have taken over the structured organization for him. As a result, Sinclair's roots can reach deep and wide through Britain's recreational heartlands without requiring his own mature corporation to balance underlying depth with outlying strength.

FROM PIONEERING TO MANAGEMENT

From simple and lean, to loose-tight

The companies which expand, and grow strong are middle-sized, with powerfully structured and sophisticated systems. Where the pioneer is instinctive, the manager is refined. The excellent managed companies, like F International and Habitat/Mothercare, turn simple forms into subtly balanced loose-tight structures. Conran's group financial director, Ian Peacock, conveys this attitude very well. 'I have to ensure that creativity is allied with good common sense and adequate discipline. . . . You have to take account of the local nuances in different companies and countries. . . . The important thing is to ensure that systems are there, but to serve rather than dictate.' Once a middle-sized company matures, of course, subtlety has to blend with complexity and sophistication.

From hunch and intuition to design for wholeness

Hunch and intuition, as structures and management become more conscious and explicit, turn to ambiguity and paradox, design and wholeness. Peters and Waterman refer to the company's willingness to be sailed rather than driven. In other words, it should respond to wind and current, rather than cruise ahead in a straight line. That leads to behaviour which might appear ambiguous and paradoxical, rather than straightforward and sensible.

Again, Ian Peacock has something useful to say in this respect.

> The best deals are the opportunistic ones. Mothercare, Richard Shops, Heal's. What is important is that the opportunity fits in with the group strategy, which I see as the creation of a federation of speciality retailers. It is our sensitivity to the marketplace, to people's changing needs, which gives us the edge.

This market sensitivity comes as no accident. It is part of the designer's stock in trade as John Stephenson, Habitat/Mothercare's design and marketing director, told me. 'When you're involved with design you've got to deliver a whole package. You put it into one envelope. All you need for a home. All together. All sympathetic. An amalgam of style that holds things together. . . . Design, merchandising and promotion must be seen as a whole.'

From personal creativity to corporate mission

The middle-sized, expanding organization characteristically loses its personal creativity and gains, if successful, a strong corporate mission. Personal creativity becomes channelled and transformed in the sense that, for example, Conran's mission of beauty and self-sufficiency becomes Peacock's 'federation of speciality retailers'. A perfect example of this is contained in F International's charter. In order for the company to outgrow its founder and develop an enduring and impersonal mission, Steve Shirley created a charter. One particular section says:

> F International is a group of companies which have sprung from seeing an opportunity in a problem; one woman's ability to work in an office has turned into hundreds of people's opportunity to work in a non-office environment. Because of its unusual origin F International has a clear sense of its mission, its strategy, and its values.

This statement clearly illustrates the progression from personal creativity to company policy, mission and strategy. The trouble with business policy, so often, is that it bypasses rather than transforms the originator's purposes. Habitat/Mothercare and F International are both clear examples of companies where this has not happened. The trouble with the maxim 'stay with what you know best' is that it fails to capture that particular dynamic. That is why I prefer to think in terms of business mission transcending individual imagination, rather than business strategy or policy. It is also more closely associated with cultural identity.

From hard work to hands on

Opportunism and image lift us into the upper echelons of the managed organization. At a more basic level, plain hard work is replaced by hands-on, value-driven activity. The founding father, or his management successors, are no longer able to be actively involved in everything. Yet their physical presence continues to be important, symbolically if not literally. Hence the importance of the 'management by walkabout'. By being there to help towards the opening of the new Habitat/Mothercare headquarters, Conran was reinforcing such values as 'team spirit' and 'attention to detail'. It also served to remind his people that work was not a thing of the past. Conran was still hard at it! Symbol replaced fact as the criteria for excellence.

From closeness to the customer or employee to productivity through people

As a business expands and develops it is no longer possible for the pioneer to maintain personal contact with everyone. So individual employees become personnel, customers become target markets. This is inevitable. In the excellent companies, though, emphasis shifts not from person to bureaucracy, from from individual motivation to team spirit. There is plenty of evidence of this in Habitat.

Beyond team spirit, and particularly in the last few years, companies have paid particular attention to their so-called 'corporate culture', the myths, the rituals, the homely touches that bond people. As a company expands, that homely touch needs to be consciously nurtured; it no longer comes of its own accord. So people have to be consciously noticed, acknowledged, united, to enhance productivity. They will no longer naturally pull together.

From fleet of foot to flexibility and experimentation

While F International is not especially noted for team spirit, it is noted for its F-lexibility. Virtually from the outset, Steve Shirley built up a system of flexible project management that would serve the company well, even after she was no longer at the helm. At Habitat/Mothercare, they have also turned Conran's fast footwork into continuing flexibility. Ian Peacock has consciously kept his controls simple and versatile, so that people can respond quickly to change.

The excellent managed organization has this capacity to rise above the very structures that it has been obliged to create and proclaim, as Habitat's marketing director, Tony Maynard, says: 'We need to develop sensitive and adaptive structures to retain that ability to respond quickly, as the need arises.' We are conscious all the time that as the managed organization develops out of its pioneering origins, it has to evolve systems and structures to deal explicitly with what was previously implicit. If you like, it attains a higher state of consciousness, but at the cost of a loss of spontaneity. The best of these organizations remain aware of that prospective loss.

From entrepreneurial flair to autonomy and entrepreneurship

The excellent middle-sized company is not able, nor should it try, to accommodate entrepreneurs in their original form. What it does is to create an organization and the right incentives for a degree of autonomy and entrepreneurship. Brian Codling, who manages ICI Paints, put it this way: 'Basically I believe in helping the individual to stand on his own two feet, and face up to the consequences. If you can do that, within the framework of where the business is going, you're on the right track.' So there needs to be a framework within which autonomy and initiative are encouraged. Ian Peacock told me that 'We always have believed in share incentives for people running subsidiaries', and Conran, too, is very proud of his share-owning scheme for employees, which he introduced at an early stage in his company's expansion.

So much for the managed organization. In the same way as the pioneering enterprise draws its greatest strength from entrepreneurial flair, so it draws its strongest influence from strategy and structure. But the excellent organization is able to link up with its origins in a way which transforms it. Here I am reminded of John Harvey-Jones's words, that 'the art of amalgamation is to produce a third, entirely new form'. The features of excellence that Peters and Waterman discovered amount absolutely to such an amalgamation. Out of two old forms, entrepreneurial on the one hand, and managerial on the other, they have produced a third, transcendent form.

THE MATURE CORPORATION

I was moved by *In Search of Excellence* to discover its roots because Peters and Waterman have virtually ignored the third stage of a business's development. This is not surprising, because few academics have paid it any attention at all. The reason, perhaps, is because it lies in the future. Only very few, enlightened executives understand its wide-ranging implications. John Harvey-Jones is one of them. Perhaps that is why ICI has become the first British non-oil business to make one billion pounds profit! We need now to look ahead, towards the genuinely mature corporation.

From image and identity to a transforming vision

Habitat/Mothercare stands poised between middle age and maturity. Though I have characterized it as the former it has some of the attributes of the latter. I vividly recall Habitat's marketing director, for example, telling me, 'We feel that we're part of a major, influential change in the human environment.' That is the stuff of which visions are made, rooted within this country's creative soil. What, then, is holding the company back?

One thing is its age and size. A corporation must have accumulated huge assets, and be employing many thousands, before it is capable of transforming a whole industry. Conran has certainly caused something of a retailing revolution, but the likes of Sainsbury and Marks and Spencer remain largely untouched. ICI's position, like BP's, or IBM's, however, is different. Each is international; each transforms the world's physical resources; each has a history stretching back between 50 and 150 years.

A company like ICI knows no national boundaries. Its history stretches across Germany and Sweden, as well as Switzerland and Great Britain. Secondly, the whole of at least one nation is caught up in its development. And there is a third point. People in ICI often refer to 'our seam of technology'. To me that is a rather neutral way of saying something of great transforming power. We get the flavour much better from Alfred Nobel, so I shall repeat a quote from the early days of his explosives business:

> Back in England he invited mine owners, railway builders and engineers to a demonstration. He ignited charges of nitroglycerine and powder mixture. A case with these contents was dropped from sixty feet high. The onlookers were stunned, as they followed the frail, small body of the scientist, moving fearlessly. One explosion after another shook the earth.

Here we are offered a superb vision of physical transformation. Harvey-Jones's belief that ICI should become 'the chemical problem-solvers of the world' is a watered-down, rather than an updated and transcendent, vision. How, then, do the ICIs of this world ensure that they convert personal creativity and company image into something much greater?

Alfred Mond gave us a clue in the 1920s. He proclaimed that the chemists of the day were the new pioneers and that ICI was paving the way towards a new form of industrial organization. Those were visionary words. What is their equivalent today? What are the new scientific frontiers that ICI is probing? What is the new form of industrial organization that it is spearheading? This leads us towards our final chapter and towards business recreation.

10. Economic Recreation: a Future for Britain

Over the past few years I have become convinced that the path to economic revitalization in Great Britain passes neither through the regeneration of manufacturing industry nor through the City of London. It lies, more fundamentally, within our national and economic self-image. If we are to develop ourselves as a successful postindustrial nation, we have, first of all, to change the way we see ourselves.

If Britain is to discover a future that works, it has to uncover that uniquely fertile soil in which its businesses can take successful root. There is no point in this country trying to become what it cannot be. Thousands of years of history cannot and should not be bypassed, but it can be reinterpreted and thus renewed.

Underneath the British psyche, I have discovered a spirit of tolerance, a creative vigour, a strong individuality, and a love of recreation. The respective seeds that Nobel and Mond, Terence Conran, Steve Shirley and Clive Sinclair planted have taken firm root in their intrinsically British soil. This gives each company, in some shape or form, long-lasting potential. When roots are deeply and widely spread in fertile soil, they are extremely difficult to dislodge.

THE BUSINESS CORE

There is no point in Britain trying to become better organized than the Germans or more enthusiastic than the Americans. They have their fertile ground and we have ours. What we can do is collaborate with them more effectively, as the world becomes a smaller place. But, more importantly, it is my belief that British business is more naturally geared to the first and third stages of business development, than to the phase in between.

PIONEERING

The first stage is pioneering. There is (and always has been) a pioneering spirit in the UK. But it has been diverted in recent years from the mainstream of business into physical, social and cultural tributaries. There are more voluntary groups *per capita* in Britain than anywhere else in the world. Explorers, mountaineers and itinerant travellers there have been and always will be. Artistic enterprises, whether in the theatre or television, in music or in art and design, are flourishing now as they never have done before.

As a result, a myriad of associated small enterprises, in industries ranging from climbing to motor racing, pop music to commercial design, women's fashions to computer games, are leading the world. Britain has never lost its pioneering spirit. Rather, it has been channelled into areas where individuality, variety, creativity and a love of recreation come together.

The enterprising spirit that results cuts across the arts, science and industry. If it is narrowly confined within a purely commercial enclave, its impact will be substantially lost. The influence of Sinclair or Steve Shirley extends far beyond business. They are preparing our society for the twenty-first century.

PROFESSIONAL MANAGEMENT

It is my conviction, based on fifteen years' experience working with Germans, Swedes and Americans, and comparing them with the British, that we will never become superb professional managers 'en business masse'.

Interestingly enough, when Clutterbuck and Goldsmith went looking for the 'winning streak' in British businesses, the one common denominator that they found was the family influence. Marks and Spencer and Sainsbury are two well-known examples. It seems that in order to maintain a tight and professional rein, a patriarchal influence is all-important.

As a nation we are not naturally attuned to formal structures. Consequently, when we impose them they become counter-productive. They bring out the worst in us. They become rigid and stultifying rather than resilient and channelling. I saw all too much evidence of this even within an excellent company like ICI.

We all know what can happen in the Civil Service and in other large and traditional British institutions. They tend to draw out our weaknesses rather than our strengths. In our self-critical way we then dwell on the resulting inertia, rigidity, class barriers and bureaucracy. It all becomes a self-fulfilling prophecy.
 and got on with the work gets British business nowhere fast.

It is not surprising that the two professionally managed organizations that I have cited for their excellence in this book are 'managed' with a difference. F International combines structured organization with built-in flexibility. Habitat/Mothercare combines professional management with a crucial design awareness.

That is not to say that Marks and Spencer, to take a prominent example, is not an excellent, professionally managed company. But unless its roots probe more deeply into contemporary and fertile British ground, it is in danger of losing its way. Companies like British Leyland lost their way, in the past, because they blatantly ignored the individuality, variety, creativity and love of recreation within the British psyche. Standardized, large-scale production is the very antithesis of all this, which brings us to the developing corporation.

THE DEVELOPING CORPORATION

Britain never lost her pioneering spirit. It has merely been diverted. What we must do now is to convert that diversion into a new mainstream, rather than relegate it to the sidelines. In other words, postindustrial Britain needs to become the 'recreation' centre of the world.

By 'recreation' I do not just mean leisure activity in the conventional sense, although that is certainly a part of it. The performing arts, hotels and restaurants, the travel business, computer games and so on are playing an ever more important role in the British economy. But I am going far beyond that. In my terms, any activity that is intrinsically pleasurable and fulfilling is re-creational.

Management can be a so-called recreation. Certainly much of the fast-moving activity undertaken in the City is of such a nature. Recreational activity is varied, creative and personally fulfilling. It can be differentiated from 'mundane' activity which is standard-ized, routine and personally degrading.

Harold Geneen, the much-renowned chairman of ITT, wrote an excellent book recently on managing. 'I always enjoyed', he said, 'going to work. In fact, I never thought of it as work. It was a part of my life, a part of the environment in which I lived and breathed. I often told colleagues that business was as much fun as golf, tennis, sailing, dancing. . . . The pleasures were different from those of eating an ice cream sundae. Business provided intellectual challenges that stimulated and fed one's mind. They were every bit as good in their own way as the momentary pleasures of gobbling down one's dessert, and they were more durable. The sweetness lasted longer. Business could be a great adventure, a lot of fun, something to look forward to every day.'

The British, with their sense of humour, their love of games, and their creative talent in so many diverse fields, should be ideally suited to put into practice what Geneen, in this particular instance, represents. The problem and challenge that remains is how to incorporate all of this into our major corporations. In the words that Andrew Pettigrew uses in *The Awakening Giant*, his recent book on ICI, how might our 'giants awake'?

What does it mean, for a business corporation in Britain, to be awake? In my view it means three things. Firstly, the corporation needs to be closely in touch with Britain's underlying being, our *national psyche*. According to the extent to which the corporation becomes in touch, it will look very different from its traditional self. Individuality, variety, creativity and recreation will become the norm, and uniformity and standardization, routine and un-fulfilling work the exception. A lot of this sort of activity is essential in business, but, increasingly, it can and should be taken over by machines. Far-sighted business leaders in this country have already seen the light. The question that still remains is how to convert the light into recreational and useful energy!

Secondly, the corporations have to rediscover their own individual roots, which must encompass both their originating spirit and the contemporary environment. Many a large corporation has 'lost its soul', and it can only be refound after a conscious search through its technological, cultural and economic history books. What is crucial, then, is to be able to reinterpret this historical evolution in a contemporary light. Historical consciousness is all-important to a large corporation, as it is to a nation. It only becomes an energy drain rather than an energy source when it is not continually renewed.

The *corporate universe*, unlike the more narrowly based company culture, represents a fusion between the whole individual and the total environment. Nowhere is this more clearly stated than within the Bank of Commerce and Credit International. Although only twelve years old, it is already reaching maturity. It operates in 65 countries, has 12,000 employees, and made a profit last year of $350 million. Although its origins lie in Pakistan, its mission is universal and its operational headquarters are in London.

Every corporation, according to the bank's founder and president, Agha Hasan Abedi, 'like nature, has its own psyche and spirit which is created by and through the relationship and interfusion of its parts and parts, its parts and totality. . . . Nature operates as a dynamic system in its dynamic state. All parts of the system are interrelated and interdependent. They interfuse and through the phenomenon of change, assume their dynamic shape in the form of evolution.'

John Hilbury, one of the bank's founder directors, told me that the reason for their phenomenal growth was that they were in touch with the fundamental laws of nature, and were able to relate these to economics and finance. At the same time they have always understood that, in John's words, 'Vision is the synthesis of the individual psyche with the psyche of the environment and the purpose of the business.'

Now, in its emerging maturity, the bank is embarking on a conscious process of communicating this underlying purpose, in an operational context, to all the members of its corporate universe. It will be doing this through an internationally based development unit. This unit will be simultaneously concerned with the development of people, products, nations and a new, naturally based theory of economics.

This gives you some idea of what needs to be done in order for the developing corporation to uncover its corporate universe. As in the case of the Bank of Commerce and Credit, the UK is uniquely placed to operate on an international scale. Much more than either the United States or Japan this country has a tradition of international business, cultural and political activity. It is also true to say that a significant proportion of its entrepreneurial thrust, in business, has drawn on European, Jewish and Asian immigrants.

l   I would like to see this country become the base for a majority of international companies, including those which are in foreign control. In our global village we can no longer afford to adopt a parochial attitude. After all variety, especially in the light of our multicultural heritage, must be the spice of life! It is also the spice of business.

THE BUSINESS BRANCHES

So, if our national economy is to be successfully recreated, then British business needs to be firmly rooted in fertile soil. In Britain our recreational gounds are particularly fertile, being a nation of hobbyists, comics, tinkerers and do-it-yourselfers, volunteer workers, travellers and explorers, gifted amateurs, games players, creative artists and scientists. These oft-considered sidestreams could become an economic mainstream if we turned into the recreational capital of the world.

The more closely individual companies get in touch with their historical, geographical, personal and economic identities, the more economically fulfilled Britain would become. In the process we should rediscover our pioneering spirit and exploit the full potential of the new technology, in order to take over much of the routine management which fits uncomfortably within our national psyche.

The role of the developing corporation is to renew itself consciously by participating in the evolution of its individual people and of its national, and international, environment.

302

The developing corporation needs to grow branches quite unlike those of its professionally managed predecessors. That is the nub of the matter. This is where ICI and Habitat/Mothercare fundamentally differ. This is also where Britain should be coming into its own again.

The truly mature business should be growing branches that are both close to the individual and close to the environment. In that sense, the laws of personal psychology and natural ecology assume particular importance, with economics coming in between. The branch implications are as follows:

● Hard work and hands-on activity is replaced by *energy*, a physical quality that has both personal and environmental attributes. John Hilbury, at the Bank of Commerce and Credit, visualizes his organization as 'a vast stream of energy to which all contribute and from which all draw'.

● Personal enthusiasm, and productivity through people, is replaced by a *community* of interests. Communities are to be found in all walks of life, and a mature corporation has to find a social force that binds them all. The force that binds has to link employees, freelancers and subcontractors, as well as customers, collaborators and shareholders. It has to accommodate variety and yet create unity. Interlingua's matriarchal model, in which individual freedom and social cohesion coexisted, provides us with some good food for thought.

● Mental agility, and organizational flexibility, is replaced by *networking*, with all its social, technical and structural implications. Computerized networks, in the context of 'the office of the future', are becoming almost commonplace. We saw evidence of it with Interlingua, in ICI and, most particularly, in Rank Xerox. Their new headquarters in Marlow is likely to be an architectural/technological innovation. Economic networks, like those characterizing Sinclair Research, its subcontractors, software producers and magazine publishers, are spreading fast, together with the joint ventures that have become an ever-increasing part of ICI's activities.

Finally, the advent of homeworking, so clearly reflected in F

International's operations, is no flash in the pan. Technological and economic networks, like their ecological counterparts, are here to stay, because they are more consistent with individual freedom and variety than traditional hierarchies. They are also making increasing economic sense, serving to cut transport costs and central overheads.

- Individual and entrepreneurial flair, as well as organizational autonomy and entrepreneurship, is replaced by a *spirit of enterprise*. What finally counts, for the developing corporation, is not the one-off entrepreneur, nor even, in isolation, autonomous profit centres.

The real challenge, which John Harvey-Jones has responded to so well, is to stimulate initiative of all kinds, all over the company. The result in ICI is what I described as six different varieties of 'intrapreneurs'. These range from the high-flier, product champion and marketeer to the less well-known entrepreneurial manager, gamesman and enventurer.

- An improvised organizational form, and the subsequent loose-tight structure, is replaced by a structure that is complex enough to accommodate individual and intrapreneurial variety. If, as John Harvey-Jones, Hamish Orr Ewing and Adrian Cadbury have all publicly advocated, the organization is to cater for the individual, rather than vice versa, its structure has to become *organic* and *complex*.

The 'business tree of life' is hopefully such a structure. I have deliberately connected up the foundations of the business's being, with its root identity, its central core, its activity branches, and the fruits of its endeavours. In that sense, the business's origins, organization, activities and products are tightly interwoven. The formal structure is a mere part of a living whole.

The challenge for a developing corporation, like ICI, is to present inside and outside stakeholders with a picture of that integrated whole. Once they see and grasp such a picture, as a mirror of their own living individuality, the potential for development will be raised many fold. I would guess that a major corporation could multiply its profits at least tenfold if it became such an appropriately complex organism.

Until corporate man becomes the measure of such things we shall be relying on extraordinary individuals alone, like Conran and Harvey-Jones, to do what the more ordinary among us should play a much greater part in achieving. The present call for organizational simplicity results in the load of complexity being placed on a very few brave and gifted individuals' shoulders.

• An important key to understanding complexity is an appreciation of the natural laws of development. This is something that the Bank of Credit and Commerce, almost in splendid isolation, has consciously converted from natural theory into commercial practice. As a business matures, then native intuition, as in Sinclair, and design awareness, as in Habitat, needs to be turned into *conscious development*.

The time is ripe for integrated development. One of F International's senior executives has exclusive responsibility for so-called 'business development'. Companies like Sinclair and ICI are now advertising for 'business development managers'. This is a new trend, the significance of which most of us are still unaware.

A company like ICI has a distinctive reputation for both its research and development and, as Andrew Pettigrew has revealed in *The Awakening Giant*, for organization development. In more recent years it has been building up its competence in systems and process development, and in market and commercial development. But it is only in the last year or so that there has been a hint of something emerging beyond the horizons of professional management.

That new force is the 'enabling company' or truly developmental corporation, which transcends both the pioneering enterprise and the managed organization. Such a company understands, and is able to respond to, the development of people and organization, of products and markets, and even of whole environments. It understands phases, it understands formative crises, and it knows how and where to tap personal, physical and economic energy.

305

The Roots of Excellence

I have proposed, in fact, that the concept of a uniform board be dissolved, to be replaced by a board of enterprise, a board of management and a board of development. For the mature corporation, this would open up not only new channels of thought but also new career channels. The individual could effectively decide whether to pursue expansion (enterprise), promotion (management) or development (evolution or transformation).

● Ultimately, the developing corporation is in the business of *transformation*: of physical energy, materials and products, and of psychic energy, people and organization. ICI, through its chemical laboratories and plants, visibly transforms things, from a relatively simple state to a more complex one. Over the years, it has also been transforming its individual enterprises, from fledgling ventures into fully grown business divisions. What remains much less visible is how its people are transformed.

Excellent companies of the future will need to be as adept in transforming psychic energy as they are in converting physical energy from less to more advanced states. It is the abilities of people, in other words psychic resources, rather than physical or economic ones, which are ultimately most scarce. This, above all else, is what the Japanese have demonstrated to the rest of the world.

These 'psychic resources' involve more than knowledge. They include stamina, enthusiasm, intellect, willpower, method, intuition and imagination. These qualities parallel our seven branches of business excellence. To the extent that each of these is transformed from lower to higher states, so the business will have realized what the Bank of Commerce and Credit call a 'spiritual profit'. To survive over the long term, individuals, corporations and whole nations need to 'profit' spiritually as well as financially.

If Britain is to profit as a nation, in both these terms, it will have to do more than revitalize its industries, reorganize its management or retrain its workforce. It will need, in fact, to recreate its entire economy, root and branch, under the impetus of a transformed self-image. That transformation will accommodate individuality, creativity, diversity and recreation.

Index

Index

Abedi, Agha Hassan 301
Advance Technology 43–4
Andahl, Gene 55
Armitage, Dr Rodney 45, 267, 270–1
Asimov, Issac: *Futures* 73–4

Babbage, Charles 62–3
Bank of Credit and Commerce International 301–6
Barnes, Alan 271
Barnes, David 238–41
Bauhaus School 159, 162
Bayley, Stephen: *In Good Shape* 162
Beer, Stafford: *Design for Freedom* 275–6
Big K 63
Black, Jimmy 216–17
Body Shop 38, 44
Boilerhouse Project 142
British Leyland 299
British Rail 41–2, 48–9
Browne, Patrick 80
Brunner, John 211
and ICI 198, 212–13, 278
Buchtal, Vera Stephanie, *see* Shirley, Steve
Burnham, James 222

Cadbury, Sir Adrian 50–1, 304
Carluccio, Priscilla 44, 168, 170, 194–5
Caxton, William 64
Cerasoli, Albert 211–12

Cliff, Stafford 171
Clutterbuck, D. and Goldsmith, W.: *The Winning Streak* 40, 298
Clutton Brock, Arthur 162
Codling, Brian 243, 245, 251–4, 278
Cole, Sir Henry 146
Conran Advertising 144
Conran Associates 141, 144, 171, 173, 184, 193
Conran Foundation 142, 162
Conran Octopus *see* Octopus Books
Conran Shop 141, 142
Conran, Sir Terence 11, 13, 41, 179, 190–1
and design 59–61, 63, 146, 154, 159–71, 284, 291
as entrepreneur 130, 141–5, 178–83, 288, 297
and Habitat/Heal's complex 39, 150, 292
and management 50, 55, 172–3, 178, 196–7, 305
and retailing 164–7, 295
continuity workers 45–6
corporate universe 14, 16, 36–7, 60–7, 294–6
and change 50–4, 299–307
Cotton, Charles 49, 96–8
Crick, Frances 63, 201
Cutting, Richard 88–96 *passim*, 104, 289

Dangoor, Jack 43, 288–9

Davis, Garner 216
Davy, Geoff 184
Dessauer, John 56
Duncan, Bill 216–19

Eichner, Claudia 27
Eichner, Fred 23–36, 53, 55
Eichner, Iona 27, 29, 47, 288
Eichner, Mark 27
Eichner, Michael 27–8, 33–4, 49
Eichner, Nelli 23–36, 40
enablers 48, 51–2, 133, 137, 305–6
  ICI management as 206–9,
    231–4, 258–62, 280–1
entrepreneurs, role of 12–14,
  245–67, 284, 298
Eyre, Mike 48, 55

Ferranti 43
Financial Times, the 69
F-International 17–18, 111–40, 284
  beginnings and growth 111–14
  and communications 124–6
  corporate charter 127–9, 138–9,
    291–2
  customer relations 134–6, 140
  and flexibility 46, 65–6, 286, 293
  and individuality 11–15, 42, 110,
    120–4, 138
  organization 67, 114–119,
    126–34, 287–305 *passim*
  and work design 131–2
Fleck, Alexander 199, 225
French, Nigel 185–6

Gale, Jan 181, 185–8
Gardner, John: *Self-Renewal* 56
Geneen, Harold 300
Goddard, Terry 178
Good, Rosemary 184–5, 188
Goodman, Barney 156–7, 172,
  179–81

Gregory, Oliver 39, 53, 55, 146–53
  passim, 190–2
Gropius, Walter 161

Habitat
  beginnings and growth 141–6,
    152
  /Heal's complex 39, 148–51,
    191–2
  management evolution 154–6,
    284
  /Mothercare merger 142, 164–5,
    172, 180–1
  /Ryman merger 141, 164, 194
Habitat/Mothercare 141–97
  and creativity 11, 13, 17–18, 55,
    61
  design and marketing 165–72,
    183–8, 291
  organization 14–18, 44, 50, 59,
    66–7, 142–5, 172–8, 193–7,
    284–99 *passim*
  products 42–3, 52–3, 151, 286
  share-ownership scheme 174–5,
    294
  teamwork 41, 152–3, 189–93
Hamlyn, Paul 153, 165, 180
Handscombe, Philip 265
Harrison, Ernie 48
Harvey, Phil 243, 248, 268, 279
Harvey-Jones, Sir John 199, 243
  and change/innovation 42, 50–1,
    56, 201–9, 228–38, 245, 263–75
    passim, 294–6, 304–5
Heal's 142–3, 165, 166, 177–8, 184,
  191–4
  recreation of 39, 148–51
Hease, Richard 75, 101–4, 109
Henderson, Denys 243, 246–51
Hilbury, John 301–2
Hoch, Robert *see* Maxwell
Hodgson, Sir Maurice 225, 226

Hudig, Dick 209
Hughes, Alan 152, 155, 189, 191

IBM 31
ICI (Imperial Chemical
    Industries) 198–282
  beginnings and growth 198–9,
    210–15
  as corporate universe 14, 16–18,
    31, 204
  as enablers of change 206–9,
    231–4, 258–62, 280–1
  management 220–5, 235, 294,
    299
  and management of change
    226–82, 286, 294–6, 304–6
  pharmaceuticals 216–20
  and tolerance of diversity 11–12,
    66–7, 201–2
Information Technology
    Development 48
Interlingua 23–36, 47–58 *passim*,
    288–9, 303
ICL 78
'intrapreneurs', role of 13, 16–17,
    285–6

Jenkins, Ken 51–3
Jones, Kevyn 157–8, 172–82
    passim, 197

Keynes, J. M.: *Economic
    Possibilities for Our
    Grandchildren* 72–3

Land, George: *To Grow or to
    Die* 19
Latin, Bob 56
Lessem, Abe 19–22, 31–2, 35
Lessem, Jack 19–22
Levinstein, Ivan 198
Libby, Maurice 192

Lievegood, Bernard 31
Linguanet 29, 35–6
Lingwood, Gill 192
Lloyd, Tom: *Dinosaur & Co.* 120

Maccoby, Michael 43
Macleod, David 265–7
Malpas, Bob 54, 61
manager, role of 15–16, 285, 290–
    4, 298–9
Margetts, Rob 53, 231–3, 243,
    258–62
Marks and Spencer 67, 229
    and family factor 40, 298
Maxwell, Robert 69–70, 92, 104, 110
Maynard, Tony 44, 60–1, 156–9,
    189–96 *passim*, 293, 295
McGowan, Harry 67, 198, 201,
    214–20, 234, 278
Mellersh, John 39, 262–4
Micronet 125
Mills, Brian 42, 118–19
Mond, Alfred 198, 212–20
    passim, 234, 278, 286, 296
Mond, Ludwig 69, 198, 211–12
    and ICI 12, 61, 201, 212–13, 220,
    234, 278–86
Morelli, Cindy 112
Morgan Grenfell 142, 144
Mothercare 142–4, 156–9, 164–5,
    177, 181–2; *and see* Habitat/
    Mothercare

National Enterprise Board 68, 77
networking 45–6, 303–4
Newbold, Brian 216–19
Newell, Alison 112, 116–35 *passim*
Nobel, Alfred 61, 198–9, 210, 295
    and ICI 201, 220, 234, 278, 284
Nossiter, Bernard 61–2, 64
Now (Habitat/Mothercare) 142–4,
    148, 165, 185, 194

Octopus Books 142, 165–6, 180, 194
Orr Ewing, Hamish 59–60, 304

Paolozzi, Eduardo 160–1
Parker, Sir Peter 41–2, 48–9, 54
Peacock, Ian 50, 145, 172–8, 197, 290–4
Peters, T. J. and Waterman, R. H. Jr: *In Search of Excellence* 7, 11, 14, 16, 32–48 *passim*, 58, 272, 291, 294
Pettigrew, Andrew: *The Awakening Giant* 300, 305
Phillips, Bartie: *Conran: the Habitat Story* 146, 169
pioneers, role of 12–15, 19–37, 284, 288–90, 298
Potter, David 40–1, 75, 82, 87, 99–109 *passim*, 288–9
Potter, Don 159
Prestel 271
Prism group 103–4
'prosumer' 44, 85–6
Psion 40, 75, 82, 86–7, 105–6, 288–9

Quant, Mary 40, 53–9, 290

Racal Electronics 48, 106
Rank Xerox 28, 45–6, 59–60, 303
recreation, British flair for 11, 13, 63–87 *passim*, 110, 297–307
Reece, Charles 242–3, 263, 278–80
Revans, Prof. R. 11
Rhodes, Zandra 55
Richard Shops (Habitat/ Mothercare) 142, 144, 165–6, 177, 187, 194
Richards, Alison 183–5, 188, 190–1
Roddick, Anita 38–40, 44, 289

Rose, F. L. 218
Rostow, Walt 62
Rowland, John 100–1, 104, 107, 109

Sainsbury, J. and family factor 40, 298
Sayer, Ann 39, 191–2
Searle, Nigel 89–93, 97
Seelig, Roger 172
Seibu 142, 170
Shirley, Steve 13, 42, 46, 67, 69, 111–39 *passim*, 146, 284–97 *passim*
Sinclair, Bill 97
Sinclair Browne 80
Sinclair, Sir Clive
  creativity of 55–6, 89–90, 290
  as pioneer 14–15, 67, 69, 74–82, 108–10, 287–90, 297
  and recreation 11, 13, 63–87 *passim*, 110, 284
  R and D philosophy 39, 88–9, 94–6
Sinclair Research 69–110
  beginnings and growth 68–9
  C5 electric car 68, 89, 91, 108
  and computer magazines 102–5
  electronic base 17–18, 284
  flat-screen pocket television 78, 89, 95
  marketing, 96–9
  organization 49–50, 64–75, 89–95, 108, 303, 305
  Quantum Leap/Spectrum/ZX80/ ZX81 68–103
  research and development 95–6
  takeover of 69, 92, 104
Smith, W. H. 43, 83, 100–1
Software Management 123–4
Southward, David 39, 82, 93–5, 108

Stephenson, John 52–3, 151, 167–
    187 *passim*
Symons, Rosie 112, 122–4

Teague, Walter 162–3,
    192–3
teleconferences 28, 125
telecopiers 125
Thorn-EMI 91, 290
Times, The 92
Timex 91, 94, 290
Toffler, A.: *The Third Wave* 44,
    85–6
Trevelyan, G. S. 64–6

Turner, Chris 142, 152–5, 168–9,
    183
Tyler, Tony 63, 70, 82–5, 105

Vaclas, Z. (Vaci) 45, 254–8
versioning 28
visionphone 125

Wilkinson, Jane 133–4

Xikluna, Nicky 70

Zilkha, Selim 70, 153, 180
    and Mothercare 156–8, 164–6,
        177–82, 190

ATM is the only voluntary association of professionals in the UK whose work focuses exclusively on management training, education and organization development. Membership is open to anyone involved in this significant field of work. ATM's fast growth in recent years has created a lively membership of interested people in business, government, voluntary organization, academic institutions and management consultancy.

The main aim of ATM is to promote high standards of management performance so that people in organizations and communities can work with greater effectiveness. Members are therefore encouraged to meet and collaborate to improve their own professional capabilities. Activities include evening and one-day meetings, and three- to four-day events held all over the UK and in Europe. These are designed to provide members with different developmental opportunities for the various stages of their careers. They also enable members to extend their knowledge and skills, to keep in touch with frontier thinking on management, and to exchange ideas and experience.

Free publications are sent to members. These include *MEAD* (*Management Education and Development*), a journal which has three issues a year and contains articles on current management training and development; frequent focus papers on topical issues; and a monthly newsletter.

For further information, contact:

ATM
Polytechnic of Central London
35 Marylebone Road
London
NW1 5LS

01-486 5811 (ex. 259)